The Catholic Moral Tradition Today
A Synthesis

MORAL TRADITIONS & MORAL ARGUMENTS
A SERIES EDITED BY JAMES F. KEENAN, S.J.

The Evolution of Altruism and the Ordering of Love
STEPHEN J. POPE

Love, Human and Divine: The Heart of Christian Ethics
EDWARD COLLINS VACEK, S.J.

Bridging the Sacred and the Secular:
Selected Writings of John Courtney Murray, S.J.
J. LEON HOOPER, S.J., editor

The Context of Casuistry
Edited by
JAMES F. KEENAN, S.J., and THOMAS A. SHANNON

Aquinas and Empowerment:
Classical Ethics for Ordinary Lives
Edited by
G. SIMON HARAK, S.J.

The Christian Case for Virtue Ethics
JOSEPH J. KOTVA, JR.

The Fellowship of Life
Virtue Ethics and Orthodox Christianity
JOSEPH WOODILL

The Catholic Moral Tradition Today
A Synthesis

Charles E. Curran

Georgetown University Press / Washington, D.C.

Georgetown University Press, Washington, D.C.
© 1999 by Georgetown University Press. All rights reserved.
Printed in the United States of America

10   9   8   7   6   5   4   3   2   1   1999

THIS VOLUME IS PRINTED ON ACID-FREE OFFSET BOOK PAPER

Library of Congress Cataloging-in-Publication Data

Curran, Charles E.
    The Catholic moral tradition today : a synthesis / Charles E.
Curran.
        p.   cm. — (Moral traditions and moral arguments series)
    Includes index.
    1. Christian ethics—Catholic authors. I. Title. II. Series:
Moral traditions and moral arguments.
BJ1249.C79   1999
241′.042—dc21   98-44646
ISBN 0-87840-716-2 (cloth)
ISBN 0-87840-717-0 (pbk.)

To my friends in Dallas

Contents

Preface   *ix*

1 Ecclesial Context   1
What is the Church? 2,   Catholicity of the Church 4,   Mediation and
Hierarchical Structure 10,   Catholic Practice 14,   Dangers in the
Catholic Approach 15,   Contemporary Challenges to the Catholic
Approach 18,   Notes 25

2 Stance   30
Meaning of Stance 30,   Stance Based on the Fivefold Christian
Mysteries 33,   The Stance and the Catholic Tradition 34,   Stance and
Other Approaches 45,   Sources of Moral Theology 47,   Notes 56

3 Model   60
The Deontological Model 61,   The Teleological Model 66,   Relationality-
Responsibility Model 73,   The Relationality-Responsibility Model and
Catholic Moral Theology Today 77,   Notes 83

4 Person   87
Preliminary Considerations 87,   Discipleship 89,   Contemporary
Theology and the Person 91,   Contemporary Spirituality and the
Person 93,   Contemporary Moral Theology and the Person 95,   Social
and Institutional Involvements of the Person 98,   Notes 106

5 Virtues   110
Virtue in the Catholic Tradition 111,   General Virtues 113,
Particular Virtues 118,   Power 130,   Notes 133

6 **Principles   137**
The Approach of the Hierarchical Magisterium 138,   Criticisms of the
Hierarchical Approach 144,   Role of Principles and Norms 160,
Absolute Norms 165,   Notes 166

7 **Conscience   172**
Preliminary Considerations 172,   The Catholic Moral Tradition 174,
Other Ways of Decision Making 177,   A Constructive Theory of
Conscience and Decision Making 181,   Meaning of Sin 190,
The "Law of Growth" 192,   Notes 194

8 **Church Teaching   197**
Total Church as Teacher 197,   The Hierarchical Teaching Office 199,
Justification of Dissent 215,   Present Situation 221,
Conclusion 226,   Notes 228

Afterword   235

Notes   240

Index   241

Preface

This book deals with the Catholic moral tradition. How one reflects systematically on morality is definitely influenced by one's social location and where one comes from. Morality and systematic and thematic reflection on it have always been important realities in the Catholic tradition, which in turn is embodied within the community of the Catholic Church. Thus the first chapter of this book begins with an understanding of this church community and how it goes about its living and reflecting on the moral life. In the past, however, few Catholic approaches to moral theology have given much prominence and importance to the church as the place that gives birth to and nurtures the Catholic tradition.

The Catholic moral tradition has developed over a long history. A systematic presentation of the tradition as it now is cannot also be a full history of its development. However, a systematic approach to the moral tradition must be in dialogue with the more significant aspects of its past history. This book engages in such a dialogue: it points out agreements, disagreements, and developments related to significant aspects of the Catholic moral tradition.

Four significant aspects of the Catholic moral tradition give direction and shape to this volume. First, the Catholic tradition is by definition a living tradition. Catholic self-understanding has always recognized that the Scriptures must be understood, interpreted, appropriated, and lived in the light of the ongoing life of the church under the guidance of the Holy Spirit. The Catholic tradition insists on the need for both Scripture and tradition but now rejects the older approach that spoke of them as two separate sources of revelation. Tradition is now understood as the process of the transmission of Scripture, belief, worship, and the moral life of the church. Tradition is an ongoing process that continues over time. Note here the different uses of the word tradition. In the strict theological sense, tradition refers to the transmission of the community's faith. Tradition in the title of this book refers to the distinctive characteristics of a particular community or institution such as the tradition of western democracy or the tradition of Native Americans. The Catholic theological tradition in the Catholic understanding is truly a living tradition because the church does not merely repeat the words of Scripture but appropriates them in the light of ongoing circumstances of time and space. The Catholic tradition is an evolving tradition that changes and develops over time. Attempts to explain the nature of this development have been discussed quite a bit in the last few decades. However, for our purposes, it is important to realize that the Catholic tradition is ongoing and developing, not stagnant and unchanging.

A second important characteristic of the Catholic tradition is its catholicity or universality. The moral tradition of the Catholic Church insists on its responsibility to, and care for, the whole world and all God's creation. The Catholic moral tradition in practice and in theory is concerned with the moral life of the church and the common good of the broader human society. The Catholic Church as seen, for example, in its social teaching and papal encyclicals works together with others for a just, free, participative, and sustainable society. Papal social encyclicals are now addressed to all people of good will, since Catholics are called to work with others for the good of the world in which we live. Catholic social justice is not one thing for Catholics and something different for others. Rather, the Catholic moral tradition is a particular and distinctive tradition that also has a universal concern for working with others to achieve the common good of the broader human society in all its social, cultural, economic, and political aspects.

Third, the Catholic tradition is inclusive. It uses all possible sources, both revealed and human, in the attempt to arrive at moral truth. The inclusive Catholic emphasis on "both–and" is opposed to an "either–or" approach and accepts as sources of moral knowledge and wisdom whatever is available to Christians and human beings in general. As a result of these two characteristics of universality and inclusiveness, the Catholic tradition must always be in dialogue not only with other religions but also with philosophy, human sciences, and the broader human experience in its struggle to arrive at moral truth. The Catholic tradition is not narrow but calls for dialogue and conversation with all other people and disciplines. How the Catholic tradition has learned from others is well exemplified by the influence of Aristotle on the thought of Thomas Aquinas.

A fourth important characteristic of the Catholic theological tradition that informs this book is its penchant for systematic approaches.

Ever since the university world of the twelfth and thirteenth centuries, the *Summa* has been characteristic of Catholic theology. These summas try to systematize and order the whole of theology. The medieval summas were often compared to medieval cathedrals. One of their purposes was to introduce students into the tradition. To order the parts and bring them into some kind of unity has been the goal of many Catholic theologians down through the centuries. It is in keeping with such a tradition that the present book attempts this synthesis or systematic approach to Catholic moral theology today.

A synthesis or systematic study of moral theology is a difficult task at any time but especially today. Without doubt, Catholic moral theology today is more diverse and pluralistic than ever before. Systematic approaches are surely easier when the discipline is monolithic. Ever since the Second Vatican Council in the early 1960s, Catholic moral theology has been undergoing a period of rapid change and development which makes any systematic study all the more difficult.

Having worked in the area of Catholic moral theology for forty years, however, and having published on so many different aspects of the discipline, I now feel the need, in accord with Catholic tradition itself, to propose my personal synthesis of moral theology. Though I have dealt with many of its themes in other writings, I have only now put them together in one systematic volume. In the process I have discovered the problem of trying to order and condense such a huge amount of material. As the synthetic approach cannot treat individual parts in depth, the danger of superficiality is always present. This danger, however, and other frustrating aspects are built into any attempt at writing a synthesis.

This synthesis of Catholic moral tradition is analogous to fundamental moral theology. Fundamental moral theology deals with aspects of morality that are common to all instances of moral living. Special moral theology, on the other hand, addresses specific experiences, for example, personal, sexual, bioethical, social, or political morality. This book does not intend to deal directly with each of those different areas, but to use examples from each of them to flesh out and explain the general ethical aspects common to all moral inquiry.

The writing of a systematic and synthetic moral theology is very similar to the work of an architect in designing a building. A building, whether it is a church, an office building, or a home, must fulfill certain basic purposes. A house, for example, needs living space, sleeping space, kitchen and bathroom facilities, storage space, heating, cooling and electrical services, and a garage. But how do you put all these together in a unified way that gives a distinctive shape to the whole house? Moral theology or ethics deals with persons, institutions, and their actions. Catholic moral theology considers these realities from the Christian and Catholic perspective. But how should the various aspects be organized and put together? This book attempts such a systematic and synthetic study of Catholic moral theology.

A brief overview of the synthesis to be developed in this book should help orient the reader who will only see the final synthesis at the end of the book. Since Catholic moral life and reflection take place in the community of the church, the first chapter discusses how the Catholic understanding of church gives shape and direction to Catholic moral life and to systematic reflection on it.

The second chapter develops the perspective or the stance of moral theology. Stance is the next logical consideration because it is the perspective from which one views all moral reality. Experience reminds us that things look quite different from different perspectives. The stance gives us a basic orientation and way of looking at the moral life.

The third chapter then considers the best model for understanding the moral life. Different models have been proposed in the past and different models are available today from other theologians. This volume develops a relationality–responsibility model—it sees the person in multiple relationships with God, neighbor, world, and self. This book recognizes that morality is a very complex reality which includes the person who acts and the persons, communities, institutions, and environment that affect and are affected by one's actions. Some refer to these distinctions as the subject pole and the object pole of morality. In this light chapter four discusses the human person who is both subject and agent. By my actions I shape my character and my moral person, and I also affect other persons, communities, and the environment. The person is obviously a central category in moral theology. The fifth chapter focuses on the virtues—the attitudes that characterize Christian persons and guide them in their actions affecting the world.

Chapters four and five deal with persons and the virtues of persons that directly describe or constitute the subject pole of morality, but the person as agent forms the bridge going to the object pole—the world in which we live. Chapter six considers the object pole of morality, the values and principles that guide our actions in our multiple relationships with God, neighbor, world, and self. The subject and the object poles of morality come together in decision making. Everything in the earlier chapters plays a role in the theory of conscience and decision making proposed in the seventh chapter. How do we decide what to do? How do we know if we have made the right decision? The last chapter deals with role of the church in teaching moral matters and concentrates finally on the hierarchical magisterium or teaching office that is such a distinctive aspect of the Catholic moral tradition.

This book is, as I have said, only a personal synthesis of moral theology. Some Catholic moral theologians will disagree with positions taken in these pages. Others would put together the various parts in a somewhat different manner. The tradition of Catholic moral theology is not monolithic. It is my hope that this synthesis will help introduce students to the Catholic moral tradition for the first time and encourage others to enter the dialogue with other moral theologians about these positions and the best way to organize and synthesize the Catholic moral tradition today.

Theologians writing from within a church community and its theological tradition know how dependent we are on those who have gone before and those who accompany us today in our faith and theological journeys. I have learned from all who are mentioned in this book and many other contemporary theological friends and colleagues.

In a special way I express my gratitude to all who have helped me in writing this particular book. Southern Methodist University has given me a congenial academic home and many good colleagues. Jack S. and Laura Lee Blanton, exemplary patrons of higher education, have generously endowed the chair I hold—the Elizabeth Scurlock University Professor of Human Values—named in honor of Laura Lee Blanton's mother. The Bridwell Library and its accomplished, friendly librarians continue to facilitate my research. Richard M. Gula, Christine Firer Hinze, and Richard C. Sparks (the latter two are former students) painstakingly read the manuscript and made many helpful suggestions. John Samples, the editor of Georgetown University Press, and his efficient staff have been most cooperative and eased the road to publication. My associate, Carol Swartz, with her accustomed cheerfulness and alacrity prepared the manuscript for publication. Rosemarie Gorman skillfully prepared the index.

1

Ecclesial Context

Catholic moral theology in the past has paid little or no explicit attention to the church and its influence on the discipline.[1] Two central strands of Catholic moral theology illustrate this lack of attention. On the one hand, the manuals of moral theology, which practically became identified with the whole discipline of moral theology during their existence from the late sixteenth century to the Second Vatican Council (1962–1965), aimed at preparing confessors (and indirectly penitents) for the sacrament of penance. Sins, according to the Council of Trent (1545), had to be confessed according to number and species, and all the faithful were obliged to confess their mortal sins at least once a year. These very practical manuals dealt with the narrow question raised by the practice of the sacrament of penance of what constituted sinful acts and the degree of sinfulness. Such manuals presumed but never explicitly developed the broader context of the church for moral life and moral theology.[2]

A second and more theoretical strand of Catholic moral theology has been identified with the approach of Thomas Aquinas (d. 1274) whose *Summa theologiae* became the textbook for theology in the sixteenth century. Pope Leo XIII's imposition of Thomism in the late nineteenth century as *the* Catholic philosophy and theology insured the hegemony of the Thomistic method until Vatican II. Both the religious culture of the time in which Aquinas wrote and his philosophical bent called for a universal ethic, and his treatment of moral theology pays no explicit attention to the church.[3]

However, since moral theology deals with the systematic study of moral life and actions within the Christian community, this discipline must recognize the primary context of the church community. It is with the church, therefore, that we must begin. This chapter will discuss the nature of the church, in particular, its characteristic catholicity and how that affects the moral life of Christians. It also seeks to understand some possible problems and contemporary challenges connected with this catholicity.

WHAT IS THE CHURCH?

What is the church in Catholic understanding? It is the community within which the triune God comes to people, and in which people respond to God's gracious gift. Vatican II describes the church as the sign and instrument of communion with God and of unity among all humankind. Through the Spirit, the church continues in time and space the salvific work of the risen Jesus and the one he called Abba. In response the people of God, the church, give praise and thanks for the triune God's salvific work and live out their new lives as children of God, brothers and sisters of Jesus. The church community is called to be the light of the world and the salt of the earth.[4] An early name for the community of the disciples of Jesus was "The Way."[5]

The members of the church are truly the community of Jesus' disciples. Discipleship is a word often used to describe the life of members of the church. Vatican II's Constitution on the Church insists that all members of the church are called to holiness. Jesus called each and every disciple to be perfect even as the heavenly Father is perfect. All Christians in whatever state or walk of life are called to the fullness of Christian life and to the perfection of love.[6] Christian moral life thus arises within the context of the church, the community called to nurture and foster the life of discipleship.

The ecclesial or church dimension of the Christian moral life has not been explicitly developed in the two main approaches to Catholic moral theology. The moral dimension of the church has also been ignored in systematic treatments of the church in Catholic theology. Modern theologies of the church developed in the light of the controversies following the Reformation and stressed aspects that differ from Protestant approaches, for example, the Petrine office in the church and the structural elements in Roman Catholicism. Subsequent developments especially in the context of the dialogue of Vatican II put these aspects into a wider and broader framework. But even contemporary and reforming theologies of the church do not develop the moral life of the disciples of Jesus.[7]

The situation is paradoxical. Catholic theology stresses the importance of the visible community of the church, but existing systematic theologies of moral life and of the church fail to develop the ecclesial context of the moral life. At best, the teaching role of the church is emphasized in the discussion of various acts in moral theology (e.g., birth control, distributive justice issues) where church teaching authority has taken a position.

The ecclesial aspect of Catholic moral life needs to be developed in depth. God wills to make human beings holy and to save them, not as isolated individuals without any bond or link among themselves, but as a people who acknowledge and serve God in holiness. God chose the Israelites as God's own people. The church is the new Israel with whom God keeps covenant, but contemporary Catholic theology also recognizes the enduring reality of the first covenant. The messianic people of God, the church, are "a chosen race, a royal priesthood, a holy nation . . . who at times past were not a people but now are the people of God (1 Pet 2:9-10)."[8]

Most Americans tend to think of the church as a voluntary society in which like-minded individuals come together to sustain, nurture, and develop their spiritual lives. But this understanding is not the Catholic understanding and betrays individualistic presuppositions. We are not saved as individuals who then come together to deepen our spiritual lives within the community of the church. The saving love of God comes to us in and through the church. The church is the way in which God has chosen to come to us with God's saving love. We are saved by belonging to the people of God. Such is the way Catholics believe God comes to us; we find God's saving love in and through belonging to the people of God.[9]

One good illustration of this understanding of the church as the community in which God wants to encounter human beings comes from the continued practice of infant baptism. Many pastoral and practical problems arise from the practice of infant baptism, but this practice reminds us that we are not individuals first saved by God in the depths of our own hearts who only then form a community of like-minded individuals. The church is not a voluntary society like the Elks or the Lions. One does not belong to the church because one admires the pastor or the preacher or the choir or the people. One belongs to the church, the community of disciples, because it is the way that God has chosen to enter into saving love with us.

At times in its history the Catholic tradition so stressed the communitarian aspect of the church that it did not give enough importance to the individual and the individual's experience of God's saving gift. Partly in response to such deficiencies in Catholic practice, the

Protestant Reformation put more emphasis on the individual's relationship to God and downplayed the role of the church. Over time the
Catholic Church has attempted to recognize more fully the importance
and role of the individual person within the community, but even today
Catholics often criticize their church for not giving enough importance
to the needs and rights of individuals.[10] However, a truly Catholic
ecclesiology can never reduce the church to a voluntary society in the
sense that individuals join the group merely to nurture and sustain
their Christian life. The church is the way God has chosen for us, not
the means we voluntarily embrace to help ourselves as individuals.

CATHOLICITY OF THE CHURCH

The theory and practice of the church will thus greatly affect and shape
the moral life of its members. The Roman Catholic Church calls itself
catholic. The very word elucidates the reality of the church. Catholic
(with a small c) means universal and all-inclusive. The Catholic Church
is Catholic with a large C and catholic with a small c. Large C Catholic
Church refers to the totality of its Catholicity including its origins and
unique history as the Roman Catholic Church and its difference from
other churches. Catholic with a small c refers to the broader catholicity
that the Roman Catholic Church shares with many other churches. The
Nicene–Constantinopolitan Creed professes belief in the church as one,
holy, catholic, and apostolic. Ecumenical discussions within the World
Council of Churches (to which the Roman Catholic Church does not
belong) have emphasized the need for the church to be catholic in
this sense.[11]

The catholicity (small c) of the church involves four important
characteristics for our understanding of the church and how it shapes
the moral life of its members. In these four areas the Roman Catholic
Church is not necessarily different from other small c catholic churches.
These aspects can thus serve as the basis for ecumenical discussion.[12]
They spell out the church's basic catholicity—its universality and all-
inclusiveness.

INCLUSIVE IN MEMBERSHIP. First, the Catholic Church is an inclusive
community open to all and appealing to all. In the early centuries, the
church's openness to gentiles was a very significant development (Acts
10). Indeed, the ideal of catholicity is the meaning of Galatians 3:28—

there is neither Jew nor Greek, slave nor free, male nor female in Christ Jesus. The church catholic goes beyond ethnic, racial, gender, political, and economic differences. It thus differs from any and every community whose unity is based on human bonds.

The church catholic is all-embracing. Some religious groups restrict membership to the spiritually elite and perfect. But the church catholic recognizes that its members are also sinners. The Catholic tradition has distinguished two kinds of sin—mortal and venial sin. Mortal sin, from the Latin word for death, involves spiritual death and separation from God (thus meriting eternal punishment). Venial sin comes from the Latin word for pardon and refers to sin that does not destroy one's relationship to God and which can therefore be more readily pardoned and forgiven. No one in the world is perfect; venial sin exists in all. But the Catholic tradition recognizes that even people in mortal sin still belong to the church. Yes, boundaries exist but the church catholic is inclusive and recognizes that among its members, all of whom are sinful, are some who have even broken their relationship with God.[13]

If the church were the home of only the perfect, it would have a different moral ethos and a very different moral tone. One of the perennial problems in the church catholic comes precisely from this tension between its need to include sinners and the call to follow Jesus. Before Vatican II Catholics generally accepted a two-tiered division in the church between the ordinary Catholic who lived in the world and obeyed the ten commandments and those who sought perfection and followed the evangelical counsels. In this view, one who wanted to be perfect left the world and entered religion—a life based on the evangelical counsels of poverty, chastity, and obedience. But Vatican II insisted that all Christians are called to holiness, not only priests, sisters, or monks. The tension, however, remains between the call to holiness and the recognition that sinners belong to the church. The danger always persists that the church catholic will fail to be the light of the world and the salt of the earth; however, its characteristic of being open to all, including sinners, is intimately linked to the catholic understanding of the church as the way in which God offers salvation to human persons.[14]

INCLUSIVE IN ITS CONCERNS. A second characteristic of the church catholic is that its faith and moral life are inclusive and touch all aspects of reality in the world. The church catholic does not withdraw from the world but lives in the world and is directly involved with it. The Pastoral Constitution on the Church in the Modern World makes this point clear in its opening words: "The joy and hope, the grief and anguish of the people of our time, especially of those who are poor or afflicted in any way, are the joy and hope, the grief and anguish of the followers of Christ as well. Nothing that is genuinely human fails to find an echo in their hearts."[15]

Thus the church catholic has traditionally been distinguished from communities called sects. According to the now classic discussion of Ernst Troeltsch, the sect proposes a radical and perfectionist ethic, tends to have a small and limited membership, and does not become directly involved in the world but tends to withdraw from the world. Many traditional Christian sects make themselves different by insisting on the literal interpretation of the sayings of Jesus found in the Sermon on the Mount. For example, they will take no oaths. Since living in the world makes it impossible to live out this radical ethic of Jesus, sectarians generally withdraw from the world. The church, on the other hand, accepts that its members are saints and sinners living in and trying to change the world. In Troeltsch's discussion, one sees clearly the difference between models of the church and sect and how different characteristics cohere within a systematic understanding of each model.[16] The Catholic Church, according to Troeltsch and many others, best illustrates the church model although mainstream Protestant churches exemplify the same model.[17]

The church catholic also differs from an interpretation of the church and Christian community recently proposed by Stanley Hauerwas and the late John Howard Yoder. In general Hauerwas and Yoder are not strict sectarians. However, in their approach the church is primarily concerned with its own internal moral life and not directly and immediately concerned with the world. The church's witness and example can and should have some effect on the world.[18] Hauerwas begins by considering that there cannot and should not be a universal ethic. Moral identity is tradition-dependent. Consequently, his moral theology is directed at the church community itself.[19] Such an approach has appealing aspects but it is not the approach of the church catholic. The U.S. Catholic bishops' 1986 pastoral letter on the economy exemplifies the catholic approach. The letter addresses two different audiences—church members and the broader public, so that the bishops can specifically add their voice to the public debate about the direction of the U.S. economy. Church members and all human beings are called to work for a just economy.[20]

INCLUSIVE OF OTHER REALITIES. A third characteristic of the church catholic, along with its universality and all-inclusiveness, is its recognition that church members also belong to other communities, institutions, and groupings. In the past the church had a tendency to absorb these other institutions in a subordinate relationship. Think, for example, of the relationship between church and state. In the post-Constantinian era the church recognized the state as a separate reality with its own ends and means, but insisted that the state serve the higher reality of the church. One sees here the danger and temptation of subsuming the church's universality and all-inclusiveness to a hierarchical ordering.

In the twentieth century, the relationship that prevails between church and state illustrates that the Catholic Church now recognizes the proper domain of other institutions and no longer makes them directly subordinate to the church. Vatican II's Declaration on Religious Liberty clearly sets out the proper relationship of the church and state, recognizing the legitimate and independent role of each but also avoiding the total separation between them that would privatize the church and religion. The church, through its members who are both Christians and citizens, can and should work for justice in society and the state.[21] The Pastoral Constitution on the Church in the Modern World devotes a section to the rightful autonomy of earthly affairs: "If by the autonomy of earthly affairs is meant the gradual discovery, exploitation, and ordering of the laws and values of matter and society, then the demand for autonomy is perfectly in order: it is at once the claim of modernity and the desire of the Creator."[22] The last sentence is fascinating. The emphasis on rightful autonomy has obviously come to the fore with modernity and that has not always been the case. Yet this autonomy is now understood to express the desire of the Creator.

The pastoral constitution also says that methodological research in all branches of knowledge, provided it is carried out in a truly scientific manner and does not override moral laws, can never conflict with faith because the things of this world and the things of faith both derive from the same God. The footnote to this section of the constitution refers to a book on Galileo. It is the only footnote in the document that does not come from Scripture, a father or doctor of the church, a recognized theologian in the church, or a document of the magisterium.[23] The claim that faith and reason cannot contradict one another has been emphasized in Catholic tradition since the rise of scholasticism in the middle ages although in practice the Catholic Church has not always lived up to that axiom. The next chapter will develop the role of reason as a source of moral wisdom and knowledge for the Christian.

The individual Christian is a member of the church but also lives and labors in the world—with family, friends, and co-workers in the midst of cultural, political, and economic institutions. Whereas Christian faith should permeate life in all these spheres, relationships, and institutions, such institutions have their own structures and meanings that are not derived directly from faith. The Christian thus belongs to many institutions and groups that have a rightful autonomy from the church. Once again the catholic nature of the church is completely unsympathetic to a sectarian view of the world as an evil opposed to the church and the Gospel. The church catholic recognizes that it exists in the world among many other institutions and further that it must be in dialogue with these realities and even learn from them.

This understanding of catholicity also imbues the nature and role of theology in general and of moral theology in particular. Catholic theology serves three different publics—the church, the academy, and the larger world. Different emphases can be given to these different audiences, but Catholic theology is related to all. Theology is aware of and learns from other academic disciplines. Likewise, the notion that theology is in dialogue with the world is well illustrated in the Pastoral Constitution on the Church in the Modern World. The church catholic and its theology are not isolated from the academy and the world.

A sharply debated question within Roman Catholicism in the last decades is ultimately connected with the notion of catholicity: Is there a unique moral content for the Christian that differs from the moral content of other persons living in the world? The question does not concern individual vocations or functions in the church but life in the world. All admit that Christian intentionality and motivation are quite different. Many non-Christians love their enemies, forgive others, and work for social justice as Christians are called to do. Moreover, the older, natural law Catholic approach claims no unique status for its teaching other than the human nature and reason common to all humankind. Ever since *Pacem in terris* in 1963, papal social encyclicals have been addressed not only to Catholics but to all persons of good will. Thus all admit that the moral obligations of Christians and others in the world have much in common. I defend the thesis that in principle, in any given situation Christians and non-Christians can come to the same decision, but this discussion lies beyond the purpose of this book.[24]

INCLUSIVE OF DIFFERENT LEVELS. A fourth characteristic of the church catholic with its emphasis on universality and inclusiveness concerns the various embodiments of the church. The church catholic is obviously universal, but it is also very much local.

Without doubt, the Roman Catholic Church has often overemphasized the universal aspect of the church at the expense of the local church. The growing importance of the role of the papacy in the church, abetted by the First Vatican Council's definition of papal infallibility and discussion limited only to the papal role in the church, continued until Vatican II. This council then tried to overcome the one-sided development of the papacy and the universal church by spelling out the role of the college of bishops and the importance of the local or residential bishop. All bishops, with the bishop of Rome as their head, form the college of bishops which has "supreme and full authority over the universal church."[25] The local bishop is not merely a delegate of the pope but exercises a proper, ordinary, and immediate power over his diocese.[26] Vatican II also recognized that the local church is not simply a portion or branch office of the church, but that the ecclesial body of Christ is truly present in each local eucharistic community.[27] The term "local community" remains somewhat ambiguous and can refer to the church in a particular nation, a particular diocese, or even a particular parish. Today the Catholic Church recognizes that the church exists on the universal, regional, national, diocesan, and local levels, but gives much greater emphasis to the local eucharistic community. [28]

Although Vatican II offered a well-rounded understanding of the different levels of church, the new code of canon law (1983) has failed to give enough importance and independence to regional and national churches. Catholic ecclesiology and canon law need to better incorporate the principle of subsidiarity into their understanding of the church. This principle plays an important role in Catholic social ethics. According to this principle, the higher level should help the lower level do all that it can and only take for itself that which cannot be done properly on the lower level.[29]

Finally, recent discussions about inculturation call for the church to be more truly incarnated in the local culture. In the past, a false universalism too readily identified the church with western culture.[30] This process of inculturation will have significant ramifications for moral theology.

MEDIATION AND HIERARCHICAL STRUCTURE

Roman Catholic ecclesiology shares the foregoing characteristics with all churches that accept the mark of catholicity. There are, however, two important ecclesial characteristics that are distinctive of Roman Catholicism—the emphasis on mediation and the hierarchical structure and organization of the church.

MEDIATION. The Roman Catholic emphasis on mediation is somewhat connected with the church's catholicity, but it is also the most distinctive aspect of Roman Catholic theology and self-understanding. Sometimes the word "sacramentality"[31] or the term "analogical imagination"[32] is used to describe the same basic reality. Mediation refers to the fact that the divine is mediated in and through the human and the natural. All creation shows forth the work of the Creator and gives us a glimpse of the Creator. The created, the natural, and the human are not evil but basically good and contain within themselves a reflection of their Creator.

The Catholic understanding of the church illustrates the reality and importance of human mediation. As in Jesus the divine became incarnate in the human, so too in the church, the divine works in and through the human. The church is not primarily an invisible reality involving a relationship between God and the saved. Nor is the external aspect of the church merely a coat or a garment to cover over the divine element. The divine aspect and the human, the invisible and the visible, are united. The church is a visible community with visible structures that mediate God's loving presence in our world. Many other churches do not attach as much significance to the human or visible and structural aspects of the church as perhaps they should. However, the problem in the Catholic tradition is a tendency to identify the human church too closely with Jesus.

The church carries out its mission and function primarily through the sacraments which again illustrate the reality of mediation. As Vatican II's Constitution on the Liturgy affirms, the liturgy is the summit toward which the activity of the church is directed; it is also the fount from which all her power flows.[33] The eucharist is the heart and center of the liturgy and the place where the church most fully expresses its true reality.[34] But the eucharist is primarily a meal. The solemn or celebratory meal is the primary way in which human families and friends gather to celebrate their love and make themselves present to one another. They share food, converse, remember the past, tell stories, and sustain one another in love and friendship. So the liturgy takes this fundamental human way of family and friends coming together in love to remember, to sustain, and to nurture one another and makes it the sign of the reality of God's presence among them. Jesus is present to us in and through the celebratory meal. Each eucharistic celebration recalls the many meals Jesus shared with his own disciples and the final meal that came to be known as the Last Supper. The other sacraments also illustrate how the divine is mediated through natural and created things. Baptism is conferred with water—the natural significance and meaning of water (life-sustaining, refreshing, cleansing) merging with the historical and salvific (Noah's Ark, the Israelites passing through the Red Sea). Oil is used in the sacraments to anoint certain ministers in the church and to symbolize the healing love of Jesus for the sick.

The Catholic tradition, especially in its Thomistic philosophical expression, insisted that reason can prove the existence of God by going from the natural and the created world to the divine. Analogy or mediation forms the basis for claiming that one can reason from the order of the universe back to the all-knowing orderer whom we call God. The shadow of God is present in all creation, and we can see something of God in all that is. God not only tells us something about creation and the human, but creation and the human tell us something about God.[35] Catholicism in the past gave great importance to natural theology or theodicy as an understanding of God based totally on human reason. Today some people question this emphasis on proving God's existence strictly from reason, but natural theology's existence and role in Catholic tradition exemplifies the Catholic insistence on mediation.[36]

Karl Barth once claimed that his major problem with Roman Catholicism was its *and*. Catholics believe in Scripture and tradition, faith and reason, grace and works, Jesus and the church, Mary and the saints. I disagree with Barth's conclusion, but he is correct in pointing to the distinctive Catholic emphasis on mediation, which is the reason for the *and* in all these pairs.[37]

This emphasis on mediation has important ramifications for moral life and moral theology. A very important manifestation of mediation is the Catholic understanding of grace and works. Some Protestants have spoken about grace only, but the Catholic tradition recognizes the importance of the human response. The conjunction between grace and works serves as the whole basis for the importance of the moral life and for theoretical and systematic reflection on it.[38]

The Catholic tradition recognizes the role of the church and the disciples of Jesus in mediating the mission and work of the risen Jesus in time and space. This work involves not only the internal life of the church but also activity in the broader human community. According to the 1971 international synod of bishops, action on behalf of justice and the transformation of the world are a necessary element of preaching the Gospel—that is, of the church's mission to redeem the human race and liberate it from every oppressive situation.[39] Thus the Christian and the church continue through their actions the redeeming work of Jesus.

The importance of works and the role of human response in the reality of grace are also illustrated in the sacrament of penance. By our sins we offend God and need the mercy and forgiveness of the loving parent and the community. The sacrament of penance thus shows the great importance and significance of human actions—contrition and absolution coalescing in forgiveness.

The Roman Catholic insistence on mediation strongly grounds the basic goodness of the natural world and human reason and experience. Whatever is created is good and can even tell us something about God. Another example of the Catholic *and* is the insistence on both faith and reason and the assertion that there can be no conflict between the two.[40] Thus, human reason and all that is created constitute important sources of Christian moral wisdom and knowledge. Catholic moral theology is not sectarian; it shares this much with other human approaches to ethics.

Andrew M. Greeley maintains, on the basis of his sociological studies, that Catholics have a distinctive imagination different from the Protestant imagination. This perduring Catholic imagination is grounded in what he calls the analogical imagination and what I have called mediation. Greeley has designed surveys that demonstrate the existence and importance of the Catholic imagination with its emphasis on the sacramental presence of God in all things and on a communitarian understanding of the human person. This Catholic imagination helps to explain why Catholics like being Catholic and remain in the Catholic Church despite problems with church leadership and disagreements with some official church teachings. Thus, Greeley's sociological findings support the distinctive Catholic emphasis on mediation developed here.[41]

POSSIBLE PROBLEMS OF MEDIATION. The Catholic emphasis on mediation with its acceptance of basic human goodness is replete with problems that have not always been avoided in the past. The primary danger comes from the tendency to identify the divine with the human. This error has occurred especially in ecclesiology. Too often the church was seen as only divine or as fully embodying the reign of God. The church was thought to be perfect, holy, and without spot. Vatican II recognized that the danger of triumphalism is a practical illustration of the harm inherent in this error. It therefore emphasized the pilgrim nature of the church—the notion that the church itself is continually growing and developing to overcome its own sinfulness.[42] In the light of the teaching of Vatican II, the church is no longer identified as the reign of God but as a sign or sacrament of the reign of God. The problem of too closely relating the church to Jesus also comes from seeing the church exclusively in the light of carrying on the mission of Jesus. The church is the body of Christ but also the people of God—fallible and weak but sustained, nourished, and guided by the Holy Spirit in its pilgrim existence.[43]

A related danger or problem comes from a poor understanding of mediation which tends to absolutize or give too much importance to the second element or the aspect after the *and*. Thus in understanding Jesus and the church, the church has at times seemed to be more important than Jesus. Likewise in the phrase "Scripture and tradition," tradition can seem to have an independent value apart from Scripture. And in morality Catholics have at times emphasized human works at the expense of grace. But this interpretation is Pelagianism or semi-Pelagianism—the heresy that claims we save ourselves by our own works and not by the grace of God. Invariably, even today, Protestants and Catholics give different answers to the question of how the Christian is saved. Protestants usually respond by saying we are saved by faith, while Catholics often say that we are saved by obeying God's law or keeping the commandments. This popular testimony shows how at times the Catholic tradition has overstressed works at the expense of grace.

HIERARCHICAL STRUCTURE. A second unique characteristic of Roman Catholicism involves the hierarchical nature of the church. Ecclesiology in the Roman Catholic Church includes the role of pope and bishops in the church. As mentioned, Vatican II tried to overcome the one-sided emphasis on the papacy in the pre-Vatican II church by insisting on the collegiality of bishops with the pope in governing the whole church and by emphasizing the bishop's role as a proper and immediate shepherd in his own diocese. The hierarchical nature of the church also has significant ramifications for moral theology because of the authoritative nature of church teaching. Catholic teaching recognizes the role of the magisterium (more accurately, the hierarchical magisterium) or teaching office of pope and bishops. The teaching authority and role of pope and bishops is usually described as referring to matters of both faith and morals.[44] The papal magisterium has issued authoritative teachings in many areas of personal and social morality. A 1962 textbook in medical ethics, for example, refers to the authoritative teaching of Pope Pius XII on almost forty different issues.[45]

However, within the church, one cannot reserve the role of teaching and formation to those who hold hierarchical offices. Vatican II has insisted that the church is primarily the people of God. Through baptism all Christians share in the threefold office of Jesus as priest, teacher, and ruler.[46] Thus, through baptismal commitment everyone in the church is called to teach and share the good news of faith and its implications for life with others. Such an understanding affects the way in which the whole church goes about its moral teaching and learning. Before Vatican II a distinction was often made between the teaching church and the learning church. The teaching church was the hierarchical magisterium and the learning church was everyone else. Truth trickled down from the teaching church to the learning church. However, this distinction can no longer be maintained in the light of the role of the whole people of God.[47] In addition the Catholic Church has long recognized the role that theologians play in the church. Perhaps the most heated discussions within the Catholic Church in the last two decades have centered about the exact relationship between the hierarchical teaching office, the experience of the people of God, and the role of theologians. Our final chapter will discuss this question in great detail.

CATHOLIC PRACTICE

In theory the Roman Catholic Church is truly catholic in the sense of being universal, inclusive, and in dialogue with all others. The practice of the Catholic Church well illustrates this approach. The Catholic Church borrowed some of its structural aspects from the institutions of the Roman Empire.[48] For example, Thomas Aquinas (d. 1274), the greatest figure in the history of Catholic theology, borrowed heavily from the works of Aristotle.[49] Or—for an example closer to home—

look at how the Catholic Church in the United States has structured its social mission. Education, social service, and care for the sick have always formed an important aspect of the church's mission. Now, however, Catholic higher education, health care, and social services are institutionalized in a way that is truly catholic. These institutions include in their governing bodies, their employees, and their clients both Catholics and non-Catholics. In addition such institutions could not survive in their present form without money from the government. Catholic Charities, for example, receives about two-thirds of its budget from government money.[50]

Since Vatican II, the Catholic Church in the United States has structured its social mission in another way which also shows the catholic influence. The Campaign for Human Development started by the U.S. Catholic bishops over twenty-five years ago recognizes that social change involves more than providing services for those in need. Structural change is absolutely necessary. This campaign helps finance and support community action programs in which members of local, pluralistic communities can come together, determine their needs, and work together for the structural changes that will fulfill these basic needs. Here the church supports community groups comprising people of all religions or none to help people help themselves. The direction and action of the group come from the people themselves and not from the church.[51] The Catholic Church strives to be inclusive and universal in theory and in its work with all people of good will to obtain a greater justice in our world.

DANGERS IN THE CATHOLIC APPROACH

The Catholic Church has many strengths in theory and in practice, and also some potential dangers. The primary danger arises from a temptation to conform the church too much to the *Zeitgeist* or world around it. Historically, the Roman Catholic Church has not always avoided this danger. Often the church has aligned itself with those in power and with people of affluence and influence. Many, for example, have pointed to the church's failure to condemn the Holocaust for fear it would harm the church.[52] In the United States the fear has always been that the church might too readily accommodate itself to the American ethos and culture.

The basis for these temptations comes from the positive Catholic understanding that whatever God made is good. The church catholic must always be in dialogue with reality, willing and open to learn about God and human actions from all that exists in our world. But an inclusive church open to all and living in the world must not lose the dynamism and commitment that distinguish it as the disciples of Jesus. Specifically, the church must not be so conformed to the world that it forgets that God's goodness in the world is still confined by human finitude, sinfulness, and nonconformity to the fullness of God's reign.

An old axiom of the spiritual life counsels the individual to act against the predominant vice or fault. In an analogous way the church catholic must confront the dangers inherent in catholicity. A number of important steps can help to alleviate such dangers.

First, the universal call of all to holiness and the fullness of Christian life, which was so clearly taught at Vatican II, must become more central in the teaching and life of the church. This call serves as the primary antidote to the danger of a church that can too easily lose the flavor of its salt. All are called to be perfect even as the gracious God is perfect. Perfection or holiness does not mean that we must leave the world and our many obligations in the world, but faith should permeate all our relations and actions in daily life.

Second, and intimately connected with the call to holiness, is the call for continual conversion. No one has fully responded to the gift of God; we all fall short. No one who meditates seriously on the Sermon on the Mount can ever say: "All these things I have kept since my youth." The call to continual conversion means that the individual Christian and the church must always be self-critical. We must continually be alert to the danger of too easily buying into the reigning *Zeitgeist*. The Roman Catholic Church has had a perennial difficulty in recognizing and acknowledging its own sin and failings. Recall our tendency to identify the church totally with the divine. However, recent emphasis on the pilgrim church provides an antidote; it underscores the need for the church to be constantly self-critical and always willing to confess its sins, ask for forgiveness, and strive to be a more faithful witness to the reign of God.

Third, the church catholic must recognize and foster a prophetic element in the church. Prophecy has always played an important role in the Judeo-Christian tradition. The prophets of the Hebrew Bible constantly upbraided the people of God for their infidelity and inveighed against their failure to hear the cry of the poor and the oppressed. The prophetic voice is always disturbing. Prophets are not the easiest people to live with, but the church must encourage the prophetic voice no matter how disturbing it might be. Without the prophet's voice and witness, the church will never hear the calls to holiness and continual conversion. However, as there are dangers and temptations for the church catholic, so also are there dangers and temptations for prophets. The prophet, too, must always be self-critical and quick to recognize temptations of delusion and self-righteousness. But the church catholic is always willing to encourage and listen to the prophetic voice no matter how painful or difficult it might be.

Fourth, the church must recognize different vocations and callings within the church—and their close association with the prophetic function. The church catholic, has traditionally recognized that in this imperfect world justice and peace do not always lie together. Sometimes violence is the only way to insure that some measure of justice is achieved. Nations in this imperfect world cannot always be pacifist; however, individuals within the church can be and (thanks be to God) are sometimes called to be pacifists.[53] How can both pacifism and just war (or its equivalent) be acceptable positions within the church? Yes, there is some overlap between them in that the just war theory clearly contains a presumption against violence. Ultimately, however, from a moral perspective, the two positions are contradictory.[54] Nonetheless, from an ecclesial perspective the church catholic can and does recognize both positions as exemplified in hierarchical teachings. Nations cannot be pacifists today, and many individuals will accept some use of violence, but there are also pacifists in the church. Peace is an important value in human existence that is too often forgotten about or discarded. Pacifists are called by God to bear witness to this very significant value.

The church catholic recognizes many important moral values that are not absolute but exist in relationship with many other values. Among them, however, certain values are so important that individuals are called to bear witness to these values for the sake of the church and the larger world. Such, in my judgment are those values included in the tradition of religious life as we have known it until now. The vows of poverty, chastity, and obedience do not make monks or nuns better Christians than those who do not take these vows. More precisely, they are not called to a higher state of life or holiness but to bear witness to these important values.

Many people, especially in the Protestant tradition, have understood monasticism as a flight from the world and religious communities as very similar to sects.[55] However, such is not the case. Religious life serves the world. Humorously we can note that some of the best liqueurs in the world are named after monks, but more seriously, Thomas Cahill has recently pointed out the role the Irish monks played in preserving western civilization during the so-called Dark Ages.[56] Thomas Merton, too, has shown that contemporary monasticism is not a flight from the world.[57] Monks and religious strive to bear witness to the world concerning the significance of poverty, chastity, and obedience; they do not necessarily flee the world.

Today the calling or vocation to bear witness to particular virtues must be extended to all Christians. A significant number of Christians bear witness to voluntary poverty. The whole church cannot embrace such poverty, but the church as a whole and all Christians living in the world must guard against becoming entrapped by the allure of wealth. Today other Christians voluntarily make themselves one with the oppressed and powerless—a magnificent witness that serves the church and the world. We in the church must recognize and support this vocational witness that is not a flight *from* the world but an important witness *for* it. The church catholic must make room for and encourage such witness. Those who accept this call give their lives for the life of the world and prevent the church catholic from becoming too conformed to the world around us.

CONTEMPORARY CHALLENGES TO THE CATHOLIC APPROACH

The morality of the Catholic Church is an inclusive and universal morality that seeks to affect the whole world. The Catholic Church is concerned about what happens to people everywhere and not just about what goes on within the church. Many reasons justify this catholic or universal social ethics. The belief in creation reminds us that we are brothers and sisters of all human beings since we recognize God as mother and father to us all. In Genesis the name given to the first human being is Adam which means "man" or, for us today, "human being." The first human being is not identified as belonging to a tribe or clan or race but simply as "human." The papal social encyclicals, beginning with Pope Leo XIII in 1891, promulgate the Catholic understanding of morality. The popes propose a social teaching not only for Catholics and all Christians; Catholic social teaching is directed to all people of good will.

POSTMODERNISM AND LIBERATION THEOLOGIES. Universalism and inclusivism in morality and ethics have been strongly challenged in recent years. Postmodernism attacks the theory of universality in morality; in practice struggles for justice and equality by groups that have been marginalized and oppressed by the larger society also bring to light the dangers of universalism and essentialism.

Postmodernism has disagreed with modernism's acceptance of the rational, objective, neutral, value-free, universalist perspective of the ideal knower. This understanding, which was intimately connected with the Enlightenment, has been the major and perhaps the only way of approaching knowledge and education in the modern western world. The ideal scientist is the person who has these characteristics and can therefore better understand and judge more objectively what is occurring.

On both the theoretical and practical levels liberation theology in all its embodiments (e.g., South American, African-American, feminist) challenges this understanding of the ideal knower. There is no such thing as a neutral, objective, value-free, universalist perspective. Everyone comes to the scene with his or her own background, commitments, and history. We have often been reminded lately that history is not the objective science we once thought it was. History has always been written by the winners. If Native Americans were still the predominant group in this country, we would not accept as a historical fact the notion that Columbus discovered America.

The universalism and essentialism connected with the Enlightenment have had disastrous effects on the needs and concerns of the poor, the marginalized, and the oppressed. These people have either been forgotten or totally absorbed by the dominant ideology. Liberation theology in Latin America begins with the experience of the oppressed and the marginalized in society. But such an approach also recognizes that the Christian God is not a neutral, value-free observer. God is prejudiced. In our culture, and often for good reasons, prejudice is a pejorative term. However, the root meaning of the word is simply a prejudgment. The Judeo-Christian tradition recognizes that God is definitely on the side of the poor. Although others will oppress the poor, God will be their defender and supporter. The psalmist reminds us that God hears the cry of the poor. The prophetic books of the Hebrew Bible strongly support such an understanding of God's prejudice. Our God has a special love and concern for the poor and is neither neutral nor value-free.[58]

Feminist theology and ethics, especially as developed in this country, show how a universal and essentialist approach has distorted commonly held perceptions of reality. The claim to offer a universally valid, neutral, and objective approach to the role of women in society (and the church) was in reality the imposition of patriarchy by the dominant group in society. Women were assigned a subordinate, private, and generally passive role. Patriarchy has seriously affected the Catholic Church and its tradition. Feminist ethics begins with the experience and particularity of women. Most feminists in the beginning of this movement were white, middle and upper class American women. Some African-American women pointed out that their experience was quite different, and womanist theology and ethics emerged from this experience.[59] Hispanic women, too, recognized that their experience was different from both the middle class white women and African-American women and began developing a *mujerista* theology and ethics.[60] To their credit most feminist theologians and ethicists recognize the need for these varying approaches. Feminist theology and ethics in general are still too universal and continue to struggle to be accountable to the experiences of particular women in diverse cultures and situations.

In theory, and in conjunction with feminism and other defenders of the marginalized, postmodernism insists on the particular and diverse, not the universal and the all-inclusive. Modernism's emphasis on the universal had provided a means to further subordinate and even eradicate the "other" who is not like us. Postmodernism deconstructs the self and glories in emphasizing the particular and the different.[61] But as a result, postmodernism often has no place for the universal and even denies the possibility of a universal ethics or morality.

RESPONSE OF CATHOLIC ETHICS. Where does and should Catholic ethics stand with regard to these developments? Catholic moral theology has also opposed the Enlightenment, especially its stress on individualism, autonomy, and freedom.[62] However, the Catholic tradition has, in its own way, stressed universalism and essentialism. The essential nature of human beings, according to this tradition, can be known by reflecting on its sameness all over the world. From this universal nature, reason can deduce how human beings should act. Manuals of moral theology stress this essentialist, universalist, and deductive approach to moral theology which has recently been described as classicism. Classicism emphasizes the universal, the immutable, and the unchanging, while employing a deductive methodology well illustrated in the syllogism. The syllogism contains a major premise (all humans are rational); a minor premise (Mary is a human); and a conclusion (therefore, Mary is rational). The conclusion is just as certain as the premises if the logic is correct. Certitude was thus the goal of a deductive methodology.[63]

Many commentators, following Bernard Lonergan, have pointed out that the most significant change at Vatican II was the shift from classicism to historical consciousness. Vatican II brought about important changes in the Catholic Church and Catholic self-understanding, but the church still has the same Scripture and the same tradition it has always had. What has changed is the way we look at reality. Historical consciousness gives more importance to the particular, the individual, and the contingent. In addition, historical consciousness pays greater attention to human subjectivity. Such an understanding employs a more inductive methodology—one that searches for the best hypothesis, rather than absolute certitude. Historical consciousness avoids the extreme dangers of classicism on the one hand and sheer existentialism on the other. Sheer existentialism sees the particular human person with no real connection to the past and future and with no binding relationships to other human beings and the world.[64] Chapter six will elaborate in greater detail the change from classicism to historical consciousness in Catholic social teaching.

Post-Vatican II historical consciousness wants to give more weight to the particular, the individual, and the historical, but it does not want to give up or deny some aspects of universality. Postmodernism seems at times to deny the universal in the name of protecting the particular and the diverse which appear to be threatened by the universal. Catholics have addressed the challenge of postmodernism especially in the area of liberation theology and feminist theology. Most Catholic thinkers in these areas recognize the great failure to give enough importance to the particular, the other, and the diverse in the past, but they do not deny some universalism today.

Liberation theology, especially in the Roman Catholic tradition, holds on to particularity, diversity and also the universal by insisting on a preferential option for the poor, not an exclusive option. God loves all people, but God has a preferential option for the poor.[65] Liberation theology's Christology and soteriology also stress the particular and the concrete. The pre-Vatican II manuals of dogmatic theology neglected soteriology and stressed rather the metaphysical and ontological aspects of Christ (one person—two natures) rather than the saving work of Jesus. Liberation theology emphasizes that Jesus is savior and liberator; in the process liberation theology develops a Christology from below as differentiated from the older Christology from above. Christology from above begins with the preexisting *Logos* who is consubstantial with the Father. The *Logos* then takes on a human nature and saves us by dying and rising for all. Without denying the divinity of Jesus or the fact that salvation is open to all, the liberation approach puts more emphasis on the humanity of Jesus and the historical circumstances surrounding his life and death. Salvation and redemption thus become more particular and concrete. As Jesus was a victim who was unjustly put to death, he stands in solidarity with all victims of oppression and injustice. Jesus sides with the poor, the outcast, and the oppressed. Redemption is thus particular and concrete and not merely abstract with no particular differentiations. But still, Jesus came to save all.[66]

Feminist ethicists in the United States have been dealing with the problem of the particular and the universal for the last few years. Attention to diversity, otherness, and difference is the essential methodological concern of contemporary feminist theologies. Their method calls for attention to women's experiences, differences in the analysis of subjectivity and language, and the need for a hermeneutic of suspicion with regard to past traditions since they have been so deeply affected by patriarchy.[67] Feminists are very aware of the social construction of moral norms, the grave inadequacy of past views of women's nature, and the need to appreciate diversity and particularity, though Catholic feminists also realize the need to avoid total relativism. Margaret Farley, for instance, is conscious of the problems that result from an essentialism and abstract universalism that all too readily ignore particularity and the diversity of persons in their concrete context. Farley tries to develop a feminist version of respect for persons that is the same for all persons, male or female, whatever their diversity and particularity. She proposes a revised understanding of autonomy and of relationality as obligating features of persons. An obligation to respect persons requires that we honor their freedom and respond to their needs, that we value difference as well as sameness, and that we attend to the concrete realities of our own and others' lives.[68]

Anne E. Patrick appreciates many of the chief points of postmodernism with its attention to discourse, its recognition of plurality and ambiguity, and its acknowledgment of the moral significance of linguistic forms and the politics of discourse. Epistemology can never again claim to reach the abstract certainty and stability expected of it in the past. It offers instead a relatively adequate knowledge within given historical circumstances. In discussing the moral self, attention must be paid to a critical analysis of social, historical, political, psychological, and economic factors. For Patrick, however, feminist ethics can never become relativistic.[69]

Lisa Sowle Cahill, in her presidential address to the Catholic Theological Society of America, insisted that feminist theology is thoroughly particular, historical, and concrete, but it is also committed to equal personal dignity, equal mutual respect, and equal social power for women and men. Some feminists often rely too uncritically on postmodern understandings. Cahill's view of postmodernism is more negative than Patrick's precisely because she feels many postmodernists seem to deny any possibility of the universal. Such feminists either retreat romantically into tradition-bound and limited approaches that do not allow for any intercultural comparison or evaluation, or buy a no-holds-barred deconstruction of all social reality so that any communality is lost. Cahill wants to retain the importance of objectivity and some universality while rejecting the Enlightenment ideal of abstract reason and ahistorical universalism. She therefore revises somewhat the Roman Catholic natural law tradition accepting an objective moral order, which involves the basic goods that constitute human flourishing, that can be known by reasonable reflection on human experience.

Like Patrick, Cahill appeals to Roman Catholic theologian David Tracy who expresses the reliability and generalizability of truth judgments in ethics in terms of analogy. In such an approach we can understand and evaluate justice and injustice in different cultures by virtue of their resemblance to our own experience. Cahill wants to combine the historical consciousness of postmodernism with the inductive ethical approach of the Aristotelian-Thomistic tradition. Truth claims, especially through praxis and prudence, can be grounded in the culturally mediated but reliable stratum of common human experience. Cahill wants to move away from the manualistic natural law approach often associated with Catholic moral theology before Vatican II with its emphasis on abstract essentialism, a priori reasoning, and deduction, and toward a renewal of ethics in an objective moral order discovered through experience, praxis, and classical reason set within an intercultural context.[70]

The signs of the times point to the imperative of recognizing particularity and diversity while at the same time maintaining some universality and unity. On the political scene countries today are being torn apart by religious and tribal differences, and in the United States the divisions among races and cultures are becoming more acute—

especially in many large cities. Likewise the economic gap between the wealthy and the poor is ever growing in this country. In the midst of all these differences and divisions it is hard to maintain universality and unity. Can people with so many differences live together in peace and harmony in a particular country, in a hemisphere, and on the globe? This practical question is facing all societies but is obviously more acute in some countries than in others. On the economic scene we are beginning to experience a global economy, but we desperately need a global ethic to bring about greater justice. We have been conscious for so long of the great economic gap between the first world and the two-thirds world, but we have done little or nothing to close that gap. In the light of these needs and with the greater emphasis on the global aspect of human realities, the World Parliament of Religions tried to develop a global ethic in Chicago in 1993.[71] International organizations now stress the importance of universal human rights that are applicable to all people in all places, but they—and we—must also acknowledge the great difficulty in agreeing on what these rights are.[72] The challenge for all humanity today, as well as for the church catholic, is to hold on to particularity and diversity while still claiming some universality and unity.

In the past there can be no doubt that the Roman Catholic Church, in both ecclesiology and ethics, put too much emphasis on the essential and universal and not enough on the particular, the individual, and the contingent. Now the challenge for us as church is to recognize greater particularity and diversity while also maintaining some universality and unity. The shift to historical consciousness and the dialogue with postmodernism as illustrated in Catholic feminist thought can help us recognize fewer certainties and greater ambiguities than were found in the older Catholic approaches.

This chapter has shown how the reality of the church guides and directs moral life in the church and our reflection on that morality. The Catholic Church is not a sect but a gathering of saints and sinners all of whom are called to holiness. The Catholic Church lives in the world and cooperates with other people of good will in working for a freer, more just, participative, and sustainable world. The temptation for Catholics is that they might forget the call to holiness and too easily conform themselves to cultural understandings. The Catholic tradition needs to be aware of this temptation and to struggle against it. Inclusiveness and universality constitute two important characteristics of the morality rooted in the Catholic Church. Contemporary developments, for example, postmodernism and liberation theologies, have rightly criticized too great an emphasis on universality. More attention must be paid to the particular, the individual, and the diverse. However, Catholic morality must resist relativism and retain a chastened and more nuanced universality and inclusiveness.

The Roman Catholic understanding of the church provides very significant direction and parameters for Catholic moral practice and theology.

N O T E S

1. No one has written a definitive history of moral theology. Louis Vereecke, the recognized authority in the field, has not published a general history, though he has published four volumes of printed notes for his students at the Accademia Alfonsiana in Rome. Entitled *Storia della teologia morale moderna*, these volumes have been widely diffused and cited, and they are for public sale. They cover the period from 1300 to 1789—*Storia della teologia morale dal XIV° al XVI° secolo: da Guglielmo d' Ockham a Martin Lutero* (1300–1520); *Storia della teologia morale in spagna nel XVI° secolo e origine delle "Institutiones Morales"* (1520–1600); *Storia della teologia morale nel XVII° secolo: la crisi della teologia morale* (1600–1700); *Storia della teologia morale nel XVIII° secolo: Concina e S. Alfonso de' Liguori, l'Aufklarung* (1700–1789). Summaries of Vereecke's historical research have appeared—L. Vereecke, "Moral Theology, History of (700 to Vatican Council I)," *New Catholic Encyclopedia* (New York: McGraw-Hill, 1967), 9, pp. 1119–22; L. Vereecke, "Storia della teologia morale," *Nuovo dizionario di teologia morale* (Milano: Paoline, 1990), pp. 1314–38. A very helpful collection of his essays has been published—Louis Vereecke, *De Guillaume d'Ockham à Saint Alphonse de Liguori: Études d'histoire de la théologie morale moderne* 1300–1787 (Rome: Collegium S. Alfonsi de Urbe, 1986). The best available one volume history of moral theology is Guiseppe Angelini and Ambrogio Valsecchi, *Disegno storico della teologia morale* (Bologna: Dehoniane, 1972).

2. For my discussion of the development and approach of the manuals, see Charles E. Curran, *The Origins of Moral Theology in the United States: Three Different Approaches* (Washington, D.C.: Georgetown University Press, 1997), pp. 12–167.

3. For a classic view of Aquinas's philosophy, see Etienne Gilson, *The Christian Philosophy of St. Thomas Aquinas* (New York: Random House, 1956); for a contemporary theological perspective, see Thomas F. O'Meara, *Thomas Aquinas Theologian* (Notre Dame, Ind.: University of Notre Dame Press, 1996).

4. Constitution on the Church, nn. 1–17, in *Vatican Council II: The Conciliar and Post Conciliar Documents*, ed. Austin Flannery, rev. ed. (Collegeville, Minn.: Liturgical Press, 1992), pp. 350–69; for a summary of Vatican II's teaching on the church, see Michael A. Fahey, "Church," in *Systematic Theology: Roman Catholic Perspectives*, 2 vols., ed. Francis Schüssler Fiorenza and John P. Galvin (Minneapolis, Minn.: Fortress, 1991), 2, pp. 33–43.

5. Acts 9:2; 18:25–26; 19:9, 23; 22:4; 24:14, 22.

6. Constitution on the Church, nn. 39–42, in *Vatican Council II*, ed. Flannery, pp. 396–402.

7. Hans Küng, *The Church* (New York: Sheed and Ward, 1968); Fahey, *Systematic Theology*, eds. Fiorenza and Galvin, 2, pp. 3–74.

8. Constitution on the Church, n. 9, in *Vatican Council II*, ed. Flannery, p. 359.

9. Catholicism must, therefore, deal with the possibility of salvation outside the church. Today all recognize that God's salvific call is addressed to all, but they still have some type of relationship to the church. See Francis A. Sullivan, *Salvation Outside the Church? Tracing the History of the Catholic Response* (New York: Paulist, 1992).

10. Hans Küng and Leonard Swidler, eds., *The Church in Anguish: Has the Vatican Betrayed Vatican II?* (San Francisco: Harper & Row, 1987).

11. Norman Goodall, ed., *The Upsala Report* (Geneva: World Council of Churches, 1968), pp. 11–18. See also *Catholicity and Apostolicity*, a special issue of *One in Christ* 6, n. 3 (1970), and Patrick W. Fuerth, *The Concept of Catholicity in the Documents of the World Council of Churches* (Rome: Anselmiana, 1973).

12. Basilio Petrà, "Il dialogo etico interconfessionale: Considerazioni e prospettive," *Studia Moralia* 34 (1996): 295–321.

13. Marcellinus Zalba, *Theologiae moralis summa*, 3 vols. (Madrid: Biblioteca de autores cristianos, 1952–1958), 1, pp. 609–32, 708–13.

14. Sociological studies confirm the theological understanding of the Roman Catholic Church as embracing people with different levels of commitment. See William V. D'Antonio et al., *Laity, American and Catholic: Transforming the Church* (Kansas City, Mo.: Sheed & Ward, 1996), pp. 131–44.

15. Pastoral Constitution on the Church in the Modern World, n. 1, in *Vatican Council II*, ed. Flannery, p. 903.

16. Ernst Troeltsch, *The Social Teaching of the Christian Churches*, 2 vols. (New York: Harper Torchbooks, 1960), 2, pp. 691–729.

17. Ibid., pp. 461–65.

18. For an analysis of Yoder's approach from a Catholic perspective, see Kenneth P. Hallahan, "The Social Ethics of Non-Resistance: The Writings of Mennonite Theologian John Howard Yoder Analyzed from a Roman Catholic Perspective" (Ph.D. Diss., The Catholic University of America, 1997).

19. For his most systematic work, see Stanley Hauerwas, *The Peaceable Kingdom: A Primer in Christian Ethics* (Notre Dame, Ind.: University of Notre Dame Press, 1983); also Stanley Hauerwas, *Where Resident Aliens Live: Exercises for Christian Practice* (Nashville, Tenn.: Abingdon, 1996).

20. National Conference of Catholic Bishops, *Economic Justice for All: Pastoral Letter on Catholic Social Teaching and the U.S. Economy* (Washington: National Conference of Catholic Bishops, 1986), n. 27, pp. 12–13.

21. Declaration on Religious Liberty, in *Vatican Council II*, ed. Flannery, pp. 799–812.

22. Pastoral Constitution on the Church in the Modern World, n. 36, in *Vatican Council II*, ed. Flannery, p. 935.

23. Ibid.

24. Charles E. Curran and Richard A. McCormick, eds., *Readings in Moral Theology No. 2: The Distinctiveness of Christian Ethics* (New York: Paulist, 1980); Vincent MacNamara, *Faith and Ethics: Recent Roman Catholicism* (Washington, D.C.: Georgetown University Press, 1985).

25. Constitution on the Church, n. 22, in *Vatican Council II*, ed. Flannery, p. 375.

26. Ibid., n. 27, p. 383.

27. Ibid., n. 26, p. 381.

28. Fahey, in *Systematic Theololgy*, ed. Fiorenza and Galvin, 2, p. 39.

29. John Mahoney, "Subsidiarity in the Church," *Month* 21 (1988): 968–74.

30. S. Iniobong Udoidem, *Pope John Paul II on Inculturation: Theory and Practice* (Lanham, Md.: University Press of America, 1996): Eugene Hillman, *Toward an African Christianity: Inculturation Applied* (New York: Paulist, 1993).

31. Richard P. McBrien, *Catholicism*, rev. ed. (San Francisco: Harper, 1994), pp. 9–12.

32. David Tracy, *The Analogical Imagination: Christian Theology and the Culture of Pluralism* (New York: Crossroad, 1981).

33. Constitution on the Sacred Liturgy, n. 10, in *Vatican Council II*, ed. Flannery, p. 6.

34. Ibid., nn. 47–58, pp. 16–19.

35. Thomas Aquinas, *Summa theologiae*, 4 vols. (Rome: Marietti, 1952), *Ia*, q. 2, a. 3.

36. McBrien, *Catholicism*, pp. 209–23.

37. From a Catholic perspective see Hans Urs von Balthasar, *The Theology of Karl Barth* (New York: Holt, Rinehart, and Winston, 1971), pp. 40–41.

38. Joseph P. Wawrykow, *God's Grace and Human Action: "Merit" in the Theology of Thomas Aquinas* (Notre Dame, Ind.: University of Notre Dame Press, 1995).

39. Synod of Bishops, 1971, *Justita in mundo*, in *Catholic Social Thought: The Documentary Heritage*, ed. David J. O'Brien and Thomas A. Shannon (Maryknoll, N.Y.: Orbis, 1992), p. 289.

40. Robert Sokolowski, *The God of Faith and Reason: Foundations of Christian Theology* (Washington, D.C.: Catholic University of America Press, 1995).

41. Andrew M. Greeley, *The Catholic Myth: The Behavior and Beliefs of American Catholics* (New York: Charles Scribner's Sons, 1990), especially pp. 34–64.

42. Constitution on the Church, nn. 48–51, in *Vatican Council II*, ed. Flannery, pp. 407–13.

43. Ibid., n. 3, p. 351.

44. Ibid., nn. 18–29, pp. 369–87.

45. John P. Kenny, *Principles of Medical Ethics*, 2d ed. (Westminster, Md.: Newman, 1962), p. 272.

46. Constitution on the Church, nn. 9–12, in *Vatican Council II*, ed. Flannery, pp. 359–64.

47. Fahey, in *Systematic Theology*, ed. Fiorenza and Galvin, 2, pp. 49–50.

48. James A. Coriden, *An Introduction to Canon Law* (New York: Paulist, 1991), pp. 65–99.

49. See, for example, Dennis J. Billy and Terence Kennedy, eds., *Some Philosophical Issues in Moral Matters: The Collected Ethical Writings of Joseph Owens* (Rome: Editiones Academiae Alphonsianae, 1996); Daniel Westberg, *Right Practical Reason: Aristotle, Action, and Prudence in Aquinas* (New York: Oxford University Press, 1994).

50. Charles E. Curran, "The Catholic Identity of Catholic Institutions," *Theological Studies* 58 (1997): 90–108.

51. Cardinal Joseph Bernardin, "The Campaign for Human Development at Age 25" *Origins* 25 (1995): 196–99; The Campaign for Human Development, *Empowerment and Hope: 25 Years of Turning Lives Around* (Washington, D.C.: U.S. Catholic Conference, 1996).

52. Robert G. Weisbord, *The Chief Rabbi, the Pope, and the Holocaust: An Era in Vatican-Jewish Relations* (New Brunswick, N.J.: Transaction Publishers, 1992).

53. National Conference of Catholic Bishops, "The Challenge of Peace: God's Promise and Our Response," nn. 56–121, in *Catholic Social Thought*, ed. O'Brien and Shannon, pp. 504–18.

54. Kenneth R. Himes, "Pacifisim and the Just War Tradition in Roman Catholic Social Teaching," in *One Hundred Years of Catholic Social Thought: Celebration and Challenge*, ed. John A. Coleman (Maryknoll, N.Y.: Orbis, 1991), pp. 329–44.

55. For example, H. Richard Niebuhr, *Christ and Culture* (New York: Harper Torchbook, 1956), p. 56.

56. Thomas Cahill, *How the Irish Saved Civilization: The Untold Story of Ireland's Heroic Role from the Fall of Rome to the Rise of Medieval Europe* (New York: Doubleday, 1995).

57. William H. Shannon, *Silent Lamp: The Thomas Merton Story* (New York: Crossroad, 1992).

58. For the thought of the father of liberation theology in South America, see Gustavo Gutiérrez, *Essential Writings* (Minneapolis, Minn.: Fortress, 1996).

59. Diana L. Hayes, *Hagar's Daughters: Womanist Ways of Being in the World* (New York: Paulist, 1995).

60. Ada Maria Isasi-Diaz, *Mujerista Theology: A Theology for the Twenty-First Century* (Maryknoll, N.Y.: Orbis, 1996).

61. Zygmunt Bauman, *Life in Fragments: Essays in Postmodern Morality* (Oxford: Blackwell, 1995).

62. R. Bruce Douglass and David Hollenbach, eds., *Catholicism and Liberalism: Contributions to American Public Philosophy* (New York: Cambridge University Press, 1994).

63. Richard M. Gula, *Reason Informed by Faith: Foundations of Catholic Morality* (New York: Paulist, 1989), pp. 30–39.

64. For my development of historical consciousness, see Charles E. Curran, *Directions in Fundamental Moral Theology* (Notre Dame, Ind.: University of Notre Dame Press, 1985), pp. 137–55.

65. Stephen J. Pope, "Proper and Improper Partiality and the Preferential Option for the Poor," *Theological Studies* 54 (1993): 242–71.

66. Jon Sobrino, *Jesus the Liberator: A Historical-Theological Reading of Jesus of Nazareth* (Maryknoll, N.Y.: Orbis, 1993).

67. Susan A. Ross, "Feminist Theology: A Review of the Literature," *Theological Studies* 56 (1995): 327–30.

68. Margaret A. Farley, "A Feminist Version of Respect for Persons," in *Feminist Ethics and the Catholic Tradition: Readings in Moral Theology No. 9*, ed. Charles E. Curran, Margaret A. Farley, and Richard A. McCormick (New York: Paulist, 1996), 164–83; Farley, "Feminism and Universal Morality," in *Prospects for a Common Morality*, ed. Gene Outka and John P. Reeder, Jr. (Princeton, N.J.: Princeton University Press, 1993), pp. 170–90.

69. Anne E. Patrick, *Liberating Conscience: Feminist Explorations in Catholic Moral Theology* (New York: Continuum, 1996), pp. 40–71.

70. Lisa Sowle Cahill, "Feminist Ethics, Differences, and Common Ground: A Catholic Perspective," in *Feminist Ethics and the Catholic Moral Tradition*, ed. Curran, Farley, and McCormick, pp. 184–204; Cahill, *Sex, Gender, and Christian Ethics* (New York: Cambridge University Press, 1996), pp. 14–72.

71. Hans Küng and Karl-Josef Kuschei, eds., *A Global Ethic: The Declaration of the Parliament of the World's Religions* (New York: Continuum, 1993).

72. A. H. Robertson, *Human Rights in the World: An Introduction to the Study of the International Protection of Human Rights*, 4th ed. (New York: St. Martin's, 1996).

2

Stance

The Catholic Church constitutes the location and ground of Catholic morality and moral theology. Still, the logical first question for moral theology as a systemic and thematic discipline, is what comes first, or where do we start?

MEANING OF STANCE

Moral theology does not often explicitly address the question of its own starting point, but some Protestant Christian ethicists have talked about the logical first step that the discipline should take. Some years ago, James Sellers referred to the stance of moral theology as being the logically prior first step in the discipline which thus becomes a source for other criteria.[1]

EXPLANATION OF STANCE. James M. Gustafson also refers to the logical first step or starting point as the perspective, posture, or fundamental angle of vision. "Perspective" is drawn from the visual experience and expresses the way we look at something that puts everything else into focus.[2] Horizon is a more philosophical word used to help explain the same reality—to refer to the maximum field of vision from a determined viewpoint.[3] In the light of these approaches "stance" is the logical first step in moral theology: it gives us a perspective on reality and is a critical source for further steps. The most important factor is how we perceive and view the world around us. Perspective gives us the angle of vision from which we can put all the aspects of reality together and give some unity and order to what we see. As the logical first step stance must be broad enough to encompass all reality but narrow enough to provide some critical understanding of how all aspects of reality fit together.

We have no a priori reason to say that one stance is correct and others are false. The proof of the stance is pragmatic; it all depends on whether the proposed stance really is a logical first step that encompasses all other aspects and gives some critical direction.

SOME PROPOSED STANCES. For James Sellers the stance of Christian ethics is an understanding of salvation or wholeness, which involves a movement from promise to fulfillment and which takes place in this world of time and space. Such a stance seems to fit the basic purpose of being a starting point that provides a perspective on reality and a critical understanding of all that is happening.[4] In my judgment, however, such a stance is much too optimistic. Fulfillment or wholeness can never completely take place in this world. There is much more brokenness, suffering, and irrationality present in our world than such a stance is willing to recognize. Sellers was writing in very optimistic times, but today we are much more conscious of the world's brokenness.

James Gustafson has proposed Jesus Christ as the stance or perspective for Christian ethics.[5] Such a stance seems quite logical because we are dealing with the Christian moral life and in some sense Jesus Christ must be central to the discipline of moral theology. However, I do not employ Jesus Christ as the stance for moral theology. First, one would have to unpack what is meant by Jesus Christ. Gustafson himself points out that Jesus Christ's role in the moral life has been understood as Lord, sanctifier, justifier, pattern, and teacher.[6] Catholic writers have recently expressed strong and very different positions on the identity of the historical Jesus.[7] We now have many different understandings of Jesus Christ. We all know the temptation for Christians to make Jesus Christ into their own image and likeness. After all, everyone wants Jesus on her or his own side. Consequently, Jesus has been proposed as a capitalist and a socialist, a revolutionary and a law abiding citizen, a nonviolent pacifist and a guerilla. Yes, problems abound in the effort to spell out or unpack the meaning of Jesus, and it may be difficult to find agreement. I also have problems using Jesus Christ as stance because this approach has been used by some in the past to ground a very narrow Christology or Christomonism that gives little or no independent room or importance to the human. One question that the church catholic must always deal with is what Christians share with others who are not Christian.[8] So because of the need to unpack the meaning of Jesus and the danger of a narrow Christology, Jesus Christ does not seem to be the best stance for moral theology.

The moral life of Christians has most often been associated with the virtue of love. Love is the heart and center of the Christian moral life. Should love not be the stance of moral theology? But there are some problems with love as the stance for moral theology. The first problem recognizes the various meanings of love and the difficulty in finding agreement on what love means and entails. The New Testament has many different meanings of love. The synoptic Gospels stress the twofold commandment of love of God and love of neighbor (Mark 12:28–34, Matt 22:34–40, Luke 10:25–37). Paul, however, seldom if ever, refers to our relationship to God as love. The basic Christian law is to love our neighbor not God (e.g., Rom 13:8–10). A moment's reflection reminds us of the great difference between God's love for us and our love for God. God's love for us involves total and complete giving that in no way depends on the response that we as human beings offer. God takes the first step. Our love for God is precisely a response to the one who has first loved us and calls us to love. There seem to be two very different realities involved in these two kinds of love. Even in neighbor love the reality of love differs depending on who the neighbor is. Is the love of spouse or family the same as love of enemies? If the divine model of love is the Trinity or Jesus, what different understandings of love result? Coming from the Trinity, love involves relationship and mutuality; but for Jesus, love is the total giving of self as illustrated by the cross without necessarily any return or mutuality. Love of God, love of neighbor, and love of self are not the same reality. Thus, love is a very complex reality, and Christians have found it hard to agree on the precise meaning of Christian love.[9]

But a second problem arises with regard to love as stance. No one content virtue or value can ever serve as the stance of moral theology because it will always be related to other content virtues or values. In other words a substantive reality cannot encompass all the other realities, but by definition is distinguished from them and constitutes only a part of moral reality. In the Catholic Thomistic tradition the theological virtue of charity was looked on as encompassing all things, but love was seen as the form or formal element of the virtues, not as their material or content aspect.[10] Thus, in that sense love can be understood as the formal aspect of all reality.[11] But no content virtue can ever be the stance of moral theology because by definition it will not include all the other moral realities. This recognition points us to a stance that is more formal than material or content oriented. Remember that the stance has to be broadly catholic so that it includes all reality, and at the same time gives us some critical direction for understanding and ordering all moral reality.

STANCE BASED ON THE FIVEFOLD CHRISTIAN MYSTERIES

I propose a horizon involving the fivefold Christian mysteries of creation, sin, incarnation, redemption, and resurrection destiny as the stance for moral theology, the church, and the individual Christian. The stance constituted by these mysteries and the relationship among them well fulfills the description of what the stance should be and do.

First, the explanation of the stance. The church catholic believes in God as the Creator of the world and the one who saw that it was good. A fundamental goodness characterizes whatever God has made. The world and everything in it, although finite and limited, is not fundamentally evil but basically good.

Sin and evil came into the world through human beings. Most Christians think that the book of Genesis deals primarily with the mystery and reality of the world's creation by God because it is the first book in the canon of Scripture and because it begins with the story of creation. Genesis deals primarily with sin and evil. The authors of Genesis, many years after the creation event was thought to have occurred, dealt with the existential problem that faces all believers in God. Why is there so much evil and suffering in our world despite the goodness of God who made everything? The answer: sin and evil come from human beings and not from God. Not only Scripture but our human experience testifies to the presence of sin in our world.

Sin and evil are present in our world, but in the Roman Catholic tradition sin does not completely destroy the fundamental goodness of creation. Sin does not even take away the basic humanness of the sinner. In the famous words of Thomas Aquinas sin does not destroy our basic humanity, but it does wound it in some respects.[12]

The mystery of the incarnation contends that the divine and the human are joined together in the one person of Jesus. Consequently, the human and all its aspects including the bodily or the corporeal and material are in no way connected with evil. The incarnation supports and strengthens the fundamental goodness of everything human. The divine is not in opposition to the human. Dualistic oppositions such as spirit and flesh or body and soul are ruled out by the implications of the incarnation.

Incarnation is linked with redemption: Jesus came into the world to free us from sin and evil. Redemption involves the successful struggle of Jesus against the power of sin and evil. The cross and the resurrection show forth the reality of redemption. The cross is at once the victory of sin, evil, and death and the redeeming love of Jesus. The resurrection represents the triumph of Jesus over all enemies, primarily evil, sin, and death. The triune God offers us salvation and reconciliation through the redemptive love of Jesus.

However, resurrection as destiny—as the fullness of the triumph of Jesus—has not yet taken place. The fullness of the reign of God is not yet here. Resurrection destiny, understood as the fullness of the reign of God, will never take place within this world. Christian fulfillment lies outside history. The Catholic Church believes in an afterlife in which individual happiness in community with others and the fullness of the reign of God will flourish as God's gracious gift.

Thus, redemption as the "already" and resurrection destiny as the "not yet" will always be in some tension. The Christian temptation has always been to eliminate the tension either by a collapsed eschatology in which the fullness of redemption is already occurring in time and space and usually close to the present or by reducing the present time to a mere waiting for the future of resurrection destiny which will then come to us. Christians and moral theology must, however, live with an eschatological tension between the present time of redemption and the unrealized future of resurrection destiny. We are called to improve on and change what exists here and now but also to realize that the fullness of redemption will never be here.

These fivefold Christian mysteries constitute the stance or vision that moral theology employs as it sets about its work of systematically, comprehensively, and synthetically understanding Christian moral life within the context of the church. From its vantage point, we can now analyze and criticize various approaches to moral theology that have been proposed historically and at the present time with special attention to the Catholic tradition.

THE STANCE AND THE CATHOLIC TRADITION

The Roman Catholic tradition recognizes the fundamental and basic goodness of the human world, human reason, and all that God has created. In the development of moral theology this insistence on the goodness of creation and the human has come to the fore in the recognition that the human can be an important source of moral wisdom and knowledge for the Christian. This viewpoint, traditionally called the natural law theory, has been distinctive of the Catholic approach though it is often rejected to some extent by other Christians. It has two important aspects. The first is the theological aspect—the one which concerns us here. Are human reason and human experience sources of moral wisdom and knowledge for the Christian, or can the Christian find true moral wisdom and knowledge only in Jesus Christ and in revelation? The second, more philosophical aspect of the natural law then asks what we mean by human reason, human nature, and the created; but this question will be discussed later.[13]

THE THEOLOGICAL ASPECT OF NATURAL LAW. Creation serves as the foundation for the Roman Catholic insistence that human reason, reflecting on what God has made, can arrive at moral wisdom and knowledge. God the Creator made the world and all human beings. God's plan for the world came forth from divine reason and has been imprinted in everything that God has made. God has given human beings reason so that we may discover the plan that God put into creation, and on the basis of that, know how human beings should act and how creation should be treated. Note again the emphasis on mediation. To find out what God wants us to do, we do not immediately go to God and ask. Rather, human reason reflecting on what God has made, discovers the plan that God has put into the world and how God wants us to act. The eternal law is understood as God's plan and design for creation; the natural law is the participation of the eternal law in the rational creature. Human reason reflecting on human nature and creation can discern how God wants us to live. This natural law emphasis was a strong, though by no means central, part of Thomas Aquinas's approach to moral theology.[14]

The hierarchical magisterium in the Catholic Church has always insisted on the importance of human reason in its moral teachings. All students of Catholic moral theology recognize that it has given a very central and important role to reason. A number of examples from the recent teaching of the hierarchical magisterium well illustrate such an approach. In 1963 John XXIII wrote his famous encyclical *Pacem in terris*—"Peace on Earth." One might expect a Christian approach to peace in this world to have unique Christian aspects. Jesus, after the resurrection, offered his disciples the gift of peace—a peace that the world cannot give. True peace will only come about in the context of the love of Jesus that forgives, that puts down all the barriers that separate and divide us, and that extends to all people especially those most in need. Such was the redeeming love of Jesus and the love Jesus now calls us to make present in the world.

But *Pacem in terris* does not follow such an approach. Jesus and redemption do not constitute the basis for its methodology. The encyclical begins by claiming that "Peace on earth . . . can be firmly established only if the order laid down by God be dutifully observed." The Creator of the world has imprinted an order on the human heart that conscience reveals to us and enjoins us to obey. The laws governing the relationships between human beings and states are to be sought where the Father of all things wrote them, that is, in human nature.[15] The encyclical thus in its very beginning sets out the direction and the methodology that it will follow. Jesus and redemption or grace are not mentioned, but human reason reflecting on creation will provide the basis for understanding the laws that govern the relationships existing in our world. The four parts of the encyclical then develop the various laws that govern different types of relationships.

The Declaration on Religious Liberty of Vatican II (passed in 1965) illustrates the same approach. Recall that Catholics arrived at their acceptance of religious liberty much later than Protestants. Protestants, however, often developed their arguments for religious liberty by seeing it as an implication of the Christian faith itself, as an outward protection for the freedom with which Christ has set us free.[16] But the Declaration on Religious Liberty proposes a different basis for religious freedom—a natural law approach. The right to religious freedom is based on the dignity of the human person, the demands of which have become more fully known to human reason through centuries of experience.[17] The document on religious liberty is divided into two parts with the first part proving and developing the concept of religious liberty based only on reason. The second part of the document brings in revelation and claims: "Furthermore, this doctrine of freedom is rooted in divine revelation, and for this reason Christians are bound to respect it all the more conscientiously."[18] Thus the teaching of religious liberty is grounded primarily in human reason.

Even the more controversial teachings of the hierarchical magisterium of the Catholic Church have claimed to be based on human reason and natural law. In 1968 Paul VI issued his encyclical *Humanae vitae* which reasserted the Catholic Church's condemnation of the immorality of artificial contraception for all spouses whether they are Catholic or not. The methodology of the encyclical is clear. Spouses "must conform their activity to the creative intention of God, expressed in the very nature of marriage and of its acts. . . ."[19] This natural law teaching of the church is founded on the inseparable connection, willed by God and unable to be broken by human beings, between the unitive and the procreative meaning of the sexual act. The pope believes that people today "are particularly capable of seizing the deeply reasonable and human character of this fundamental principle."[20] Our concern here is with the theological aspect of natural law and its insistence on human reason as a primary source of wisdom and knowledge for the Christian. Note that those who disagree with the pope, both inside and outside the Catholic Church, also frequently use human reason reflecting on creation to arrive at a different conclusion.[21] The disagreement of these critics with the pope is not over the theological aspect of natural law but the philosophical aspect—the meaning of human reason and human nature.

All recognize the historical insistence of the Roman Catholic tradition on the theological aspect of natural law with its basis in the doctrine of creation. However, criticisms have been raised against this theological construal of natural law from a number of different sources. We will first consider the objections that have been raised primarily from classical Protestant writings and sources.

PROTESTANT OBJECTIONS TO NATURAL LAW. A first reason for some Protestants to deny the theological aspect of natural law comes from an insistence on *Sola Scriptura*—the Scripture alone. A strict insistence on Scripture alone would deny that human reason is a starting point or reliable source of wisdom and knowledge for the Christian. However, even though the axiom has been associated with traditional Protestantism, Jaroslav Pelikan has pointed out that the axiom has seldom, in practice, been taken in an absolutistic way.[22] Thus, some Protestants claim to find a natural law approach in many of the Reformation figures themselves, especially John Calvin.[23]

A second Protestant challenge to natural law comes from the emphasis on sin. Sin has deeply affected human reason, human nature, and all of creation. How can a sinful human reason reflecting on a sinful creation ever arrive at true moral wisdom and knowledge?[24] One example of natural law teaching proposed by Roman Catholics and many others in the past is the just war theory. According to this theory criteria exist for determining if war as a last reasonable resort can be just. But, one must ask, why do Christians living in this country usually claim our wars are just whereas the wars of our opponents are unjust? Sin obviously affects how we human beings understand and judge what is occurring; from the point of view of these critics, sin's effects radically distort and incapacitate reason's grasp of natural law.

I cannot accept this objection as denying any possibility of human reason discerning what God wants us to do, but it rightly points up a problem with the Roman Catholic tradition and ethics. Generally speaking, Catholic tradition has not given enough importance to the reality of sin. Recall the 1963 encyclical *Pacem in terris*. It would have been as appropriate to write an encyclical entitled *Bellum in terris*— war on earth. We have never known a time when there have not been wars and rumors of war in our world. Some are major wars, some minor; some are revolutions; others are wars of imperialism. The optimistic, even idealistic, tone of this encyclical illustrates the penchant in Catholic tradition for not giving enough importance to the reality of sin in our world.

The Roman Catholic tradition in its moral theology has not, in my judgment, given enough importance to the reality of sin. However, I still want to affirm the tradition's basic insistence that human reason reflecting on creation can arrive at moral wisdom and knowledge. The realization of the presence and influence of sin results in a more chastened natural law approach. Sin does not destroy or annul the created and the natural but definitely affects both human reason and human nature. The recognition that sin affects but does not destroy the goodness of creation and of the human accounts for the presence of sin in our stance. In the contemporary ecumenical climate, Protestants and Catholics often agree on recognizing both the human and the sinful.

Why did Roman Catholic moral theology give too little importance to the role of sin? Three historical reasons contribute to an answer. First, Catholic moral theology was, from the time of Thomas Aquinas, intrinsically connected with moral philosophy which by definition makes reason supreme and does not acknowledge the theological category of sin.[25] Second, in the unecumenical climate that prevailed prior to the 1960s, both Catholics and Protestants tended to emphasize their differences and failed to recognize nuances and even common assumptions. Some Protestants so stressed sin as to insist on total human depravity, while Catholics, so insisting that sin did not destroy the human, underplayed the role of sin.

The Catholic position was to maintain a fundamental goodness of the human even after sin. Pre-Vatican II Catholics often said that sin destroys the supernatural in us but leaves the natural intact. However, sin definitely affects and weakens human reason, human nature, and creation. In more recent days Protestants and Catholics have been listening to and learning from each other. Catholics need to impute a greater role to sin than they have traditionally done. The Catholic insistence on the natural as unaffected by sin is theoretically closely connected to the Catholic distinction between the realm of the supernatural and the realm of the natural, which we will discuss later.[26]

While theologians and scholars are generally aware of this so-called Catholic natural law optimism, many Catholics in the pew, trained in a pre-Vatican II catechesis, have difficulty accepting the fact that Roman Catholicism did not attach sufficient importance to sin. "What do you mean by saying that the Catholic Church did not think sin important? That's wrong. From the time I was young I was taught it is a sin to do this, a sin to do that, a sin to do the other thing. We learned a whole list of sins. I think that the Catholic Church overplayed the importance of sin, and I do not want to go back to the past with all its negativity." What about such an objection?

Without doubt pre-Vatican II Roman Catholicism, especially in the United States, emphasized sinful acts. But sin was perceived as *only* an act, not as a power or force that deeply affected the individual person or the world. Protestantism more rightly saw sin as a power. If sin is only an act, it does not have much influence and can easily be eradicated. Catholics in the pre-Vatican II era who overemphasized sin as an act tended to forget about sin as a reality affecting every person and the world. The somewhat easy availability of forgiveness for sinful acts in the sacrament of penance contributed to lessening Catholics' apprehension of the enduring power and force of sin.

A third criticism proposed by some Protestants against the natural law approach concerns the illegitimacy of moving from knowledge of the human to the divine which, as mentioned earlier, is a characteristic Catholic approach based on an understanding of mediation and the analogy of being. On the basis of the human one can know something about God and how God wants us to act. Karl Barth, on the other hand, coming from the Calvinist or Reformed tradition, strongly objected to starting with the human. One begins, he said, with God and God's self-revelation. Otherwise, by beginning with the human in theology, one ultimately commits the great idolatry of making God into one's own image and likeness.[27]

Some truth resides in this Barthian claim. We all have a tendency to make God into our image and likeness. Those who know me recognize that I often refer to God as "she." Too often in the past our male-dominated society has made God into its own image and likeness. Most of my life I thought God was a white male—just like me. In like manner, the Catholic approach of the past tended to identify the divine too readily with the human. This tendency is one of the dangers of the Catholic emphasis on mediation. At times Roman Catholicism has presumed to know too much about God and moved too readily from the finite human to the infinite divine. The truth is that creation is both similar and dissimilar to God. God is both present and absent.[28] Barth's objection, then, does not totally invalidate the Catholic insistence on human reason and the created in understanding the moral life, but it does chasten such an approach. It calls us to be always conscious of the danger of moving too quickly, rapidly, and easily from the human to the divine.

VATICAN II AND NATURAL LAW. The renewal of Roman Catholicism at Vatican II also entailed criticism of the older theological approach to natural law with its almost exclusive emphasis on human reason and creation as sources of moral wisdom and knowledge. First, Vatican II in open dialogue with Protestantism began to appreciate more clearly the centrality of the Scriptures in the life and thought of the church.[29] The renewed emphasis on the liturgy of the word resulted in Catholics recognizing how word and sacrament must be seen together in the liturgy.[30] The council also encouraged individuals and groups to begin the practice of reading Scripture. The word of God, according to Vatican II, should become the very soul of theology.[31] In its document on the training of priests Vatican II declared that special care should be given to perfecting moral theology. Its scientific presentation should rely more heavily on the teaching of Scripture.[32] Reason could no longer remain the primary (if not the only) source for Catholic moral theology.

Pre-Vatican II theology had clearly distinguished the natural from the supernatural. The natural primarily concerns life in this world and is governed by reason and natural law. Recall the natural law approach in the 1963 encyclical *Pacem in terris*. The Pastoral Constitution on the Church in the Modern World lamented: "One of the gravest errors of our time is the dichotomy between the faith that many people profess and the practice of their daily lives."[33] Both in theory and in practice, said Vatican II, faith, grace, and Jesus Christ must have a greater role in Christian moral life.

The Pastoral Constitution on the Church in the Modern World deals with the moral life of the church and the Christian in the world and employs a methodology that attempts to overcome the separation between the supernatural and the natural, between faith and daily life. In its consideration of the human person, human community, human action, and the role of the church in the modern world (part one, chapters one to four), the document employs a more inclusive methodology appealing to creation, sin, Jesus Christ, and grace. Vatican II confirmed and in no way denied the traditional Catholic emphasis on human reason and creation as sources of moral wisdom and knowledge, but it also integrated these realities within a broader approach that recognizes the presence of sin and grace.[34]

Vatican II's effort to overcome the natural-supernatural dichotomy had problems of its own, however. In trying to relate Jesus Christ, grace, and faith immediately to daily life, the danger arises of forgetting that the fullness of resurrection destiny comes only at the end of time. The emphasis on redemption now frequently results in a too optimistic approach especially in the light of tradition's earlier failure to fully weigh the importance of sin. To some extent, the Pastoral Constitution on the Church in the Modern World and the Catholic theology it inspired is too optimistic. From the viewpoint of our stance, the constitution did not give enough emphasis to sin or the future aspects of resurrection destiny. Recall that the early and mid-1960s were very optimistic times generally, and Protestant and Catholic theology often imbibed too much of this optimism as illustrated in the death of God theology and the secular city theology.[35]

The drafters of the Pastoral Constitution on the Church in the Modern World recognized in some places the danger of excessive optimism and explicitly tried to avoid it. The consideration of the human person begins with a section on creation, includes a section on sin, and closes with a section on "Christ as the New Man [sic]."[36] The second chapter on human community is somewhat similar and ends with a section on "The Incarnate Word and Human Solidarity."[37] The chapter on human activity in the world—after dealing with creation and sin—includes a section on "Human Activity Finds Perfection in the Paschal Mystery" and a final section on "A New Earth and a New Heaven."[38]

This chapter explicitly combats the danger of overoptimism by stressing that resurrection destiny, or the future reign of God, will come outside history and at the end of the world. The danger in attempting to overcome a false dichotomy between the supernatural and the natural, between grace and the human, is to have no distinction—that is, that the eschaton will be collapsed and human sin forgotten. One acts as if the fullness of God's reign is already present in this world.

A word should be said about the concept of "the natural." Catholic theology developed the concept of the natural in the context of insuring the gratuity of grace, but "the natural" is a category that never historically existed. It is a metaphysical abstraction—a "remainder concept." The natural simply means that God could have created human beings as human without necessarily calling them to share God's life now and in eternity. In reality, the purely natural has never existed.[39] In moral theology, however, it was an easy step for Catholic tradition to identify the natural with life in this world and the supernatural with the spiritual life. Since Vatican II, moral theologians and others have been downplaying the concept of the "purely natural" as it once existed in moral theology. In contemporary thinking, the natural is that which is related to creation. However, creation, too, is only one dimension of the Christian understanding of what is present in the world. The stance proposed here tries, then, to include other aspects, for example, sin, incarnation, redemption, and resurrection destiny.[40]

The previous paragraphs show how a particular stance can be used to analyze and criticize theology—in this case the Catholic natural law approach that insists on creation but neglects other aspects of reality that undergirds the stance. Frequently the natural law tradition has not appreciated the importance of sin even though it correctly insists that sin can never totally destroy the goodness of creation. The same stance also helps us understand and correct instances of an overoptimistic theology that overstresses redemption and fails to recognize the future aspect of resurrection destiny. In helping illumine critiques of this sort, I believe that our stance is very much in accord with the inclusiveness of the Catholic tradition and serves as a helpful tool in evaluating different approaches to moral theology or Christian ethics.

THE STANCE AND SPECIFIC POSITIONS.   The stance coheres with and helps to explain some specific positions taken in the Catholic tradition. Take, for example, killing. The Catholic tradition has not condemned all killing. Severe conflict situations can always arise in a sinful world that is not yet at the fullness of God's reign. Tradition has recognized, for example, that one can kill an unjust aggressor seeking one's own life if the killing is the only way to save one's own life. However, as a tradition that accepts the goodness of the human and the fact of redemption having already occurred, the Catholic tradition also severely limits the conflict situations in which killing can be accepted. In the same vein, the Catholic tradition has accepted the just war theory; that is, it recognizes that violence may be acceptable in some situations to defend and achieve justice. Tradition rejects absolute pacifism because pacifism fails to appreciate that conflict situations can arise in our finite and sinful world. But the Catholic tradition also puts severe limits on a nation's going to war and on what it can do in the event of war. Not all is fair in love and war. The attention to sin and to the lack of eschatological fullness in the stance supports the use of violence as a last resort in limited situations, but the stance's inclusion of creation, incarnation, and redemption requires strict limits on when violence can be accepted.

This stance also sheds light on two other significant aspects of Christian life—suffering and death. Every Christian will experience the cross at some time in this life. The Christian life does not always involve suffering, but suffering will generally be a part of every Christian life. For some, the cross emphasizes the paradoxical relationship between the divine and the human. God's life is made known in the midst of human death, God's joy in human sorrow, God's power in human powerlessness. The Catholic perspective with its emphasis on mediation can never adopt a totally paradoxical understanding of the relationship between the divine and the human. However, the role of redemption and resurrection destiny highlights the need to transform the limited and sinful realities of the present. In Catholic perspective, the cross and resurrection are not paradoxical but transformationist. The cross is always seen in connection with the resurrection. The Christian believes that suffering is redemptive. However, resurrection destiny remains in the future; therefore, not all suffering in this world is redemptive here and now. There are no easy answers in the face of suffering. All of us will experience it, some more than others. Some people will grow in and through suffering in this world, but other people will seem to be overcome by their suffering. Christians see suffering in the light of the cross and resurrection of Jesus, but the fullness of the resurrection is not yet here. Our stance indicates the proper Christian approach to suffering. The Christian is not asked to seek suffering, but suffering will come and should be borne in the light of the suffering and transforming love of Jesus.

The stance also helps us understand death. In the light of creation all finite reality eventually dies. The Scriptures, especially Genesis and Romans, project an intimate connection between sin and death. This sinful aspect of reality accounts for the fear of death that we experience. Death is experienced as loss and separation, and most of us cry at the death of a loved one precisely because we suffer loss. Christians believe that Jesus has transformed death into life; and, for those who are baptized into the death and resurrection of Jesus, death is the way to eternal life. But again, the fullness of resurrection destiny lies beyond the present. Thus, death is experienced as natural, as breach or loss, and as the way to eternal life. All these aspects of human finitude, sin, redemption, and resurrection destiny can help Christians better understand the complex reality of death.

The stance also helps modify some distinctive Catholic approaches. Mediation, for example, is distinctive of the Catholic world view (see chapter one). Thus the Catholic cannot put creation and the world in opposition to God and the divine. At times God's love, beauty, and truth are experienced in human love, beauty, and truth; however, finitude, sinfulness, and the lack of eschatological fullness prevent the human from being fully identified with the divine. Nevertheless, and especially in pre-Vatican II ecclesiology, a triumphalistic Catholic approach paints the church as a perfect society—as the kingdom of God on earth. Against this overvaluation, Vatican II rightly insisted on the sinful and pilgrim nature of the church. Even as the body of Christ, the church always falls short of eschatological fullness and is consequently always in need of change and reform.

That in moral matters the traditional Catholic approach often failed to adequately recognize the reality of sin has already been pointed out. Sometimes the presence of sin in the world forces us to do what we would not do if sin were not present. Yes, we must struggle against sin, but we may also have to live with sin's consequences. Many medieval Catholic theologians, for instance, recognized that without sin there would be no need for private property. At times the presence of sin will justify some compromises in what should be done, but there are also dangers of caving in too readily and easily to the presence of sin. Reason and experience must try to determine when compromise is justified. For example, moral theologians have always justified spying in war-time situations and even at other times. Many moral theologians recognize that if everyone else who is taking the exam is cheating, then an individual is justified in doing the same thing. Thus the presence of sin in the world can at times influence the proper moral response.

STANCE AND OTHER APPROACHES

To understand better the meaning and role of the stance and to show how it can be used to analyze and criticize other theological method-ologies, this chapter will now consider very briefly some of these other approaches in the light of the stance. The Social Gospel school (1890–1920) represented especially in the work of Walter Rauschenbusch (1861–1918) had an important impact on American Protestantism. It stressed the social dimension of the kingdom of God and the need for that kingdom to be more present in our world. The Social Gospel maintained that the principles of the historical Jesus could serve as guidelines for social life in this world. Rauschenbusch was the best exponent of this position. He recognized the presence of sin but de-scribed sin as selfishness, at times implying that such selfishness could be overcome through education and other means. Rauschenbusch, however, was not as naively optimistic as some others in the movement and did not expect God's reign to be fully realized in this world.[41]

According to our stance the two biggest problems with the Social Gospel as a whole were its failure to take sin more seriously (sin is basically alienation from God and others and not merely selfishness) and the danger of forgetting resurrection destiny as future and beyond the present world. As a result the Social Gospel approach was much too optimistic. Note that here we are dealing with theological ethics as a second order discipline. The Social Gospel made many very important contributions to life in the United States and to Protestantism in particu-lar. Martin Luther King claimed that Walter Rauschenbusch left an indelible imprint on his thinking, despite Rauschenbusch's over-optimism.[42]

In Protestant circles in the United States, Reinhold Niebuhr's Christian realism followed in the wake of the Social Gospel, and criti-cized the latter for its easy optimism.[43] It is interesting to note that the Social Gospel flourished especially in the optimistic climate before the First World War and illustrated the progressivism of the times. How-ever, after the war and during the Depression, times were not so opti-mistic and theology recognized the change. In this context Reinhold Niebuhr proposed Christian realism—a methodology that recognizes all the aspects in my stance. I would, however, give slightly more emphasis to creation, slightly less to sin, and I would be more insistent that true redemption is already present though not fully realized in our world.

Liberation theology originally arose in a South American context and has had a tremendous influence on recent Catholic life and thought. The emphasis here is on praxis—truth is not arrived at merely through theory, contemplation, and work in the library but also requires involvement and participation in life's struggle. Salvation and liberation affect the whole person and all the institutions of life. Sin is personal and structural. Salvation involves liberation at all levels—political, economic, cultural, social, and religious. The exodus of God's people from the slavery of Egypt is the paradigmatic event of liberation and a reminder of the multidimensional aspects of God's grace and salvation.[44]

I am very much in favor of the struggle for liberation and of the need to see grace and sin in their social and individual dimensions. Liberation theology has raised an admirable prophetic voice that the whole church needs to hear. However, from the theological-ethical perspective of the stance, I want to suggest some friendly amendments to the theory of liberation theology—some of which are already occurring. The need for liberation now is so pressing that some forget the future aspect of our goal. The fullness of liberation will elude us until the end of time, but meanwhile we must struggle mightily to make liberation more present in our persons and in the structures and institutions of our society. One can understand why liberation theologians want to emphasize liberation in the present as a strong motivating force for Christians to do something about oppression. In the long run, however, theory and practice will be better served if one also recognizes that the fullness of liberation will only occur at the end of time. Absent this recognition, people may commit to the struggle for a short time but will quickly burn out or turn off when progress does not result that quickly from their efforts.

Liberation theology also needs to pay greater attention to the human and rational aspects proposed in the creation part of the stance. Liberation approaches rightly condemn the existing structures of injustice and oppression. But a further step is needed. What structures and institutions do we need? Human reason, using all the available sciences, must devise better and more just structures. The Gospel message of liberation needs to be mediated through institutions that are just and equitable.

Finally, recall our earlier remarks about the work of Protestant ethicist Stanley Hauerwas. Hauerwas's approach to Christian ethics has many positives from my perspective. He strongly opposes the individualism of contemporary liberalism and insists on a more communitarian approach. The Duke University ethicist rightly emphasizes the importance of virtue, character, and the role of the Christian community. However, for Hauerwas morality is not universal but is limited and bound to a particular tradition. Christian morality and ethics must address primarily the church and not directly the world. The church must not try to change the world and the structures of society directly but by its own example, the church does hope to have some influence on the world.[45]

From the perspective of our stance, Hauerwas does not give enough importance to creation and incarnation. The created order, the world at large, and the human cannot be separated from the direct responsibility of the church. The incarnation reminds us that the human cannot be cut off from the divine. The church catholic and the proposed stance are inclusive. The church directly affects the world, and church members are called to contribute to a better world and a more just society. In so emphasizing the importance and role of the church community, Hauerwas at times does not seem to recognize sufficiently the continuing sinfulness and imperfection of the church. In this sense Hauerwas, like pre-Vatican II Catholic theology, tends toward a triumphalistic understanding of the church.

In the above section I have tried to explain my stance primarily by using it as a tool to criticize other approaches to moral theology and Christian ethics. However, in the process the positive way in which the stance functions has also come through. Based on the fivefold Christian mysteries, this stance avoids the danger of both optimism and pessimism. It is realistically hopeful about humanity and what humanity can hope to accomplish, but it also recognizes that human limitation, sinfulness, and the lack of eschatological fullness will always characterize life in this world. The Christian is called to ongoing personal conversion and development in moral life and to work for institutional and social justice and peace in the world. On the other hand, the struggle for growth in personal moral life and worldly justice will never be fully accomplished. We can and must work for progress, but we must also accept defeats and backsliding along the way.

SOURCES OF MORAL THEOLOGY

The church's catholicity and this stance throw important light on the sources of moral wisdom and knowledge for the church and Christians.

Where do we find such knowledge? The inclusiveness of catholicity and the creation and incarnational aspects of the stance ground our recognition that the sources of moral theology include the human sources of knowledge, as well as Scripture and tradition. Today one can speak of four major sources of wisdom for moral theology—Scripture, tradition, reason, and experience. From an ecumenical perspective, churches that accept catholicity can readily accept these four sources of moral theology or Christian ethics. In fact, the four sources are generally known as the Wesleyan Quadrilateral.[46] In addition, the Roman Catholic tradition has always insisted that the church, itself relying on these sources, is an important teacher of morality. The church's role in teaching morality was briefly mentioned in the previous chapter and will be discussed at length in the final chapter.

SCRIPTURE. Revelation is the saving self-communication of God to us by words and deeds. Revelation is thus broader than the Scripture and not completely identified with it.[47] The written Christian Scriptures incorporate the Hebrew Bible (Old Testament) and the New Testament, (the Gospels and letters written in the generations after Jesus). Finally the canon or definitive list of these various books was accepted by the early church as the Christian Bible or Scripture.

A significant question for Christians is how to interpret Scripture. The Catholic tradition sees the church as the primary and authoritative interpreter of Scripture since the church, through the power of the Spirit, carries on in time and space the work of the risen Jesus.[48] However, theologians and individual Christians in their own way must also interpret Scripture.

American Christianity, especially U.S. Protestantism, is sharply divided over this question. Fundamentalists insist on a literal interpretation of the Scripture, which is seen as free from all error since it is the word of God, true for all times and places. God reveals God's self and will in and through the propositions found in Scripture.[49] Liberal or mainstream Protestants reject such an approach, as does Roman Catholicism.[50] Vatican II's Dogmatic Constitution on Divine Revelation insists that God's revelation does not consist in God's revealing propositions but is the saving self-communication of God in word and deed. In the Scriptures, God speaks through human authors who work in a truly human fashion and not merely as secretaries taking down God's dictation. To interpret the Scriptures properly, we need to understand the meaning that the human author had in mind. One must attend especially to the different literary forms such as historical, poetic, or prophetic. The human authors were also conditioned by the times and circumstances of their lives.[51] Thus for the proper interpretation of Scripture, one must use all the tools: historical, form, source, redaction, and literary criticism. The Catholic approach to interpretation recognizes both the authoritative role of the church and the need for everyone to employ the requisite critical tools in determining the meaning of the Scriptures.

Catholic moral theology has only recently begun to ask explicit questions about the use of Scripture in moral theology. In the manuals of moral theology before Vatican II the primary source of moral wisdom and knowledge was human reason, and the Scriptures were often used in a very uncritical way primarily as proof texts to support a point that was grounded in human reason. One example of this uncritical use of the Scripture concerns the question of killing in self-defense. The tradition generally accepted one's right to kill another who attacks or threatens one's life. In defense of what other goods could one kill the attacker (assuming one has no other way to preserve these goods)? Some manualists proposed that one could, as a last resort, kill a person who insulted one by attacking one's honor, especially if the person so attacked was a noble person. (Note how culturally conditioned realities of hierarchy and honor operate in this justification.) To justify the possibility of killing the attacker in this case, appeal was also made to scriptural passages maintaining that the tongue can do more harm than the sword. However, Innocent XI, without commenting on this text, condemned the possibility of justly killing the attacker of one's honor even as a last resort.[52]

Today, moral theology recognizes the need to give Scripture a greater role in its development. This recognition was made explicitly at Vatican II; but even before that Bernard Häring, a renowned German theologian then teaching in Rome, had proposed a more biblically centered approach in his groundbreaking systematic moral theology— *The Law of Christ*.[53] However, Scripture is not the whole of revelation or the only source of moral wisdom for the church and Christians. It is even difficult to speak about "the Scripture" as a whole, especially in dealing with morality. Scripture is comprised of many different books written in different historical and cultural circumstances over a long period of time. Recall, for example, that we can find no unified concept of love in Scripture even in the New Testament. In addition moral theology is a scientific, synthetic, and critical study, whereas Scripture is primarily a narrative.

The New Testament also bears the imprint of eschatological

coloring. Protestant ethics has often grappled with the fact that Jesus and the early disciples thought that the end was going to come very quickly.[54] Such eschatological expectation greatly affected their understanding of morality. If the end time is coming quickly, one should not be concerned about storing goods in the barn. There is no need to work or to worry about the future. On the other hand, 2 Thessalonians 3:10 strongly insists that those who do not work will not eat. The expectation of the coming end time even in the New Testament period gave way to the realities of day-to-day living.

We have noted Scripture's historical and cultural conditioning. But feminists and others properly point out that Scripture has also incorporated many cultural meanings over time—and even some that are erroneous. As a matter of fact, the Bible incorporates the patriarchy of the times in which it was written. For example, the New Testament took over its so-called "household codes" from the contemporary culture. These codes are found primarily in Colossians 3:18–4:1 and Ephesians 5:22–6:9. These passages among other things teach the inferiority and subordination of women to men. Man is, they claim, the head of the household, and a woman is to obey her husband. For centuries the Christian Church has repeated these teachings. But now we recognize that such teaching is wrong and must be corrected.[55] That biblical teaching on specific moral points can be wrong and in need of correction is also illustrated in the New Testament's failure to condemn slavery.

Moreover, Scripture obviously does not and cannot deal with the new issues that we are facing in different historical and cultural circumstances. It does not address issues of nuclear power, reproductive technologies, or the proper role and function of government; it does, however, say important things about the needs of the poor, the dangers of wealth, and the arrogance of power.

Moral theology recognizes the importance of Scripture and its limitations in the development of a systematic moral theology. The question is further complicated by the tension between the universal and the particular, especially the different social locations of people. How can the same Scripture provide moral wisdom and knowledge for people living in divergent cultures now and in very different historical and cultural circumstances from those that prevailed in scriptural times?

In discerning the proper role of Scripture in moral theology, the catholic perspective recognizes the many different levels involved in the systematic study of moral theology. In the past for many reasons the manuals of moral theology dealt primarily with the morality of particular acts or what has been called quandary ethics. But moral theology involves more than the consideration of particular acts, for example, the virtues. Virtues as the dispositions of persons are very important; in fact, more important than acts because virtues are perduring and ultimately have an influence on many actions. However, by their very nature virtues are somewhat general and therefore applicable to people living in diverse circumstances. For example, despite all diversity among Christians, we can agree that the fundamental theological virtues of faith, hope, and love must be present in all Christians. These virtues have a rather general content and will be incarnated in different ways and different settings, but there can be no Christian morality or ethics if we do not recognize that all Christians must have these basic theological virtues.

This volume will distinguish various levels of morality and maintain that Scripture has more to say at general levels and less immediate input as the matter under discussion becomes more specific and concrete and thus subject to the diverse interpretations of culture and history. Our proposed stance, the fivefold Christian mysteries of creation, sin, incarnation, redemption, and resurrection destiny, depends heavily on biblical data. The next chapter will discuss a person's basic orientation by appealing to the general biblical narrative as modifying the person's identity and by employing such biblical concepts as conversion. However, later discussions of norms and concrete actions will not directly appeal to biblical materials.

One important aspect of biblical morality that moral theology must deal with concerns the radical teachings of Jesus as summarized especially in Matthew's Sermon on the Mount. How do we deal with the so-called hard sayings of Jesus—take no oaths; let your speech be yes or no; turn the other cheek; give to whoever asks; do not worry about what you will eat or drink; walk the extra mile; forgive seventy times seven times?

In a recent book on the use of Scripture in ethics, Jeffrey Siker analyzes how eight different Christian ethicists have employed it in their work and compares their different approaches to the focal passage of the Sermon on the Mount in Matthew 5–7. Generally speaking authors see the Sermon on the Mount as either an ideal or a realizable morality for life in this world.[56]

Using the inclusive Catholic approach with its emphasis on a "big church" and the stance proposed here, the Sermon on the Mount is clearly an ideal. The eschatological coloring of Scripture also supports such an understanding. Christians living in this world cannot follow in a practical way the radical ethical teaching of the Sermon on the Mount. However, this radical ethic is not "merely an ideal" in the sense of having no practical ramifications. Rather, it gives a quality and a direction toward which we strive. Recall the danger in the church catholic of too readily conforming ourselves to the *Zeitgeist*. The quality and direction coming from the Sermon on the Mount reminds us of our need for growth and conversion.

This view of the Sermon on the Mount has some important ramifications. For instance, authoritative Catholic teaching and theology has seen the Matthean condemnation of divorce and remarriage in Matthew 5:32 and 19:9 as the basis for the church's teaching opposing divorce and remarriage.[57] I understand this teaching as a true ideal and not an absolute norm. It could very well be that there was an original absolute saying, perhaps even uttered by Jesus himself, against divorce and remarriage. However, the Matthean church recognized the need for some exception to that absolute teaching. Notice the famous exception clauses in Matthew 5:32 and Matthew 19:9 which involve the case of the Greek word *porneia*. Many different proposals have been made to interpret *porneia*; but whatever it means, it constitutes an exception to the radical teaching on divorce and remarriage. In 1 Corinthians 7:12–16, Paul also recognizes an exception to the radical ethic by allowing divorce and remarriage in the case of the spouse whose unbelieving partner wants to separate. The Catholic Church itself allows a non-consummated marriage to be dissolved. In my judgment, the ideal of indissolubility would allow more exceptions today within the church.[58]

TRADITION. Tradition is linked to the fundamental reality of the church as the people of God living in new times and places and handing on their lived faith. The church, through the Holy Spirit, tries to be faithful to the word and work of Jesus in the changed times and circumstances in which it lives. Tradition involves the handing on of beliefs, doctrines, practices, rituals, and church life. Many today follow the approach of the Faith and Order Movement of the World Council of Churches in distinguishing three realities—Tradition (capital T) is the process of handing over; tradition (with a small t) is the content that is handed over; and traditions (small t and plural) refer to the distinctive inheritances of particular churches or denominations.[59]

Catholic theology, in keeping with its emphasis on mediation, has stressed its reliance on Scripture and tradition and not just Scripture alone. Today many theologians recognize that Scripture itself depended for its existence on the life of the early church. Many Counter-Reformation theologians, in reaction to the reformers' insistence on Scripture alone, maintained that revelation is found in two parallel and distinct sources—Scripture and tradition. Vatican II rejected this two-source theory of Scripture and tradition and spoke of a single deposit of the word of God, expressed in written form and in tradition. Scripture and tradition are not opposed but their relationship is correlative. The Catholic emphasis on tradition recognizes a living tradition that is not merely a mechanical handing over of the past but the work of the Holy Spirit in and through the lived experience of the church.[60] From an ecumenical perspective, Catholics and Protestants today are finding much common ground in their approaches to tradition.[61]

Earlier manuals of moral theology gave little thought to tradition. However, pre-Vatican II manuals of dogmatic theology assigned an important role to tradition, with an emphasis on church councils and authoritative church teaching. The early councils of the church said much about Christology, Trinity, and grace. No such comparable conciliar statements are found in matters of morality. It seems to me that historically a general agreement often prevailed within the church on moral matters or else the recognition that legitimate diversity could take place on specific issues. Authoritative papal teaching on moral matters first prominently appeared in the seventeenth and eighteenth centuries with the condemnations of the specific positions taken by the two extremes of laxism and rigorism.[62] Eastern Orthodoxy, on the other hand, has given much greater consideration to tradition in moral matters, especially in the form of the teachings of the fathers of the church.[63] In the context of this volume I can only point out the need for Roman Catholic moral theology to give more emphasis to tradition in all its forms. In dealing with tradition, the hermeneutic problem is to discern the difference between continuing a content that expresses divine revelation and a teaching that merely reflects the sociological and cultural circumstances of a particular time and place. This discernment is the nub of a number of contemporary controversies in Roman Catholicism including debate about the ordination of women.

Traditions (small t and plural) refer to the inheritances of a particular church. This book deals with the Catholic tradition in moral theology. Here too one sees a living tradition which is open to the new but in continuity with the ongoing distinctive life and thought of the Roman Catholic community.

REASON AND EXPERIENCE. The Catholic tradition and stance recognize that Christians share with all others the human sources of knowledge coming from reason and experience. However, faith and grace also help these sources without taking away their basic human character. Creation and the incarnation ground these sources of moral wisdom in the Catholic tradition. In the past, this tradition has talked primarily about reason, but today we add experience which recognizes more than the rational and also includes an a posteriori way of moral learning. So strong was the Catholic commitment to reason that it has insisted that faith and reason cannot contradict one another.[64] In practice, however, moral theology gave primary place to reason in discussing the morality of particular actions.

Our stance has pointed out not only the goodness of human reason but also its limitations. From a theological perspective, these limits are two—finitude and the susceptibility to sin. We are all conscious of finitude and how it affects our decisions. How often do we hear it said, "If only I knew then what I know now, I would have done things differently." None of us sees the total picture and knows all that is involved. We all have to live within our limits, which also means that we will at times make mistakes and be wrong. We also know that nobody is a totally objective, neutral observer of the human scene. Second, all human reason and experience can be affected by sin. History and the daily news both testify to the effect of sin on human reason and experience.

Reason, however, can mean different things. Earlier some clarifications have been made. Today, reason is employed more inductively than deductively as it was in an older approach to moral theology. Postmodernity and the experience of the oppressed have made people more suspicious of sweeping universal claims of reason. However, some communality and universality are necessary to maintain life in this world. The contemporary emphasis on praxis reminds us that our practical involvements and commitments also help us discover wisdom and truth.

The concept of experience needs similar unpacking. Whose experience? How is it evaluated? How do we determine if experience is correct or not? Here again we must recognize the dangers of finitude and sinfulness and work against them. More will be said about reason and experience in subsequent chapters.

In addition to human experience, moral theology also recognizes our experience of the presence of God and the Holy Spirit in our lives as a source of moral wisdom and knowledge. The Catholic tradition's lengthy discussion on the discernment of spirits will come into play in a later section.

How do these four sources—Scripture, tradition, reason, and experience—relate to one another? Each of these four sources can underwrite wrong judgments on moral matters. First one tries to correct the limitations and problems that might get in the way of each of these sources in their quest for moral truth. Second, since each one of these sources might be wrong on a particular moral issue, we must not allow any of them to be the final arbiter. For example, contemporary experience challenges the biblical teaching on slavery and women, but Scripture also strongly criticizes the American experience of individualism. Thus we must look for a type of hermeneutic circle in which all four sources relate to one another and mutually correct one another.

In the Roman Catholic tradition the church is the primary teacher and the source of moral wisdom and knowledge. The whole church plays this role through the gift of the Spirit as the church tries to carry on in time and space the word and work of the risen Jesus. In addition, Catholic teaching recognizes a special hierarchical teaching office of pope and bishops to teach authoritatively in the church on matters of faith and morals. The whole church and the hierarchical teaching office are searching for truth in the areas of faith and morals. The whole church and the hierarchical teaching office must critically use and integrate the sources mentioned here. The role of the church as teacher and learner will be discussed in the last chapter.

This chapter has explored the role and function of stance as the logical first step in moral theology. The stance we have chosen, namely, the fivefold Christian mysteries, helps ground our recognition of the four sources of moral wisdom—Scripture, tradition, reason, and experience. Stance provides the perspective in which moral theology looks at the Christian moral life. The next logical question is how do we understand the moral life. The following chapter discusses different models for conceiving the moral life and ultimately opts for a relationality-responsibility model.

NOTES

1. James Sellers, *Theological Ethics* (New York: Macmillan, 1968), pp. 34–38.

2. James M. Gustafson, *Christ and the Moral Life* (New York: Harper and Row, 1968), pp. 240–47.

3. Stephen Duffy, *The Graced Horizon: Nature and Grace in Modern Catholic Thought* (Collegeville, Minn.: Liturgical, 1992).

4. Sellers, *Theological Ethics*, pp. 54–65.

5. Gustafson, *Christ and the Moral Life*, pp. 242–48.

6. Ibid., pp. 11–237.

7. For example, John P. Meier, *A Marginal Jew: Rethinking the Historical Jesus*, 2 vols. (New York: Doubleday, 1991–1994); John Dominic Crossan, *The Historical Jesus: The Life of a Mediterranean Jewish Peasant* (San Francisco: Harper, 1991); Crossan, *Jesus: A Revolutionary Biography* (San Francisco: Harper, 1994); Luke Timothy Johnson, *The Real Jesus: The Misguided Quest for the Historical Jesus and the Truth of the Traditional Gospels* (San Francisco: Harper, 1996).

8. This passage refers especially to the ethics of Karl Barth. See Robin W. Lovin, *Christian Faith and Public Choices: The Social Ethics of Barth, Brunner, and Bonhoeffer* (Philadelphia: Fortress, 1984).

9. For a recent attempt to develop a unified concept of love as central to moral theology, see Edward Collins Vacek, *Love, Human and Divine: The Heart of Christian Ethics* (Washington, D.C.: Georgetown University Press, 1994).

10. Aquinas, *IIaIIae*, q.23, a.8.

11. Gérard Gilleman built on the Thomistic concept of charity as the form of the virtues in a significant pre-Vatican II attempt to move away from the minimalism of the manuals of moral theology. See Gérard Gilleman, *Le primat de la charité in théologie morale: Essai methodologique* (Brussels: Desclée de Brouwer, 1954).

12. Aquinas, *IaIIae*, q.85.

13. Charles E. Curran and Richard A. McCormick, eds. *Readings in Moral Theology No. 7: Natural Law and Theology* (New York: Paulist, 1991).

14. Aquinas, *IaIIae*, q.93–94.

15. Pope John XXIII, *Pacem in terris*, nn. 1–5, in *Catholic Social Thought*, ed. O'Brien and Shannon, pp. 131–32.

16. Angel F. Carrillo de Albornoz, *The Basis of Religious Liberty* (New York: Association Press, 1963), p. 157. Carrillo de Albornoz was the head of the World Council of Churches Secretariat on Religious Liberty. For his analysis of the Vatican II document, see Angel F. Carrillo de Albornoz, *Religious Liberty* (New York: Sheed and Ward, 1967).

17. Declaration on Religious Liberty, nn. 1–3, in *Vatican Council II*, ed. Flannery, pp. 799–802.

18. Ibid., n. 9, p. 806.

19. Pope Paul VI, *On the Regulation of Birth: Humanae Vitae* (Washington, D.C.: United States Catholic Conference, 1968), n. 10, p. 7.

20. Ibid., n. 12, pp. 7–8.

21. Daniel Callahan, ed., *The Catholic Case for Contraception* (New York: Macmillan, 1969).

22. Jaroslav Pelikan, *The Vindication of Tradition* (New Haven, Conn.: Yale University Press, 1984).

23. David Little, "Calvin and the Prospect for a Christian Theory of Natural Law," in *Norm and Context in Christian Ethics*, ed. Gene H. Outka and Paul Ramsey (New York: Charles Scribner's Sons, 1968), pp. 175–97; Michael Cromartie, ed., *A Preserving Grace: Protestants, Catholics, and Natural Law* (Washington, D.C.: Ethics and Public Policy Center, 1997).

24. Helmut Thielicke, *Theological Ethics*, vol. 1, *Foundations*, ed. William H. Lazareth (Philadelphia: Fortress, 1966), p. 398.

25. For example, Ralph M. McInerny, *Ethica Thomistica: The Moral Philosophy of Thomas Aquinas* (Washington, D.C.: Catholic University of America Press, 1982).

26. Franz Böckle, *Law and Conscience* (New York: Sheed and Ward, 1996), pp. 117–31.

27. Henry Chavannes, *L'analogie entre Dieu et le monde selon saint Thomas d'Aquin et selon Karl Barth* (Paris: Cerf, 1969); Battista Mondin, *The Principle of Analogy in Protestant and Catholic Theology*, 2d ed. (Hague, Martinus Nijhoff, 1968).

28. For example, William J. Hill, *Search for the Absent God: Tradition and Modernity in Religious Understanding* (New York: Crossroad, 1992).

29. Dogmatic Constitution on Divine Revelation, nn. 21–26, in *Vatican Council II*, ed Flannery, pp. 762–65.

30. Constitution on the Sacred Liturgy, n. 24, in *Vatican Council II*, ed. Flannery, p. 10.

31. Dogmatic Constitution on Divine Revelation, n. 24, in *Vatican Council II*, ed. Flannery, p. 764.

32. Decree on the Training of Priests, n.16, in *Vatican Council II*, ed. Flannery, p. 720.

33. Pastoral Constitution on the Church in the Modern World, n. 43, in *Vatican Council II*, ed. Flannery, p. 943.

34. Ibid., nn. 12–45, pp. 913–47.

35. For example, Thomas J. J. Altizer and William Hamilton, *Radical Theology and the Death of God* (Indianapolis, Ind.: Bobbs Merrill, 1966); Daniel Callahan, ed., *The Secular City Debate* (New York: Macmillan, 1966).

36. Pastoral Constitution on the Church in the Modern World, nn. 12–22, in *Catholic Social Thought*, ed. O'Brien and Shannon, pp. 172–79.

37. Ibid., nn. 23–32, pp. 179–85.

38. Ibid., nn. 33–39, pp. 185–89. The reference in this footnote is to the document as found in *Catholic Social Thought* not to the document in *Vatican Council II*, ed. Flannery. The reason is that *Vatican Council II*, ed. Flannery, (n. 39, p. 938) omits the heading "A New Earth and a New Heaven." This heading is found in the Latin original. See *Constitutio Pastoralis de Ecclesia in Mundo Huius Temporis*, n. 39, *Acta Apostolicae Sedis* 58 (7 Decembris 1966): 1056.

39. See Duffy, *Graced Horizon*.

40. In the light of Vatican II's emphasis on the role of faith, Jesus, and grace in the moral life, one can understand how the question arose about what is distinctive and unique about Christian action in this world. The debate about this issue was mentioned in chapter one. See Vincent MacNamara, *Faith and Ethics*.

41. Walter Rauschenbusch, *Christianity and the Social Crisis* (New York: Macmillan, 1907). Westminster/John Knox of Louisville reprinted this classic in 1991. For the best available biography of Rauschenbusch, see Paul M. Minus, *Walter Rauschenbusch, American Reformer* (New York: Macmillan, 1988).

42. Martin Luther King, Jr., "Pilgrimage to Non-Violence," *Christian Century* 77 (April 13, 1960): 439.

43. Robin W. Lovin, *Reinhold Niebuhr and Christian Realism* (New York: Cambridge University Press, 1995).

44. In my judgment Gutiérrez remains the most satisfying exponent of liberation theology. See Gutiérrez, *Essential Writings*.

45. Stanley Hauerwas is a prolific author but his most systematic presentation is *The Peaceable Kingdom*.

46. In reality the term Wesleyan Quadrilateral does not come explicitly from John Wesley but from Albert Outler. See Ted A. Campbell, " 'The Wesleyan Quadrilateral': A Modern Methodist Myth," in *Theology in the United Methodist Church*, ed. Thomas G. Langford (Nashville, Tenn.: Kingswood, 1990), pp. 127–82. For the acceptance of the Wesleyan Quadrilateral by some evangelicals, see Donald A. D. Thorsen, *The Wesleyan Quadrilateral: Scripture, Tradition, Reason, and Experience as a Model of Evangelical Theology* (Grand Rapids, Mich.: Zondervan, 1990).

47. Dogmatic Constitution on Divine Revelation, nn. 2–6, in *Vatican Council II*, ed. Flannery, pp. 750–53. For a fuller discussion of revelation from the Catholic perspective, see Avery Dulles, "Faith and Revelation," in *Systematic Theology*, ed. Fiorenza and Galvin, 1, pp. 91–128.

48. Dogmatic Constitution on Divine Revelation, nn. 7–10, in *Vatican Council II*, ed. Flannery, pp. 753–56.

49. Douglas J. Moo, ed., *Biblical Authority and Conservative Perspectives* (Grand Rapids, Mich.: Kregel, 1997).

50. *Ad Hoc* Committee on Biblical Fundamentalism of the National Conference of Catholic Bishops, *A Pastoral Statement for Catholics on Biblical Fundamentalism* (Washington, D.C.: United States Catholic Conference, 1987).

51. Dogmatic Constitution on Divine Revelation, nn. 12–13, in *Vatican Council II*, ed. Flannery, pp. 757–58.

52. For a summary of this discussion, see Albert R. Jonsen and Stephen Toulmin, *The Abuse of Casuistry: A History of Moral Reasoning* (Berkeley, Calif.: University of California Press, 1988), pp. 216–27.

53. Bernhard Häring, *Das Gesetz Christi: Moral theologie dargestellt für Priester und Laien* (Freiburg I. Br.: Erich Wewel, 1954); Bernard Häring, *Free and Faithful in Christ: Moral Theology for Clergy and Laity*, 3 vols. (New York: Seabury, 1978–1981). Note that Häring first published this work in English. For an analysis of Häring's use of Scripture, see Michael Clark, "The Major Scriptural

Themes in the Moral Theology of Father Bernhard Häring," *Studia Moralia* 30 (1992): 3–16, 227–87.

54. Richard Hiers, *The Historical Jesus and the Kingdom of God: Present and Future in the Message and Ministry of Jesus* (Gainesville, Fla.: University of Florida Press, 1973).

55. Elizabeth Schüssler Fiorenza, "Discipleship and Patriarchy: Early Christian Ethos and Christian Ethics in a Feminist Theological Perspective," *Annual of the Society of Christian Ethics* (1982): 131–72.

56. Jeffrey S. Siker, *Scripture and Ethics: Twentieth Century Portraits* (New York: Oxford University Press, 1997), pp. 203–10.

57. For an in-depth discussion from the Catholic perspective, see Raymond Collins, *Divorce in the New Testament* (Collegeville, Minn.: Liturgical, 1992). I basically accept much of Collins's position.

58. Charles E. Curran, *Ongoing Revision in Moral Theology* (Notre Dame, Ind.: Fides, 1975), pp. 66–106.

59. P.C. Rodger and L. Vischer, eds., *The Fourth World Conference on Faith and Order: Montreal, 1963*, Faith and Order Papers, No. 42 (London: SCM, 1964), nn. 38–63, pp. 50–57.

60. For an overview of the Catholic understanding of tradition which is followed closely here, see George H. Tavard, "Tradition" in *The New Dictionary of Theology*, ed. Joseph A. Komonchak, Mary Collins, and Dermot A. Lane (Wilmington, Del.: Michael Glazier, 1987), pp. 1037–41; also Dogmatic Constitution on Divine Revelation, nn. 8–10 in *Vatican Council II*, ed. Flannery, pp. 754–56.

61. Harold C. Skillrud, J. Francis Stafford, and Daniel F. Martensen, eds., *Scripture and Tradition: Lutherans and Catholics in Dialogue IX* (Minneapolis, Minn.: Augsburg, 1995).

62. Vereecke, *Storia della teologia morale nel xvii secolo*, pp. 147–68.

63. For example, Stanley Samuel Harakas, *Toward Transfigured Life: Theoria of Eastern Orthodox Ethics* (Minneapolis, Minn.: Light and Life, 1983).

64. Sokolowski, *God of Faith and Reason*.

3

Model

This chapter will consider the ethical model and some of its significant implications for moral theology. Catholic moral theology has not given that much explicit attention to the question of models, which was also true with regard to the question of stance. However, in reality and implicitly, everyone doing ethics or moral theology employs a model or a way of conceptualizing ethics and the moral life. This chapter explicitly considers this important question, namely, what shall we choose as the primary model for understanding and conceiving the moral life?

Historically, and especially in the area of philosophical ethics, two models have been most prominent—the deontological and the teleological. The deontological sees the moral life primarily in terms of duty, law, or obligation. The teleological model understands the moral life as seeking ends or goals. A third and newer model was developed by H. Richard Niebuhr who spoke of it as the responsibility model.[1] I will develop this third model as a relationality–responsibility model.

A few cautionary notes are in order. If one divides all possible approaches into three categories, these categories will be quite broad. Many theories will fit under the same umbrella even though they may have significant differences among themselves. For the same reason the model that one chooses must be further developed to show how it functions specifically. In choosing a model one decides on the primary way of conceptualizing the moral life, but that does not rule out a place for other considerations. A teleological model or relationality–responsibility model, for instance, does not necessarily exclude some deontological or legal considerations. The model describes the overarching way of analyzing and understanding the moral life. These different approaches will be discussed in some detail.

THE DEONTOLOGICAL MODEL

The deontological approach employs the metaphor of duty, law, or obligation as the primary model for the moral life. In philosophical ethics the Kantian categorical imperative and principle of universalizability exemplify the deontological approach. A person can do anything, provided that he or she accepts the maxim that all persons in similar circumstances may do the same.[2] In a very popular vein the late Senator Sam Ervin, who was in charge of the committee investigating the Watergate scandal in the 1970s, illustrates such an approach. Many people were defending their actions by appealing to the good ends or goals they were trying to accomplish. Sam Ervin said he did not care about the ends or goals. All he wanted to know was, "Did you obey the Constitution or didn't you?"[3]

In popular Christianity, most people probably follow a legal model which is formally a deontological approach. Christian morality is often seen in relation to the Ten Commandments. God is the lawgiver and we are called to obey God's law. Morality is primarily obedience to the law of God.

EXAMPLES OF THE DEONTOLOGICAL MODEL. The manuals of moral theology are likewise illustrations of a deontological approach. These manuals, which became synonymous with moral theology, first appeared at the end of the sixteenth century and continued in existence until Vatican II. Until the seventeenth century, two genres of moral theology had flourished. The first, which involved a systematic study of the moral life of Christians, is found in the *Summa* of Thomas Aquinas (d. 1274) in which moral theology did not exist as a separate discipline but was integrated into the whole of theology. In fact Aquinas did not use the term moral theology to refer to these considerations. Theologians in the sixteenth and seventeenth centuries wrote commentaries on parts of the *Summa* dealing with moral theology. The second strand of moral theology was very practical and associated with the sacrament of penance. The *Libri paenitentiales* had come into existence in the sixth century in connection with the move to private penance beginning in Ireland. These books were practical tariff books that listed the penances that should be assigned for particular sins.[4] In the thirteenth century *Summae confessariorum*, texts that often avoided any systematic approach and considered their subject matter purely in alphabetical order, flourished as aids to the confessor.[5]

The manuals of moral theology emerged at the end of the sixteenth century in response to the Council of Trent's call for all Catholics to confess their mortal sins according to number and species once a year to their priest. The decrees of the Council of Trent also called for the formation of seminaries to train future priests; these seminaries needed textbooks to instruct future priests to "hear confessions" as the celebration of penance was popularly described before Vatican II. The textbooks, called the *Institutiones theologiae moralis*, developed especially among the Jesuits, then spread to all seminaries and theologates. In accord with their pragmatic purpose of delineating sins and distinguishing them by number and species, these manuals gave little consideration to theory and no great attention to other aspects of morality such as virtues.[6]

As they developed over the decades and centuries, moral theology textbooks often appeared in three volumes. Volume one began with the basic principles including a consideration of human acts in a very brief manner (sometimes a shorter section was included on the ultimate end of human beings), but the major emphasis was on law as the objective norm of morality and conscience as the subjective norm of morality. Then there usually followed a further discussion of sin and a short chapter on the virtues, but the emphasis in the presentation was primarily on the obligations and acts of the virtues. In keeping with the deontological or legal model, volume two developed moral theology on the basis of the Ten Commandments. Some manuals written in the Dominican tradition (Thomas Aquinas belonged to the Dominican order) followed the format of a treatise on the virtues, but their concern was still acts that are wrong. Volume three discussed the sacraments primarily from the perspective of canon law, spelling out all the requirements for the valid and licit celebration of the seven sacraments.[7]

In the seventeenth and eighteenth centuries a sharp dispute arose between the proponents of rigorism and laxism, that is, between opposite approaches to the Christian moral life.[8] These controversies occasioned the first heavy involvement of the papal magisterium in matters of moral theology. The Holy Office (today called the Congregation for the Doctrine of the Faith) condemned specific opinions held by the proponents of these two extreme positions. Within parameters marked off by the extremes, tensions soon came to the fore, and the ensuing probabilism controversy had a great influence on the continuing development of the manuals. The probabilism question concerns how to move from practical doubt about the law to the certitude necessary to act. Probabiliorists required that the argument for freedom from the law had to be more probable (the word here really means more proveable) than the reasons for the law's existence in order to free one from obligation. Probabilists required only that the reasons for freedom from the law be truly probable even if less probable than the position in favor of the law. Probabilism based its position on the reflex principle that a doubtful law does not oblige. If the opinion in favor of freedom from the law is truly probable, the law is doubtful and does not oblige. However, all agreed that the safest course always had to be followed in dealing with the means to a necessary end. The analogous case, maintaining that the hunter could not fire at the figure seen in the bush that might be either an animal or a human being, illustrates this need to take the safer course. In the end moderate probablism won the day.

In the wake of the probabilism controversy the legal model was firmly entrenched, and the primary question in moral theology was whether or not an opinion favoring freedom from the law was truly probable. Intrinsic probabilism was based on the reasons themselves; extrinsic probabilism existed if six serious authors held a position. From that time on, the manuals tended to cite the number of authors holding a particular position to establish its extrinsic probability. As a result, less attention was paid to the intrinsic search for the moral truth involved. The practical concerns of the discipline completely overshadowed the more theoretical aspects of the search for moral truth.[9]

St. Alphonsus Liguori (d. 1787) is credited with having proposed a sane middle course between the extremes of rigorism and laxism by defending a moderate probablism, and his approach became generally acceptable in the church. Alphonsus was beatified in 1816, canonized in 1839, declared a doctor of the church in 1871, and made the patron saint of confessors and moral theologians in 1950. The papal approbation of Alphonsus resulted in part from the practical wisdom of his moral theology; but his ultramontanist positions in favor of the papacy and heavy emphasis on the role of Mary further solidified his support. The stature of Alphonsus supported the common perception of the manuals of moral theology as synonymous with all moral theology until Vatican II.[10]

Other theologians have also adopted a deontological model of moral theology. Sectarian versions of the Gospel have seen the radical ethic of Jesus as a command that Christians are called to obey.[11] In contemporary Christian ethics the late Paul Ramsey was very fearful of teleological approaches that sought to justify means on the basis of the ends to be obtained. Ramsey insisted on the importance of norms or principles and an independent ethic of means. The center of Christian morality for him was Christian love, but Christian love was primarily understood as covenant faithfulness. Faithfulness to covenant bonds cannot be eroded to attain other particular goods or ends. Ramsey especially used this approach in his many discussions of bioethics.[12]

EVALUATION OF THE DEONTOLOGICAL MODEL. How ought we to evaluate the deontological or legal model, particularly as it was used in the manuals of moral theology? From a scriptural and theological perspective, law should not be the primary consideration in the Christian moral life. The Ten Commandments themselves should be seen in the light of the covenant and as an expression of God's people's response to the gift of the covenant. The covenant is primarily a relationship initiated by the gracious God to whom we are called to respond. Even in the Hebrew Bible, law or Torah is not the most central moral concern but must be seen in the light of the covenant. Abraham and Sarah, not Moses, are the most significant and important figures in the Hebrew Bible. Yes, there is always a place for law in the context of the covenant, but the law can never become primary.[13]

From a theological perspective our model of Christian morality says something very significant about our concept of God. In the legal model God is primarily the lawgiver. Is this the best image for God? I do not think so. God is the gracious mother and father who shares love and life with us.

More philosophical reasons also argue against the primacy and adequacy of the deontological model especially in its legal form. Law does not cover most of the actions that we perform in our daily lives. Reflect on your own life and actions. How many of your decisions are based on whether or not there is a law to guide you? Law is very helpful in pointing out the boundaries beyond which one should not go, but laws are less helpful in directing our actions in a positive manner. Choosing a spouse, a profession, or a friend is not an action based on laws.

The legal model does not attend carefully to the role of the self as moral subject and agent and especially to the role of the virtues in the moral life. In the legal model obedience becomes the primary virtue. A legal model tends toward an extrinsic morality in which something becomes good because it is commanded and not the other way around. I insist on an intrinsic morality; something is commanded because it is good.

The great complexity in modern life reminds us that conflicts will often arise between different laws or principles. The implied promise of secrecy between a physician and a patient sometimes conflicts with the rights of others and society. The physician, for example, is required to report gunshot wounds to public authorities. The exceptions in many laws and the possible conflict between principles argues against a strict deontological model. However, because some teleological models sacrifice important goods for other ends, some contemporary Christian ethicists speak of prima facie or presumptive norms or principles. There is a prima facie or presumptive moral obligation in favor of keeping secrets but other important moral values may overturn that presumption.[14] Such modified deontological approaches avoid some problems that arise from strict deontology, but they suffer from some other shortcomings of the deontological or legal model.

In terms of an overall evaluation, the *Institutiones theologiae moralis* involved a marvelous adaptation to the pastoral needs of the church at the time, but as a compendium of all moral theology, the manuals were quite inadequate. They considered only acts and even that from the minimalistic perspective of whether or not sin exists. The moral theology of the manuals was almost totally separated from scriptural, theological, and liturgical concerns and perspectives. The manuals, in the light of their legal model and pragmatic approach, became closely associated with canon law as is evident in their treatment of the sacraments. The probabilism controversy introduced a conflict between freedom and law and emphasized an extrinsic approach to morality— something is good because it is commanded. An intrinsic approach to morality understands moral obligation not as a constraining force on human freedom but as the requirement for true human living and fulfillment.

The deontological model has some significant strengths; it upholds objectivity, disagrees with subjectivism and relativism, and prevents the individual from making personal exceptions, thus combating the dangers of individualism so prevalent in our society. However, the problems intrinsic to the deontological model argue against making it the primary model for moral theology or Christian ethics.

THE TELEOLOGICAL MODEL

The teleological model emphasizes goals or ends. Something is good if it brings you to the goal and bad if it prevents your attaining that goal. In philosophical ethics Aristotle stands as a good example of the teleological approach. Teleologists often employ the moral term of the good, whereas deontologists tend to speak of the right.[15] In everyday life we often follow a teleological model. We determine what our end or goal is before we choose the means to achieve that goal or end. Such a model incorporates a commonsensical approach to making human decisions.

TELEOLOGY OF THOMAS AQUINAS. In the Roman Catholic tradition Thomas Aquinas stands as the best example of a teleological approach to morality.[16] Aquinas begins his consideration of morality with a discussion of the ultimate end of human beings, which, he maintains, is happiness. What makes us happy? Wealth and the possession of material goods do not. Aquinas says that human beings have basic drives or tendencies within us. For Aquinas the two most distinctive drives of human beings are the intellect and the will. The intellect is constantly seeking truth and the will is seeking the good. We will never be content or happy until these two fundamental human drives achieve their end. But this achievement can only occur fully in heaven when our intellect will know God who is the perfect truth and our will will love God who is the perfect good.[17] The teleological structure of such an ethic and its intrinsic character are obvious. What makes us happy is not something outside ourselves but an intrinsic good that truly fulfills us as persons. In this understanding morality is not imposed on human beings from the outside but arises from the demands of our own being as it seeks its fulfillment and perfection. Objective morality and personal happiness are not opposed to one another but are intimately related.

Thomas Aquinas is the most significant figure in the history of Catholic theology. By the sixteenth century the *Summa* had become the textbook of theology, and the neoscholastic revival in the nineteenth century authoritatively imposed Thomism on all Catholics. Leo XIII in his encyclical *Aeterni Patris* called for the restoration of Christian philosophy in Catholic institutions of higher learning according to the mind and method of Thomas Aquinas. The Code of Canon Law in 1918 required that Catholic philosophy and theology be taught according to the method, doctrine, and principles of the Angelic Doctor.[18]

Note, however, that the authoritative imposition of Thomism did not really affect or change the manuals of moral theology. The manualistic and Thomistic approaches to moral theology were quite different as illustrated by their use of different models. The fact that Leo XIII and his successors authoritatively supported both St. Thomas and St. Alphonsus left many with the impression that the manuals of moral theology were truly Thomistic. In fact, they were vastly different. The moral manuals were in place for a long time and papal approbation of Alphonsus gave them continued backing. They were never really affected by the neoscholasticism of the nineteenth and early twentieth centuries. The manuals often cited Thomas Aquinas, but from their seventeenth century beginnings they followed their own deontological model which was coherent with their practical purpose of determining what is sinful.

In my judgment the approbation and authoritative imposition of Thomas in the nineteenth and early twentieth century was very effective in Catholic philosophy and dogmatic theology, but it involved a defensive mentality that strove to avoid dialogue with contemporary thought. Ironically, if church authority before the thirteenth century had done with Augustine what nineteenth-century church authority did with Thomas Aquinas, there never would have been a Thomas Aquinas! Thomas's genius was his willingness to dialogue with the new thought of his day—Aristotelianism was then having a great impact on the university world of Europe. The authoritative imposition of his thought and method was very un-Thomistic, but it made him an even more significant figure in the Catholic tradition. Since Vatican II a pluralism of different theological methodologies has emerged in Roman Catholic theology.

The importance of Thomas Aquinas calls for a fuller explanation of his approach to moral theology in the context of his teleological model.[19] After discussing the ultimate end of human existence, Thomas considers the actions by which we arrive at our end. Acts proper to human beings are voluntary acts that can be either good or bad (*IaIIae*, q.21). Acts common to humans and all the animals come from the passions, which are principally divided into the concupiscible (e.g., temperance) and the irascible (e.g., fortitude) appetites (*IaIIae*, q.22-48). The *Summa* next discusses the principles from which our actions flow which are habits or stable dispositions to act in a certain way. Good habits are virtues; bad habits are vices. Thomas developed these aspects in great detail (*IaIIae*, q.55-89). The extrinsic principles of human acts are law (*IaIIae*, q.89-108) and grace (*IaIIae*, q.109-114).

In his discussion of law Thomas develops the teaching on natural law that has been so central in the Catholic moral tradition. Despite the section on law, Thomas does not follow a deontological or legal model. His primary model is teleological. Note that the section on law comes at the very end of his discussion of what today we call general or fundamental moral theology. Earlier and at much greater length he had developed his understanding of the ultimate end and presented the virtues as central to moral theology. In his development of what today we call special moral theology (i.e., in dealing with particular types of acts), Thomas discussed the moral life common to all human beings, following the outline of the virtues. He first considers the theological virtues of faith, hope, and charity (*IIaIIae*, q.1-46), and then the cardinal virtues of prudence, justice, fortitude, and temperance (*IIaIIae*, q.47-170). "Cardinal" does not necessarily mean the most significant virtues but rather the logical hinges on which all the other virtues can depend. Prudence is the virtue that regulates practical reason; justice directs the will; fortitude properly orders the irascible appetites; and temperance orders the concupiscible appetites. Thus Thomas clearly followed a teleological model and virtue approach to moral theology not a deontological or legal model and approach.

Yet Thomas's system not only has a place for law, it is also the classical explanation of natural law in the Catholic tradition. In his comparatively short discussion of law (*IaIIae*, q.90-108), Thomas first considers what is common to all law and then the different types of law. In particular Thomas treats five types of law—eternal law, natural law, human law, the law of the Old Testament, and the new law. Only one question (*IaIIae*, q.94) is devoted to natural law.

For Thomas law in general is not an act of the will but an act of reason. Law is a rule of action, but reason is the norm and measure of all human action (*IaIIae*, q.90). This notion is very important for understanding Thomas's approach to law, especially in the light of most legal models' association of law with the will of the legislator. Thus Christians often speak of the will of God as the most important law and of our corresponding obligation to obey God's will. But for Thomas, law belongs primarily to practical reason and not to the will. The eternal law is not God's will but rather divine wisdom directing all actions and movements to their proper end *(IaIIae,* q.93). Note again the teleological approach. Divine reason is a law insofar as it directs all things to their proper end. The natural law is the rational creature's participation in the eternal law *(IaIIae,* q.91).

Thomas's approach highlights the role of mediation in the Catholic tradition. God the Creator made all things to strive for their ultimate end in accord with the divine plan of God's practical reason. The same God gave human beings their reason so that human reason, reflecting on human nature and God's creation, can understand how God wants us to act in this world. To determine what God wants, one does not go immediately to God and ask. Rather God gives us reason, which reflecting on what God has made, can come to know how God wants us to act. Human law is then primarily an act of reason and not of the will of the legislator. An unjust law, per se, does not oblige. The lawgiver has to conform the law to human reason. In this sense Thomas asserts the legitimacy, and at times even the obligation, of disobeying unjust laws *(IaIIae,* q.95-96). This emphasis on law as reason and wisdom continues to be an aspect of Catholic and Christian tradition aside from moral theology. When Christians gather in liturgy to pray for civil authorities, the gift that is prayed for is wisdom. The wisdom of Solomon stands as the model for what human legislators should do.[20]

More will be said shortly about the Thomistic natural law approach and some of it will be critical. However, the present treatment is sufficient to show that Thomas's moral model is teleological. Natural law is not the primary moral consideration for Thomas, and even the natural law is always seen in its relationship to reason ordering things to their end.

One can find important examples of the teleological model in many modern religious and philosophical schools of thought. The Social Gospel school of Walter Rauschenbusch employed a basic teleological approach with the values taught by Jesus being the goal or ideal toward which Christians strive.[21] Joseph Fletcher, the advocate of situation ethics in the 1960s and 1970s, also embraced a teleological approach by making love the goal or end of Christian ethics and defining and identifying love with doing good. Fletcher sees his approach in terms of consequentialism or utilitarianism.[22]

CONSEQUENTIALISM AND UTILITARIANISM. In philosophical ethics consequentialism and utilitarianism are illustrations of an extrinsic teleological approach. The goodness of an action depends only on its consequences. If the consequences are good, the act is good.[23] Utilitarianism is a form of consequentialism that makes the greatest good of the greatest number the ultimate moral criterion.[24] Despite the prominence of utilitarianism in some circles, this model has three serious drawbacks. First, utilitarianism runs the risk of subordinating the individual to the good of the whole. The greatest good of the greatest number may be at the expense of the basic human rights of one or more human persons. One person should not be sacrificed for the good of the nation. In economic issues, for instance, the total gross national product is not the only factor. How the income is distributed within society remains very important.

Second, utilitarianism shares with all consequentialism the basing of morality only on consequences. But elements other than consequences enter into moral judgment. Moral obligations arise not only from what occurs after my actions but also from what occurs before my actions. Take the example of promise keeping. Obligations of fidelity come into play here. The utilitarians recognize that good consequences come from keeping promises in society, but they give no independent weight to fidelity. Thus, one can justify breaking a promise to achieve a greater good, provided that no one has to know that a promise was broken. Fidelity, however, reminds us of the commitment to others that must enter into the moral picture. When I have committed myself as a person to another person I cannot simply consider the consequences of my actions in determining whether or not to keep the promise. On the other hand, the Catholic tradition has always recognized that promise keeping is not an absolute. A substantial change in the matter of the promise or a change in the person making the promise can mean that the promise is no longer binding.[25] But here again, factors other than consequences enter into the moral calculus. Think of the moral realities and values that may have come into play before the action itself takes place, such as gratitude, fidelity, or punishment.

A third series of objections to consequentialism comes from the need to consider the way or manner in which the action is performed. This consideration often refers to the intentionality of the agent. One must consider not only the net good or evil resulting from the act but also the way in which the act is accomplished by the agent. The moral evaluation of killing differs greatly depending on how the killing was caused—for example, intentionally, accidentally, or by not acting when it was morally impossible to act.

Consequentialists and utilitarians are aware of the arguments that have been proposed against their approach, and some have modified their approach. Thus, some insist on rule utilitarianism—the rule that will result in the best over all consequences—rather than an act utilitarianism, which occasionally seems to justify actions that most people would intuitively oppose.[26] In the end, however, it seems simplistic to reduce all moral considerations only to consequences.

EVALUATION OF TELEOLOGY. The great difference between Thomistic teleology and consequentialism supports my earlier caveat. Very different ethical theories can fit under the same model. Thomistic teleology is an intrinsic teleology based on inclinations built into the human being that incline one toward particular goods. Thus, the will tends toward the good. Consequentialism is an extrinsic teleology; it reduces everything to the consequences of the act and does not consider the act itself. Thus, the objections raised against utilitarianism do not apply to Thomistic teleology. A later section will address some of the problems in the Thomistic approach, but first some comments about teleology in general.

From a biblical perspective God is not understood primarily as the ultimate end of human beings. This image of God is not entirely foreign to Scripture, but it is not a primary image in a scriptural approach. On the other hand, tradition even before Thomas Aquinas has often appealed to an understanding of God as one's ultimate end. Consider, for example, Augustine's famous dictum that God has made us for God's self and our hearts will not rest until they rest in God.[27] Still, the scriptural understanding of God is more personal, existential, and all-encompassing than the image of God as one's ultimate end.

From a theological perspective we human beings do not have complete control over our end. Christian eschatology reminds us that our ultimate end is God's gracious gift, and we will never attain it in this world. Our final end is outside and beyond history. Here we live only in the penultimate time that will always be in some discontinuity with the future. Such a criticism applies especially to an extrinsic teleology emphasizing the end or consequences that we can attain. Intimately connected with this eschatological criticism is the difficulty in all teleologies of dealing with the reality of suffering and the tragic. Human and Christian experience remind us of the tragic reality that is so often thrust upon us in our lives. We do not control all that happens. Many things occur to us that we do not want and do not seek. The Christian reality of the cross reminds us of our many limitations and that we are often passive and acted upon by others. Suffering is a mystery; we will never fully understand it, but the teleological ethical model seems to have little or no capacity to explain or address this reality.

From a philosophical perspective the teleological model in its extrinsic and intrinsic forms is too purposive and controlling. In the Thomistic tradition God has put certain ends into human nature and human faculties, ends that human beings can discover. But many things occur in history that affect us, who we are, and how we are to act. Moral reality cannot be reduced only to the ends or purposes that God has put into human nature and especially into human powers or faculties. Human beings develop over time and many other historical and cultural realities impact and influence our development and who we are. The purposiveness of extrinsic teleology can harbor the mis-guided attempt to control everything through our actions. Again, we do not have that much control over what happens in our world and even to ourselves.

The teleological approach tends to be too rational insofar as both intrinsic and extrinsic teleology rely heavily on reason but seem to exclude the affective, the emotional, and other aspects of the human. The rational is very important, but the human being is more than rational. The traditional Catholic emphasis on the discernment of spirits reminds us of these other aspects. Ignatius of Loyola talked about the light and understanding that one can discern from experiences of desolation and consolation.[28] The rational is an important aspect of human and Christian ethics, but it is not everything.

Extrinsic teleology, as illustrated in utilitarianism, suffers from two other problems associated with its emphasis on human control. This model sees the human being, in H. Richard Niebuhr's terms, as a maker.[29] Such an approach is again too one-sided and forgetful of other dimensions of human existence. The human person is also a lover, a friend, a storyteller, a listener, a comforter, an artist, a player. The person as maker is a congenial model for a technologically ad-vanced society, but our growing consciousness of the limits of technol-ogy also reminds us of the limits in this model.

Extrinsic teleology is also in danger of using the end to justify the means. The means-end relationship is one of the most significant and vexing issues in any ethics. At times the end justifies the means, but when ends or consequences are seen as primary, we are in danger of justifying any means.

RELATIONALITY-RESPONSIBILITY MODEL

The relationality-responsibility approach is my name for a third model which, in my judgment, is the most adequate model for Christian ethics. In general this approach sees the human person in multiple relationships with God, neighbor, world, and self. These multiple relationships impinge on the moral reality of the person. Notice again the catholicity of this approach which tries to be inclusive of all the relationships and different temporal realities—past, present, and future. The danger here is to so emphasize the present that we forget about the future or the past. Ecological consciousness, for instance, reminds us of the danger of sacrificing the future to the present.

H. Richard Niebuhr developed his responsibility model in a number of steps. Responsibility involves (1) response to an action upon us; (2) in accord with our interpretation of what is going on; (3) with a willingness to be accountable for any reaction to our reaction; and (4) in solidarity with the continuing community of agents.[30] I would, however, modify this model by calling on persons to initiate action as well as respond to the actions of others. The teleological model may overemphasize the creativity and initiative of persons, but some creativity needs to be incorporated into the relationality-responsibility model.

Scriptural, theological, and philosophical arguments can be made to show the centrality of a relationality-responsibility model. The scriptural witness certainly attests to the importance of these relationships. Obviously, our relationship to God is significant, but it's not our only relationship. Love of God and love of neighbor are intimately conjoined. The so-called Last Judgment scene in Matthew 25 reminds us that what we do to the least of our sisters and brothers we do to God. The Synoptic Gospels emphasize the love of enemies (Matt 5:43-48, Luke 6:27-36). The First Letter of John (4:20-21) asks how we can love the God we do not see if we do not love our neighbor whom we do see. The Catholic tradition, certainly more than the Protestant, has stressed relationship to self including a proper love of self.[31] Recall the emphasis on happiness and fulfillment in Thomas Aquinas. The dangers of selfishness and egoism are always present, but the Catholic tradition brings together love of God, love of neighbor, and love of self.[32] The biblical teaching on creation also underscores our relationship to all God's creation, but until recently this relationship has not received that much attention.

The biblical understanding of sin in the book of Genesis also illustrates a relationality-responsibility model. Since Genesis is the first book in the canon of Scripture and begins with creation, most people assume its primary purpose is creation. But the stories found here were narrated centuries after the presumed beginning and put together in their present form beginning in the tenth century B.C.E. As noted in chapter two Genesis deals not so much with creation as with the most difficult question facing any believer then and now—how can there be so much evil and suffering in our world if it has been created by a gracious God? The answer is that evil comes not from God but from human beings. God made everything good, but human sin brings about evil.

Many Catholics now recognize that Genesis is not history as we know it but a mythical account of the origins of the world. Likewise the two accounts of creation found in Genesis come from different sources—the first account from the Priestly source (Gen 1—2:4) and the second, the earlier J or Yahwist account. The description of the fall in chapter three comes from the latter source.[33] In light of our treatment of moral models, it is useful to ask: How does Genesis understand sin?

The *Catechism of the Catholic Church* reflects the main thrust of the tradition by understanding sin in the light of the deontological approach: "It [sin] has been defined as 'an utterance, a deed, or a desire contrary to the eternal law.'" The catechism cites this quotation from St. Augustine and also refers to its use by St. Thomas Aquinas.[34] Thomas accepts Augustine's definition[35] but also sees sin, especially mortal sin, as being *contra finem*—against the end. For Thomas mortal sin goes against the ultimate end which is God, whereas venial sin goes not against the ultimate end but against the means to the end.[36] In popular religious language, sin has generally been understood as disobeying or breaking God's law.

Aspects of the Genesis story support this deontological approach to sin. Clearly, sin is the breaking of God's commandment not to eat the fruit of the tree, but a deeper reality exists here. The reason for eating the fruit was that Adam and Eve wanted to be like God. They refused to accept a relationship of loving dependence on God. Other details of the story also bring out the relational aspect. When God came to walk with Adam and Eve in the garden in the cool of the day, they hid themselves. Their loving relationship with God had been broken. The third chapter ends with God's expulsion of Adam and Eve from the garden. Most see this exile as God's punishment for their sin. But it is an intrinsic, not an extrinsic, punishment. The parent, who threatens to bar the disobeying child from watching television if she continues to be uncooperative, employs an extrinsic penalty. No connection exists between the deed and the punishment. But in an intrinsic penalty the punishment is the logical and natural consequence of the deed itself. The student who does not study will be punished with a poor grade. By breaking their relationship with God, Adam and Eve could no longer stay in God's garden.

Sin also affects their relationship with one another. In the Yahwist account, Adam had no one with whom to share his life and love, so God made Eve. They were to cleave to one another and become one flesh in a union of love and life. What happened as a result of their sin? When God asked Adam in the garden what happened, Adam pointed an accusing finger at Eve—she did it, not I. Sin had affected the intimate relationship of love and life between Adam and Eve. The Yahwist account goes on to tell the story of Cain and Abel. Sin so affected the relationship between human beings that the son of Adam and Eve killed his brother. The first eleven chapters of Genesis detail the growing power and prevalence of sin.

Sin also affects human beings in their relationship with the natural, created world. As a result of sin Adam must toil and sweat to till the earth and bring forth fruit. The implication is that without sin work would not have involved such toil, sweat, and tears. Sin affected Adam in what was then considered to be the man's most characteristic aspect—his sustenance-providing work. With regard to the woman, the authors of Genesis considered childbearing to be the most distinctive characteristic of the woman. As a result of sin she will bring forth her children in pain and sorrow. The implication is that childbirth for the woman and work for the man are affected by sin. The very muscles and tissues of Eve's body which would have joyfully participated in giving life now fight her intention and cause pain and sorrow. Sin affects our relationship to created nature.

Sin also affects our relationship with ourselves. Before sin Adam and Eve were not ashamed of their nakedness. But after sin, they were ashamed. The peace and harmony of their total person is disrupted by the reality of sin. To the authors of Genesis, this disruption within the human person, involving the body and perhaps also the sexual appetite, would never have occurred if it were not for sin. Thus, Genesis shows us that sin is really a relational term; it affects our multiple relationships with God, neighbor, world, and self.

The Christian doctrine of the Trinity reminds us that this theological perspective also requires a relational understanding of persons. The divine persons are not individualistic monads but persons in relationships. This perspective is grounded in the relational reality of the three persons in the Trinity. Father, Son and Holy Spirit are subsistent relations.[37]

The fundamental Christian understanding of grace and the divine-human relationship calls for a relational model. Grace is God's gracious gift; we are called to respond. Many have acknowledged that the call-response theme is fundamental in moral theology.[38] In addition, a fuller explanation of God's grace and gracious call to us highlights another aspect of the relational model. As mentioned in chapter one, the Catholic understanding insists on a communitarian notion of our relationship to God. The covenant was not primarily with an individual as such but with a people—the people of God. The Catholic tradition emphasizes the role of the church community. Salvation comes not directly and immediately from God to the individual but in and through the community of God's people, the mystical body of Christ. By baptism we are incorporated into this saving community.

Contemporary philosophical approaches support the relationality-responsibility model. Consider the great diversity and particularity existing in our world. In the midst of such diversity the deontological and teleological models do not seem adequate. There appears to be no detailed law that all people should follow. There seem to be no built-in ends or goals that all should seek. However, in this situation, the danger arises that everyone does one's own thing. Some type of relationality-responsibility approach seems to be the best way to avoid tribalism and chaos in the midst of the particularity and diversity of our global existence today.[39] Earlier this volume recognized both the catholic emphasis on universality and the importance of a historically conscious approach. The relationality-responsibility model interpreted in the light of catholicity fits the historical consciousness approach with its greater emphasis on historicity, change, individuality, and contingency and its unwillingness to let go of some general universal morality common to all humankind. Neither the deontological nor the teleological model can account as well for the diversity, historicity, and contingency which characterize so much of our life today.

Since Kant, philosophy has turned toward the subject. Karl Rahner and Bernard Lonergan, two of the most influential Catholic theologians in the second half of the twentieth century, stressed the role of the subject in their philosophy and theology.[40] This emphasis on the subject naturally brings the concept of responsibility to the fore. However, we are very aware today that the person is not a self-creator but a person with limited creativity and initiative in the context of multiple relationships. Persons are not totally determined by these relationships, but their freedom and creativity are limited by these realities. Such an anthropology constitutes one more reason for adopting a relationality-responsibility model. Subsequent chapters will develop this model.

THE RELATIONALITY-RESPONSIBILITY MODEL AND CATHOLIC MORAL THEOLOGY TODAY

As might be expected, the Catholic tradition today, as seen in its official teachings and practices, is not consistent in adopting an ethical model. Aspects of the legal and the teleological models remain, but significant moves toward a relationality-responsibility model are also evident.

USE OF A RELATIONALITY-RESPONSIBILITY MODEL. Official Catholic social teaching has definitely moved toward a more relationality-responsibility model even though its documents never explicitly reflect on the model they are employing. *Pacem in terris* (1963) illustrates the deontological model at work. Peace on earth can be established only if the order laid down by God be dutifully observed. According to John XXIII, an astounding order reigns in our world, and the greatness of human beings is to understand that order.[41]

> But fickleness of opinion often produces this error, that many think that the relationships between human beings and states can be governed by the same laws as the forces and irrational elements of the universe, whereas the laws governing them are of quite a different kind and are to be sought elsewhere, namely, where the Father of all things wrote them, that is, in human nature. By these laws human beings are most admirably taught first of all how they should conduct their mutual dealings among themselves, then how the relationships between the citizens and the public authorities of each state should be regulated, then how states should deal with one another, and finally how, on the one hand,

individual human beings and states, and, on the other hand, the community of all peoples, should act toward each other, the establishment of such a community being urgently demanded today by the requirements of universal common good.[42]

Recent hierarchical social teaching accepts both historical consciousness and a relationality-responsibility model. *Octogesima adveniens*, the 1971 apostolic letter of Paul VI, illustrates these motifs.

> In the face of such widely varying situations it is difficult for us to utter a unified message and to put forward a solution which has universal validity. Such is not our ambition, nor is it our mission. It is up to the Christian communities to analyze with objectivity the situation which is proper to their own country, to shed on it the light of the Gospel's unalterable words, and to draw principles of reflection, norms of judgment, and directives for action from the social teaching of the church. . . . It is up to these Christian communities, with the help of the Holy Spirit, in communion with the bishops who hold responsibility and in dialogue with other Christian brethren and all people of good will, to discern the options and commitments which are called for in order to bring about the social, political, and economic changes seen in many cases to be urgently needed.[43]

The very title of the 1983 pastoral letter on peace and war issued by the U.S. Catholic bishops indicates a relationality-responsibility model at work—"The Challenge of Peace: God's Promise and Our Response."[44] The 1986 pastoral letter of the U.S. bishops on the economy begins by mentioning the three questions that need to be addressed: "What does the economy do *for* people? What does it do *to* people? How do people *participate* in it?[45]

John Paul II has also employed a relationality-responsibility model in his social teachings. *Centesimus annus,* written in 1991 on the one hundredth anniversary of Leo XIII's *Rerum novarum,* understands the human person in the light of this model.

> Man [*sic*] remains above all a being who seeks the truth and strives to live in that truth, deepening his understanding of it through a dialogue which involves past and future generations. From this open search for truth which is renewed in every generation, the culture of a nation derives its character. Indeed, the

heritage of values which has been received and handed down is always challenged by the young. To challenge does not necessarily mean to destroy or reject a priori, but above all to put these values to the test in one's own life and through the existential verification to make them more real, relevant, and personal, distinguishing the valid elements in the tradition from false and erroneous ones, or from obsolete forms which can be usefully replaced by others more suited to the times.[46]

Another illustration of the move toward a relationality-responsibility model comes from developments in the sacrament of penance. The name popularly given to this sacrament is confession because, until recently, the primary act involved in the sacrament was the confession of sins according to number and species. Such an approach was based on a legal model with its understanding of sin as an offense against the law of God. The penitent had to confess her or his sinful acts against God's law.[47] In 1973, the Congregation for Divine Worship in accord with the liturgical developments at Vatican II, issued a new rite for the sacrament of penance which is now called reconciliation. Thus, even the name of the sacrament reflects the shift toward a more relationality-responsibility model. The sacrament of penance involves the multiple reconciliations of the sinner with God, church, neighbor, self and world.[48]

However, as the evolution of sacramental penance also illustrates, the shift to a relationality-responsibility model has not been complete and all-embracing. This same Vatican document proposes three different rites or formats for the sacrament of penance. The first rite for the reconciliation of individual penitents basically follows the older format for the confession of sins according to number and species but adds more dialogue between penitent and minister, the option of a face-to-face meeting, and a greater use of Scripture. The second rite of reconciliation goes even further to create a communal setting but still with individual confession and absolution. The third rite brings the communal or community celebration together with general absolution and involves no individual confession, but this rite can only be used in emergency situations.

Tensions, ferment, and growing practical neglect mark Catholic approaches to penance today. Rome continues to restrict the sacrament to individual confession to a priest who absolves the penitent; in practice, some parishes celebrate communitarian penance without individual confession, on some occasions getting around the law by claiming that a large number of confessors cannot be found. The communal rite emphasizes the relational and communitarian dimensions of reconciliation. We are reconciled to God in and through our reconciliation with the church. As sin involves multiple relationships, so does reconciliation. Often the bishops in the United States have found themselves caught between the Roman authorities and some of their own pastors who celebrate communal penance at various times. However, all admit that the frequency of sacramental confession has declined spectacularly within Roman Catholic practice in the United States. Regular participation in sacramental penance no longer plays an important role in the lives of most Catholics.[49]

In the present circumstances I fear that Catholics are in danger of losing their sense of sin, which—in the light of our stance—remains an important factor in Christian existence. A properly celebrated community penance celebration with communal absolution would help Catholics become more conscious of the important realities of sin, penance, conversion, and reconciliation involving our relationship with God, our neighbors and families, and the larger world. The papal pastoral office, in renaming the sacrament clearly recognized the move to a relationality-responsibility approach, but it has stopped short of accepting the implications of that approach in practice.

The defects in the rite of individually confessing one's sins according to number and species illustrate the shortcomings of the legal model. Such a model accommodates the objective order but not the subjective dispositions of persons. Even the older manualists recognized that the confessor could never be certain of the penitent's real disposition. The objective act alone or any list of objective acts does not tell one about the motivation, intentionality, and disposition of the person.[50] The confession of a list of sins does not sit well with the reality of sin's effect on our multiple relationships with God, neighbor, world, and self. The greater emphasis on the relational understanding of sin and reconciliation argue against the need to include the individual confession of sins according to number and species in every celebration of penance. Such a model, especially if celebrated in a more dialogical setting can be fruitful and helpful, but it is not the best, and certainly not the only, format for the sacrament of reconciliation.

USE OF A DEONTOLOGICAL MODEL. On the other hand, hierarchical teaching on sexual matters has not yet accepted the relationality responsibility model. A classicist approach and a deontological model form the primary perspectives for documents concerning this theme.

The 1975 "Declaration on Sexual Ethics" issued by the Congregation for the Doctrine of the Faith exemplifies the Congregation's emphasis on eternal and immutable moral laws.

> Therefore there can be no true promotion of human dignity unless the essential order of human nature is respected. . . . These fundamental principles which can be grasped by reason are contained in "the divine law—eternal, objective, and universal—whereby God orders, directs, and governs the entire universe and all the ways of human community by a plan conceived in wisdom and love. Human beings have been made by God to participate in this law with a result that under the gentle disposition of divine providence they can come to perceive ever increasingly the unchanging truth." This divine law is accessible to our minds.[51]

And finally, John Paul II's 1993 encyclical *Veritatis splendor* also employs a deontological model. The first paragraph emphasizes the need for obedience to the truth but recognizes that such obedience is not always easy.[52] The problem, according to this document is that even inside the church many separate freedom from truth and thus reject the norms traditionally proposed by the church (n. 4). Human freedom and God's law are not opposed (n. 18). The biblical story of the rich young man presents Jesus as the teacher whose commandments are to be obeyed by the disciples (nn. 6-27). The first and longest of the four parts of chapter two deals with freedom and the law (nn. 35-53). Chapter two especially emphasizes the role of natural law. The negative precepts of the natural law oblige always and in every circumstance—*semper et pro semper* (n. 52). The third chapter continues this approach with its emphasis on laws and commands and the church's role in defending universal and unchanging moral norms (nn. 90-117). Without doubt *Veritatis splendor's* primary purpose is to strongly support the existence of immutable universal norms; hence, its reliance on the legal model.

PRACTICAL IMPLICATIONS OF A RELATIONALITY-RESPONSIBILITY MODEL. I have developed elsewhere at greater length the argument that significant differences in the ethical models and approaches are evident in papal social teaching, on the one hand, and papal sexual teaching, on the other.[53] If the relationality-responsibility model were used in sexual areas, some significant changes would occur. One illustration will suffice.

Catholic sexual teaching in the manuals and in contemporary documents of the hierarchical magisterium appeals explicitly to natural law as the basis for the teaching.[54] In this context one recognizes some of the teleological aspects of natural law found in Thomas Aquinas. Sexual morality is grounded in the nature, purpose, and finality of the sexual faculty. The sexual faculty has the twofold finality of procreation and love union. Every act of the faculty must remain open to these two God-given finalities. For this reason, masturbation, artificial contraception for spouses, and homosexual activity are morally wrong. The procreative finality also involves the need for the education of offspring and calls for the permanent bond of marriage.

Should sexual morality be grounded solely in the nature and finality of the sexual faculty itself? For example, consider the significant change that occurred with regard to lying in twentieth century Catholic moral theology. Traditionally, lying was judged to be morally wrong because it violated the God-given finality of the faculty of speech, which is to put on my lips what is in my mind. In the twentieth century, however, some authors proposed a different basis for the malice of lying in order to recognize and address conflicting situations. The faculty of speech must always be seen in relationship to the person and the person's relationship to others in society. The malice of lying consists in the violation of my neighbor's right to truth. If the neighbor has no right to truth, then my speech is false, but it is not a lie. The Dutch civilians hiding Jews in the Second World War could tell the Gestapo that no Jews were in their homes and still not be committing a lie.[55]

In a similar manner the sexual faculty should never be absolutized and seen only in itself but in its relationship to the person and the person's relationship to others. Thus in the matter of artificial contraception for spouses, the good of the person or the good of the marriage relationship justifies interfering with the faculty or its act. A relationality-responsibility model logically calls for a number of changes in the contemporary hierarchical sexual teaching.

A fascinating development occurred in 1997. The 1994 *Catechism of the Catholic Church* describes a lie as "to speak or act against the truth in order to lead into error someone who has the right to know the truth."[56] Thus the *Catechism* adopts the relationality-responsibility approach to lying. In conjunction with the promulgation of the definitive Latin edition of the *Catechism* in September 1997, Cardinal Joseph Ratzinger, prefect of the Congregation for the Doctrine of the Faith, issued a short list of corrections or changes to be made in the earlier version of the *Catechism* published in many different modern languages. The description of lying should read: "To lie is to speak or act against the truth in order to lead someone into error."[57] The new reading backs off from the relationality-responsibility model. Cardinal Ratzinger knew very well that some Catholic theologians have pointed out that, if you use the relationality-responsibility model to evaluate the proper use of the faculty of speech, then logically, you should also use it to evaluate the sexual faculty in which case contraception can be morally justified.

All recognize the ferment and tension that exists in contemporary Catholic moral theology. This section explains some of this tension by pointing out that official Catholic teaching and practice have accepted a relationality-responsibility model in some areas, especially social ethics, but continue to employ a legal model in areas of personal and sexual morality. The consistent acceptance of a relationality-responsibility model would permit some changes in offical Catholic sexual teaching, without, as later chapters will show, destroying the need for some universal principles and norms.

After considering the appropriate ethical model, systematic moral theology needs to consider other aspects of the moral life. Here it is helpful to distinguish (but never to separate totally) the subject and the object poles of human existence. The subject pole concerns the human person and involves one's basic orientation and the virtues or attitudes that characterize each one. The object pole considers the world, the communities, and the relationships in which people live and the values and principles that direct them in these areas. The church itself constitutes an important part of the object pole, but the primary importance of the church for Christian morality requires that the church be considered first in Catholic moral theology. The subject pole and the object pole come together in the discussion of decision making and conscience. The following chapters develop these aspects of moral theology.

N O T E S

1. H. Richard Niebuhr, *The Responsible Self: An Essay in Christian Moral Philosophy* (New York: Harper and Row, 1963), pp. 47–68.

2. Immanuel Kant, *Grounding for the Metaphysics of Morals*, with *On a Supposed Right to Lie because of Philanthropic Concerns*, 3rd. ed., trans. James W. Ellington (Indianapolis, Ind.: Hackett, 1993). For a contemporary commentary

with emphasis on the political aspects of Kant's thought, see Roger J. Sullivan, *An Introduction to Kant's Ethics* (New York: Cambridge University Press, 1994).

3. Sam J. Ervin, *Preserving the Constitution: The Autobiography of Sam Ervin, Jr.* (Charlottesville, Va.: Michie, 1984).

4. Hugh Connolly, *The Irish Penitentials and Their Significance for the Sacrament of Penance Today* (Blackrock, Ireland: Four Courts, 1995).

5. For a summary description of these books, see E. Dublanchy, "Casuistique," *Dictionnaire de théologie catholique*, 2, cols. 1859ff.; T. Deman, "Probabilisme," *Dictionnaire de théologie catholique*, 13, cols. 417ff.

6. Vereecke, *Ockham à Saint Alphonse*, pp. 495–508.

7. For a very popular pre-Vatican II manual of moral theology that illustrates this approach see Zalba, *Theologiae moralis summa*.

8. The following paragraphs heavily depend on Vereecke, *Storia*, 3; see also Deman, "Probabilisme," *Dictionnaire de théologie catholique*, 13, cols. 417–619.

9. For a late nineteenth century criticism of the manuals from the professor of moral theology at Catholic University of America, see Thomas Bouquillon, "Moral Theology at the End of the Nineteenth Century," *Catholic University Bulletin* 5 (1899): 244–68.

10. Marciano Vidal, *La morale di Sant'Alfonso: Dal rigorismo alla benignità* (Rome: Editiones Academiae Alphonsianae, 1992).

11. Troeltsch, *Social Teaching of the Churches*, 2, pp. 691–729.

12. Paul Ramsey, *The Essential Paul Ramsey: A Collection*, ed. William Werpehowski and Stephen D. Crocco (New Haven, Conn.: Yale University Press, 1994). For my evaluation of Ramsey's work, see Charles E. Curran, *Politics, Medicine, and Christian Ethics: A Dialogue with Paul Ramsey* (Philadelphia: Fortress, 1973).

13. Roland J. Faley, *Bonding with God: A Reflective Study of Biblical Covenant* (New York: Paulist, 1997); Joseph L. Allen, *Love and Conflict: A Covenantal Model of Christian Ethics* (Nashville, Tenn.: Abingdon, 1984).

14. Richard J. Mouw, *The God Who Commands* (Notre Dame, Ind.: University of Notre Dame Press, 1990); J. Philip Wogaman, *Christian Moral Judgment* (Louisville, Ky.: Westminister/John Knox, 1989).

15. D. S. Hutchinson, "Ethics," in *The Cambridge Companion to Aristotle*, ed. Jonathan Barnes (New York: Cambridge University Press, 1995), pp. 195–232.

16. For an overview of Aquinas's approach to ethics, see Gilson, *Christian Philosophy of Thomas Aquinas*, pp. 251–378.

17. Aquinas, *IaIIae*, q.1–5.

18. I. C. Brady, J. E. Gurr, and J. A. Weisheipl, "Scholasticism," *New Catholic Encyclopedia*, 12, pp. 1153–70.

19. Thomas Aquinas integrated his approach to moral theology into the totality of theology. Likewise, he did not use the term "moral theology." The term "moral theology" was first used by Alan of Lille (d. 1203). See Angelini and Valsecchi, *Disegno storico della teologia morale*, p. 88.

20. 1 Kgs 3:1–28.

21. Walter Rauschenbusch, *Christianity and the Social Crisis*, ed. Robert D. Cross (New York: Harper Torchbook, 1964).

22. Joseph Fletcher, *Situation Ethics* (Philadelphia: Westminister, 1966).

23. Samuel Scheffler, ed. *Consequentialism and Its Critics* (New York: Oxford Univerity Press, 1988).

24. Geoffrey Scarre, *Utilitarianism* (New York: Routledge, 1996).

25. Zalba, *Theologiae moralis summa*, 2, pp. 677–81.

26. Jonathan Glover, ed., *Utilitarianism and Its Critics* (New York: Macmillan, 1990).

27. John K. Ryan, ed., *The Confessions of St. Augustine* (Garden City, N.Y.: Doubleday Image, 1960), book 1, n. 1, p. 43.

28. Jules Toner, *Discerning God's Will: Ignatius of Loyola's Teaching on Christian Decision Making* (St. Louis: Institute of Jesuit Sources, 1991).

29. Niebuhr, *Responsible Self*, pp. 48–51.

30. Ibid., pp. 61ff. For an in-depth and systematic study of responsibility as encompassing much more than the ethical model, see William Schweiker, *Responsibility and Christian Ethics* (New York: Cambridge University Press, 1995).

31. For the positions of the Protestant theologians Anders Nygren and Karl Barth on self-love, see Gene Outka, *Agape: An Ethical Analysis* (New Haven, Conn.: Yale Univeristy Press, 1972), pp. 255–74, 221–29.

32. Vacek, *Love, Human and Divine*, pp. 239–79.

33. Richard J. Clifford, "Genesis," in *The New Jerome Biblical Commentary*, ed. Raymond E. Brown, Joseph A. Fitzmyer, and Roland E. Murphy (Englewood Cliffs, N.J.: Prentice Hall, 1990), pp. 10–13.

34. *Catechism of the Catholic Church* (Liguori, Mo.: Liguori, 1994), n. 1849, p. 453.

35. Aquinas, *IaIIae*, q.71, a.6.

36. Ibid., q.87, a.5.

37. For the relationship of the three persons in the Trinity to our spiritual and moral lives, see Catherine Mowry LaCugna, *God for Us: The Trinity and Christian Life* (San Francisco, Calif.: Harper, 1991).

38. Enda McDonagh, *Gift and Call: Toward a Christian Theology of Morality* (St. Meinrad, Ind.: Abbey, 1975). Note how the titles of Bernard Häring's two versions of systematic moral theology indicate the shift from a legal model to a relationality-responsibility model—Häring, *The Law of Christ* and *Free and Faithful in Christ*.

39. This contemporary context for a responsibility approach is highlighted by Schweiker, *Responsibility and Christian Ethics*, pp. 90–130.

40. See George Vass, *Understanding Karl Rahner* (London: Sheed & Ward, 1985); Frederick E. Crowe, *Lonergan* (London: Geoffrey Chapman, 1992).

41. Pope John XXIII, *Pacem in terris*, nn. 1–5, in *Catholic Social Thought*, ed. O'Brien and Shannon, pp. 131–32.

42. Ibid., nn. 6–7, p. 132.

43. Pope Paul VI, *Octogesima adveniens*, n. 4, in *Catholic Social Thought*, ed. O'Brien and Shannon, p. 266.

44. U.S. Catholic Bishops, "Challenge of Peace," in *Catholic Social Thought*, ed. O'Brien and Shannon, pp. 492–571.

45. Catholic Bishops, *Economic Justice for All*, n. 1, p. 1.

46. Pope John Paul II, *Centesimus annus*, nn. 49–50, in *Catholic Social Thought*, ed. O'Brien and Shannon, p. 477.

47. For an historical overview with emphasis on the present, see James Dallen, *The Reconciling Community: The Rite of Penance* (New York: Pueblo, 1986).

48. Sacred Congregation for Divine Worship, "Rite of Penance," in Joseph M. Champlin, *Together in Peace* (Notre Dame, Ind.: Ave Maria, 1975), pp. 163–270.

49. Robert J. Kennedy, ed., *Reconciliation: The Continuing Agenda* (Collegeville, Minn.: Liturgical, 1987); Mary Collins and David Power, eds., *The Fate of Confession*, vol. 190 of *Concilium* (Edinburgh: T & T Clark, 1987).

50. Gerald Kelly, *The Good Confessor* (Dublin: Clonmore and Reynolds, 1952), pp. 53–59.

51. Congregation for the Doctrine of the Faith, "Declaration on Sexual Ethics," *Origins* 5 (1976), n. 3, p. 485.

52. Pope John Paul II, *Veritatis splendor*, *Origins* 23 (1993): 297–334. References in the text are to the offical paragraph numbers of the document.

53. Charles E. Curran, *Tensions in Moral Theology* (Notre Dame, Ind.: University of Notre Dame Press, 1988), pp. 87–109; Curran, *History and Contemporary Issues: Studies in Moral Theology* (New York: Continuum, 1996), pp. 246–50.

54. Paul VI, *Humanae Vitae*, nn. 7–18, pp. 4–12. For the current debate about Catholic sexual ethics, see Charles E. Curran and Richard A. McCormick, eds., *Readings in Moral Theology No. 8: Dialogue about Catholic Sexual Teaching* (New York: Paulist, 1993).

55. Julius A. Dorszynski, *Catholic Teaching about the Morality of Falsehood* (Washington, D.C.: Catholic University of America Press, 1949).

56. *Catechism of the Catholic Church*, n. 2483, p. 595.

57. Cardinal Joseph Ratzinger, "Vatican List of Catechism Changes," *Origins* 27 (1997): 262.

4

Person

Some preliminary understandings of the complex role of the person in ethics and moral theology are important. The self or the person is a perduring reality. Actions come and go but the person continues and remains. The biblical metaphor reminds us that the good tree brings forth good fruit while the bad tree brings forth bad fruit. The good person tends to do good actions. The moral person and the person's character and virtues are more significant for morality than the individual particular act. This chapter develops an understanding of the person in the light of the fivefold Christian mysteries of our stance and the relationality-responsibility model.

PRELIMINARY CONSIDERATIONS

The Catholic manuals of moral theology paid comparatively little attention to the moral person because they were primarily concerned with sinful acts. However, the Catholic theological tradition in general recognizes the significance of the person and also the different aspects within the person. In the traditional Catholic approach, grace truly brings about an ontological and real change in the person. Justification or redemption is intrinsic and not merely an extrinsic reality in which God no longer imputes guilt to the person. The person is truly changed and becomes a new creation, a child of God, a sister or brother of Jesus.[1] Grace thus affects the total person, but in addition the virtues modify the individual powers or faculties of the person in the Thomistic approach. Grace or charity is mediated through different particular virtues which dispose the person to perform good acts.[2]

The Catholic emphasis on intrinsic justification and the need for each one's response to God's gracious gift accounts for the insistence on personal growth as a distinct area of spirituality. The tension in the stance between redemption and resurrection destiny grounds the call for growth in the moral life. At times the Catholic tradition has given too much emphasis to human response and growth and failed to under-score the fact that salvation is primarily God's loving gift to us, but these excesses do not deny the need for growth in the spiritual life. Spiritual writers such as Teresa of Avila and John of the Cross have recognized stages of growth in spiritual life and in prayer.[3] Textbooks in spiritual theology often refer to three stages of growth—the purga-tive, the illuminative, and the unitive way. These classical spiritual stages go back at least to the sixth century.[4]

Contemporary humanistic psychologists also stress the role of the self and the development of the self as a moral person. Catholic authors in dialogue with such psychologists as Lawrence Kohlberg and Carol Gilligan base their analysis and criticisms on psychological and theo-logical grounds.[5] Although the manuals of moral theology did not consider these aspects of the moral person, such considerations are necessary for a complete understanding of morality. They are also very much in keeping with the broader Catholic theological and spiritual tradition.

A very important distinction concerns the moral person as *subject* and as *agent*. A moment's reflection makes us aware of this distinction. By my actions I make myself the person I am; and by my actions I do things for good or for ill in this world. I am both subject and agent. How these two aspects relate specifically to each other will be devel-oped later, but the distinction itself must be recognized at the start.

This distinction has not been that explicit in the Catholic tradition, but the basic reality behind it has been recognized especially in the question of what we now call an invincibly erroneous conscience. This reality involves an individual doing a wrong act but innocently thinking and intending to do the right act. The person is invincibly ignorant. Before Thomas Aquinas, this case was interpreted in two ways. Bernard of Clairvaux insisted on an objective interpretation that bound intention and conscience to the object. Actions done through invincible ignorance were bad; they are not excused or good. On the other hand, Peter Abelard insisted that intention alone could make the action good. Thomas solved the problem by saying that the objectively wrong act was excused, but not good—the act remains wrong but the person who did it is not responsible for the wrong act. However, Alphonsus Liguori went further than Aquinas by saying that such acts were not only excused, but good and meritorious.[6] This position became the common teaching among Catholic theologians, although John Paul II in his encyclical *Veritatis splendor* did not accept this position.[7] This discussion recognizes the twofold concept of the person as subject and agent. By my actions I make myself a moral subject, but I also perform objective actions that affect others and the world for good or ill. These two aspects of the moral person must be kept in mind if we want to understand the moral person from the perspective of Catholic moral theology.

In keeping with the Catholic teaching on grace and the virtues, one distinguishes between the basic orientation of the total person and the virtues that modify and dispose the person with regard to her multiple relationships. One's basic orientation is mediated through the virtues to particular actions. This chapter will consider the person as such; the next chapter will discuss the virtues.

The basic orientation of the Christian person refers to one's acceptance (or rejection) of God's loving gift of God's self to the person. Theology often refers to this orientation as the gift of salvation or justification and our grateful response. It constitutes the basic orientation or fundamental commitment of the Christian person, and it has been described in various ways in Scripture and theology. In a relational model this commitment involves all other relationships. It cannot be limited to the relationship of the individual person to a personal, saving God because the total self encompasses other relationships.

DISCIPLESHIP

Discipleship is a biblical concept that has often been used to explain the basic orientation of one who is called to be a follower of Jesus Christ.[8] Critical biblical scholarship finds different concepts of discipleship in the four Gospels in the same way that the evangelists present different christological images. Mark views discipleship as belonging to a new and radical family—the family of Jesus. Jesus' mother, brothers, and sisters are those who respond to God's call and follow Jesus. Mark underscores the radical nature of this call. The disciples must suffer and carry the cross as Jesus did. The values and roles that people most prize often become obstacles in the way of discipleship. The followers of Jesus are to serve others rather than be served; the first shall be last and the last shall be first. The disciples are to become as little children.

In Acts, Luke uses the term "the way" to describe the followers of Jesus. Luke strongly emphasizes the correct use of material goods and possessions. He alone among the synoptic Gospels, insists that the disciples sell "all that you have" (Luke 18:22) and leave "everything" to follow Jesus (5:11). Luke's beatitudes retain the earlier understanding of the materially poor (6:20). Matthew has spiritualized and moralized the poor by referring to the poor in spirit (Matt 5:3).

Matthew, in his own way, is a catechist and teacher of morality for the community of the disciples of Jesus which he understands to be a community of justice. The Greek *dikaiosuné* (justice) plays a central role in the Matthean Sermon on the Mount. Justice refers to God's saving acts and to the Christian's response in doing the works of God. The disciples of Jesus hunger and thirst for justice, and also suffer persecution for the sake of justice. The spiritualizing and moralizing additions to the beatitudes (poor in spirit, clean of heart, hunger and thirst for justice) indicate Matthew's intent. The thrust of his Gospel in general and the Sermon on the Mount in particular is to portray Jesus as the new Moses who has come not to destroy the law but to fulfill it.

John's Gospel links discipleship with faith. Faith is the fundamental decision and change of orientation that a disciple makes when confronted with Jesus. Faith is illustrated in the figures of the sheep belonging to the shepherd and the branches that are part of the vine. Since John's community was living long after the historical Jesus, faith replaces seeing and discipleship, and the Paraclete has taken the role of Jesus.

Each of these approaches to discipleship fit the purpose and direction of the particular Gospel, but at least four features are common to each version of discipleship. First, discipleship involves God's gracious call and gift. Jesus came preaching the good news. The first step is taken by God. That the poor, the nonvaluable in the eyes of many, receive God's reign—the outcasts, children and sinners—underscores the reality of discipleship as primarily God's gracious gift to us.

Second, discipleship does not involve a narrow "me and Jesus" relationship but includes our relationship with others, ourselves, and the world. As I pointed out in chapter one, the disciple's relationship with Jesus is mediated in and through the church. Membership in the community of Jesus' disciples is how the Christian comes into contact with God's gracious love. Discipleship calls us to act toward others as God has acted toward us. Love, mercy, and forgiveness are to characterize the life of discipleship. Discipleship calls us to new relationships with the poor, the needy, and the outcast.

Third, totality and radicality characterize discipleship. The reign of God is the pearl of great price for which everything else must be sold. Discipleship affects the total person; it guides and directs who the person is and all that she does. Discipleship is the basic commitment, the fundamental orientation, that influences and directs everything else in life.

Fourth, the radicalness of discipleship grounds the reality of Christian growth. There is no doubt that the Catholic tradition with its universal appeal to all and its mission to living in and transforming the world of everyday life has not insisted on a radical morality involving a flight from the world. However, the radical aspects of discipleship are the goals and ideals that call the Christian to continued growth and development in our multiple relationships with God, neighbor, self, and the world. In this way the Catholic Church is large and open to all, living in the world and working in the world but urging all to grow in the various relationships of discipleship. The difference between the church and a sectarian approach, with its emphasis on small communities withdrawn from the world, has already been discussed. The Catholic approach to discipleship is also consistent with the eschatology proposed in our stance and its tension between the now and the not yet.

There is no doubt that Jesus and the early disciples thought that the end time was coming soon. This imminent eschatology of the early disciples greatly affected the moral attitudes of the early church. It makes no sense to marry, to store your food in barns, or to worry about what you are going to eat, if the end is coming soon. However, an eschatology in keeping with our stance was also present in the early church. Although the Gospel accounts written after the resurrection idealize the followers of Jesus, the weaknesses of the disciples still come through. They are far from perfect. They misunderstand, vacillate, and quarrel among themselves. The description of the early church in the Acts of the Apostles reminds us of the contentions, the difficulties, and the disagreements that arose among the disciples. The Pauline letters also reveal the many problems and moral deficiencies existing among the community of Jesus' disciples. The early Christian communities were not models of perfect discipleship, and that is still true of the church today. Eschatological tensions, human limitations, and human sinfulness will always be present within the community of the disciples of Jesus. No follower of Jesus can ever say "All these things I have done from my youth." Nevertheless, we strive to grow in the multiple relationships that mark our discipleship.

CONTEMPORARY THEOLOGY AND THE PERSON

Contemporary theological developments also recognize that salvation involves a basic orientation involving multiple relationships. Soteriology and grace were often presented as individualistic realities in an older Catholic theology. Individual souls shared in the salvation that Jesus won for us on the cross. Salvation was primarily a spiritual reality. A more soteriological approach to Christology and to Trinitarian theology has contributed to the understanding of salvation and grace as more social and more concrete.[9]

Until recently, Catholic Christology was primarily interested in the ontological and metaphysical mystery of Jesus. The Christological controversies of the fourth and fifth centuries centered on the nature of Jesus. The definition of the Council of Chalcedon (451) dealt primarily with the metaphysical reality of Jesus who is complete in divinity and complete in humanity, truly God and truly human. There are two natures and one person in Jesus. The Chalcedonian formula barely recognizes the soteriological aspect—one and the same Son, our Lord Jesus Christ, as regards his humanity begotten for us and for our salvation. Recent Christology has emphasized the importance of the soteriological aspect which has been developed on the basis of a Christology from below.[10]

A Christology from below begins with the work and ministry of the historical Jesus. It understands salvation in a concrete and particular perspective. In this context Jesus, a victim who was unjustly put to death, stands in solidarity with all victims of oppression and injustice. Salvation affects more than the soul as liberation theology well illustrates. Salvation and liberation embrace the whole person and all the ramifications of life. Gustavo Gutiérrez acknowledged in his seminal book on liberation theology different levels of liberation and salvation—political liberation, liberation through history, and liberation from sin. Salvation or liberation exists on all three levels.[11] It embraces the total person in all one's relationships and activities.

Trinitarian theology has also moved from an emphasis on the inner life of the Trinity to an emphasis on the soteriological function of the Trinity, in Karl Rahner's terms: the economic trinity.[12] The late Catherine LaCugna made the Trinity's relationship to us the primary aspect of trinitarian thought. We understand the three persons in God in the light of their relationships to us. The Trinity is not an esoteric intellectual mystery about the hidden life of God but an existential and saving encounter of the triune God with us. The persons of the Trinity are revealed to us for our salvation. The divine Trinity of persons in God are in relationship—for one another and for us. Through our salvific relationship with the Trinity, we too become persons in relationship for others. Salvation is not a "me and Jesus" relationship but concerns the whole person in the totality of one's relationships. The significance of the Trinity highlights the relational ontology of the human person.[13] Contemporary Christological and Trinitarian theologies insist on a soteriology that encompasses concrete persons in the totality of their relationships with a special concern for the victims of injustice and oppression.

CONTEMPORARY SPIRITUALITY AND THE PERSON

Contemporary spiritual theology builds on these more complex notions of salvation. Traditional spiritual theology often emphasized religious life and priesthood as the primary locus of spirituality. Religious life involved the call to holiness and the following of the evangelical counsels of poverty, chastity, and obedience. Spirituality seemed to call people away from their relationships with family, neighbor, and world into a life that was withdrawn from others and concentrated on God alone.[14]

The Second Vatican Council recognized that the gospel call to holiness is universal; it is directed to all the disciples of Jesus, and it is rooted in our baptismal commitment.[15] At the same time the Pastoral Constitution on the Church in the Modern World emphasizes the mission of the church in the world and calls for a critical dialogue between the church and the world. The Holy Spirit is active and present in our world, history, and culture.[16] *Justitia in mundo*, coming from the 1971 International Synod of Bishops, perhaps contains the most quoted statement of any document of the modern hierarchical magisterium. This statement deals precisely with the meaning of redemption and the mission of the church: "Action on behalf of justice and participation in the transformation of the world fully appear to us as a constitutive dimension of the preaching of the Gospel, or, in other words, of the church's mission for the redemption of the human race and its liberation from every oppressive situation."[17] Thus the Gospel and salvation involve our relationships with others and with the whole world. Responsibility for the social, cultural, political, economic, and ecological orders are essential to Christian spirituality and growth precisely because they are involved in the salvific work of God manifested in Jesus and continued through the Spirit. As a consequence, Christian spirituality can never again be reduced to a private, totally inward looking, "me and Jesus" relationship. Yes, there is still a place for contemplation and monasticism, but it can never be seen as a total flight from the world.

The concrete particularity of spirituality follows from the concrete call of God to specific persons and recognizes the pluralism existing in the church and world. Contemporary spirituality has rightly been receptive to liberationist themes and a corresponding liberationist spirituality has developed. Gustavo Gutiérrez has joined theology and spirituality in his own writings.[18] An ecological spirituality has also developed on the basis that all creation partakes of God's gracious gift. All creation must be nurtured, cared for, and brought to fulfillment.[19] Feminist spirituality has come into its own in recent years. The basis for this approach is the concrete experience of women, especially their oppression through patriarchy and their struggle for liberation. The Catholic recognition of experience as a source of moral wisdom and knowledge is well illustrated in these approaches,[20] which must also include male spirituality,[21] and Michael Downey's notions about the spirituality of the marginalized and disabled.[22] Since salvation involves the person's multiple relationships with God, neighbor, world, and self, spirituality today shows forth these same aspects and tends to be concrete and particular.

The celebration of the sacraments likewise requires the involvement of multiple relationships. Liturgical and sacramental celebration is by definition the community's celebration. In baptism we are baptized into the community of the church. The eucharist celebrates the community meal which Jesus left us as an everlasting memorial of the new covenant. The ecclesial nature of reconciliation has been recognized since Vatican II so that we are reconciled with God in and through our reconciliation with the Christian community.

The sacramental celebrations of the Christian community do not separate us from others in the world but call us to intensify and transform these relationships. The liturgical celebration of Holy Thursday incorporates into the eucharist the powerful ceremony of the washing of the feet. Love of God, sharing love and life in the Christian community, and serving the needs of all God's people are intrinsically bound together. The very structure of the eucharist, the heart and center of Christian life and celebration, exemplifies its relationship to the world's salvation. The eucharist basically has four parts. It begins with a gathering of God's people from their specific roles in families and neighborhoods, and other concrete involvements. Then this gathered community is nourished by the word of God in Scripture. The third part, the eucharistic prayer, celebrates anew the table companionship of Jesus with the disciples, especially the Last Supper and the covenant meal. In this prayer, we are one with Jesus in giving praise and thanks to

God our gracious parent and one with Jesus in our commitment to serve our sisters and brothers. The fourth part of the liturgy is the dismissal or the sending forth of the community into the world to carry on the work of Jesus. We leave the eucharistic celebration to continue God's saving work in our daily lives and activities.[23]

The very nature of the sacramental system also makes us conscious of our relationship to all creation. The divine gift is mediated in and through creation as the basic realities of bread and wine, oil and water are incorporated into the sacramental celebration.[24] The sacraments do not pull us out of the world but show us how salvation touches all of created reality.

CONTEMPORARY MORAL THEOLOGY AND THE PERSON

Contemporary moral theology has also recognized that the basic orientation and fundamental commitment of the Christian person motivates and influences who the person is as subject and what the person does as agent. Many theologians have explained this basic orientation and transformation in terms of conversion. Before Vatican II, conversion in Roman Catholic circles generally referred to the act by which nonmembers became members of the Catholic Church. However, conversion has a broader and more fundamental meaning. Mark's Gospel sees conversion as the basic response to the call and preaching of Jesus. "The time is fulfilled and the Kingdom of God is at hand; repent [change your heart, be converted], and believe in the Gospel" (Mark 1:14). Bernard Häring, the distinguished German Redemptorist theologian, developed the centrality of conversion for moral theology even before Vatican II. Häring stressed the biblical basis of conversion, the transformation of the person, its sacramental celebration, and its embrace of God's action in the world since conversion to the reign of God is not just a private or personal matter, but a call for continual renewal in the Christian life. The person is transformed from a sinner to a loving commitment to the reign of God that will grow and develop in the Christian life.[25] In keeping with the Catholic recognition of other sources of wisdom and knowledge, the meaning of conversion has been developed in dialogue with other disciplines and experience. Häring himself, in his 1978 textbook, employed the contributions of the behavioral sciences and philosophy to develop his understanding of conversion.[26]

Bernard Lonergan has elaborated the concept of conversion in the light of his transcendental philosophy. Lonergan posits four different conversions. Intellectual conversion transforms the human knower from the myth that knowing is like looking at reality out there to recognizing the world mediated by meaning. Affective conversion involves the self-transcendence by which the individual moves from narcissistic love to a self-giving love of others. Moral conversion is the transformation of the self from seeking satisfaction to seeking values. Religious conversion is being grasped by ultimate concern. It is an other-worldly falling in love involving a total and permanent self-surrender without conditions, qualifications, or reservations. In the logical order, Lonergan develops these conversions on the basis of moving from the intellectual to the religious, but in the order of experience, religious conversion generally comes first and exerts some influence on the others. Morality cannot be collapsed into religious conversion, but religious conversion can be mediated in and through the moral. The basic orientation of religious conversion expresses itself in and through the moral life, but the moral life has its own specific reality.[27]

Walter Conn has developed Lonergan's approach by incorporating the psychological insights of Erik Erikson, Jean Piaget, and Lawrence Kohlberg.[28] Stephen Happel and James J. Walter have proposed a foundational theology on the basis of conversion and discipleship.[29] Brian Johnstone insists on the importance of experience in understanding conversion and uses the experience of Edith Stein and Bartolomé de Las Casas to help understand the reality of conversion.[30]

One popular school of contemporary moral theology has developed this basic orientation and fundamental commitment in terms of the fundamental option based on a Rahnerian approach. The fundamental option theory has been developed primarily by Josef Fuchs[31] and explained in this country by Timothy O'Connell in his text, *Principles for a Catholic Morality.*[32] In many cases as exemplified by O'Connell, the theory has been applied especially to the reality of sin and the distinction between mortal and venial sin.

The theory rests on the distinction between two kinds of freedom in the human person and two kinds of knowledge. Moral theology in the past and most contemporary ethicists define freedom as freedom of choice, the choice to go to a movie or stay home and read a book. This freedom is categorical freedom because it describes the particular category of acts to be done. There is, however, a deeper level of the human person at which the person encounters one's self as a subject. Here the person as subject says yes to God who also is not a categorical object— one of a number of different objects—but a subject. The person makes this choice of God at the core of her being. This basic yes transcends all our categorical choices and becomes the fundamental option. The love of, and commitment to, God take place on this transcendental level.

These different engagements of human freedom involve different kinds of knowledge or awareness. On the categorical level, I perform this act. The act is the object, and I can be reflexively conscious of this act precisely because it is differentiated from me as an object. But on the transcendental level, the person as subject determines herself in the fundamental option. Precisely because at the core of my being I determine myself as subject, I cannot reflect on this act the same way I reflect on a categorical act. My awareness of myself as subject is different from my reflex awareness of the objects of my categorical choices. The fundamental option, my basic acceptance of God's love in Jesus through the Spirit, occurs on the transcendental level. Hence, I cannot be reflexively conscious of this as an object of choice. I cannot even know with absolute certitude that I have made such an option.

These two actuations of freedom, transcendental and categorical, are not discrete acts, but I dispose of myself as a subject in a loving relationship with God in and through my particular categorical choices. The fundamental option is not an independent act but the determination of the subject who is doing particular categorical acts. Mortal sin involves a fundamental option on the transcendental level and cannot be identified with a categorical act.

Rahner's transcendental anthropology has been criticized by Johann Baptist Metz for its failure to include the social and political dimensions of human existence.[33] There is merit in this criticism. I also think the fundamental option downplays the historical, social, cultural, and political dimensions of our lives. I want to insist on the person as subject and agent in the multiplicity of our relationships. Our multiple relationships form us as persons who are both subject and agent. Virtues modify us as subject and as agent. The person as subject is a concrete, specific person formed in and through historical relationships and realities. Proponents of the fundamental option theory claim to recognize to some degree these multiple relationships. Karl Rahner has pointed out in a now famous essay how his theory unites the love of God and the love of neighbor. This union is possible because in all our categorical acts with regard to neighbor, world, and self, our relationship to God is also present on the transcendental level.[34] However, the person as subject remains too "transcendental" in this interpretation and becomes separated from concrete social and historical reality. In this approach salvation and grace take place on the transcendental level, but salvation should involve persons totally in all their relationships and in working for justice and the transformation of the world.

My view of the person accepts the basic orientation of the person in the light of fundamental relationships. Individual acts must be seen in the light of these relationships. The spiritual and moral life of the Christian involves growth in our relationships with God, the world, and one another. Mortal sin consists in the breaking of these relationships.

Although I have some hesitations about the theory of fundamental option, I do not share John Paul II's criticism of it in the encyclical *Veritatis splendor.* The pope accuses proponents of the fundamental option of separating that option from concrete behavioral acts.[35] Such a charge distorts what its proponents are really saying. The theory distinguishes the transcendental and the categorical aspects, but it does not separate them.[36] But it does, I repeat, downplay the relational and historical aspects of salvation and of the human subject.

The discussion of the person in this section has dealt with the basic orientation and commitment of the moral person from the Christian perspective which can be described in terms of discipleship or conversion. And it has developed this basic orientation in relational terms. As the concept of conversion above all points out, the basic relational orientation of the Christian person (i.e., conversion) stands in contrast to its opposite which would make the self the center of everything and direct all one's life and activity to the service of the self. This self-centeredness and denial of basic relationships is a very good description of sin. However, the relationality-responsibility model calls for a proper love of self along a continuum of relationships. The self comes to fulfillment and happiness in and through these relationships. The call to holiness requires moral growth and development through the deepening of these basic relationships.

The basic orientation of the person is most significant from an ethical perspective because it constitutes who the person is as subject and as moral agent. Yet it remains somewhat vague and undifferentiated. The fundamental orientation is mediated in and through the particular virtues that characterize the Christian person engaged in these multiple relationships. The next chapter will discuss the virtues, but first I must say more about the Catholic approach to anthropology.

SOCIAL AND INSTITUTIONAL INVOLVEMENTS OF THE PERSON

Fundamental moral theology in the Catholic tradition has historically dealt with the aspects and principles of morality that affect the person in different situations and actions. Special moral theology deals with particular areas of morality, whether personal, social, political, economic, or bioethical. This book attempts to develop a contemporary fundamental moral theology, but the traditional division creates one significant problem. By reflecting on what is true of the person in all situations, the focus tends to be somewhat individualistic—what the individual person should be and do. However, this chapter insists on a relational understanding of the person. Catholic anthropology recognizes that the human person is social and thus is shaped by, and works together with, others in various social organizations and structures.

Such a Catholic understanding of the person is illustrated in the approach the U.S. Catholic bishops took in their bicentennial program in 1976–"A Call to Action." The purpose of this project was to convene representative Catholics in the United States to suggest ways and means by which the church in America could respond to Paul VI's 1971 apostolic letter *Octogesima adveniens* and the 1971 document of the World Synod of Bishops *Justitia in mundo*. Advance preparations narrowed the discussion not to specific issues but to eight social organisms— family, neighborhood, ethnic and racial groups, personhood, nationhood, church, humankind, and work.[37] This program demonstrates the Catholic understanding of the human person as a relational being who works with others in and through various organisms, institutions, and voluntary associations. These organisms, structures, institutions, and voluntary associations are important indicators of how the person lives and acts.

As pointed out in chapter two, the general thrust of the biblical and Christian tradition is that human beings are not isolated individuals but related to all others. Thomas Aquinas, in the light of this tradition but especially based on Aristotle, accepted the Greek philosopher's notion of the human person as a social and political animal. Human nature calls us to live together in many different social groupings including the political reality of the state.[38] Aquinas develops this concept in what appears to be an esoteric and a useless question: Would we have needed rulers in society if there had been no sin? Aquinas responds, yes. The ruler in civil society directs all things for the common good which ultimately redounds to the good of individuals. Even the angels in heaven need rulers who will direct the whole angelic choir. Aquinas then talks about the different ranks of angels. Where a society of people exists, there someone must provide direction for the common good. God has given different gifts and roles to different people. In this way, Aquinas maintains that human political society results from human nature itself and not from sin.[39] Aquinas and the Catholic tradition have a positive evaluation of the need for, and role of, the state. This chapter cannot spell out all the practical implications of the social and political nature of the human person. It can, however, consider the *family* and the *state*, the two natural societies in which human beings are destined by God to live.[40]

FAMILY The family is the very basic unit of society. People are born into, raised, and educated in families. Family relationships color and affect all that we are and do. The older pre-Vatican II approach insisted on the family as a natural society that is a fundamental institution of human existence stemming from the intention and plan of the Creator. The family provides different roles and functions for mother, father, children, and extended families. The individual cannot be properly understood without including her many familial relationships.[41]

Contemporary approaches to the family recognize two problems with the pre-Vatican II Catholic understanding. The first problem is a kind of essentialism consistent with the classicism of the older Catholic methodology. This essentialism recognizes only one model of family— the traditional model of father, mother, and children, with very defined roles. However, in reality even in the past, many single parent households counted as families. One cannot claim that all families are exactly the same.[42]

The second and even greater problem was the traditional emphasis on a hierarchical order in the family that is no longer acceptable to many people. Without doubt the Catholic tradition in many areas employs a hierarchical structuring. Consider the church itself. This hierarchical ordering especially affects the role of women. An older Catholic approach definitely subordinated the wife to the husband inside the family and the female to the male in society in general. The husband was the head of the family; the wife, at best, was the heart. Notice how the tradition identified the male with leadership and intellect and the female with emotion and caring. Today the equality and mutual labor of wife and husband are necessary. The older approach also identified women in terms of their role as wife and mother. The woman's place was in the home. Women were defined in terms of motherhood, though the husband's fatherhood was but one part of his existence. Today's theology calls for equality and cooperation, for shared parenthood and equal work opportunities for women and men.

Hierarchical Catholic teaching has made some progress in the past few decades, but there is still a tendency to see the roles of wife and husband in the family and in the world in terms of complementarity. Such an approach too often stereotypes the role of women and does not fully protect their equality and participation in freedom.[43]

Yes, the structure of families and the roles of family members have changed. But the family remains the most basic unit in society. Its role is irreplaceable and its importance to moral development cannot be too highly prized.

STATE The Catholic understanding of the role of the state or the political order also illustrates the Catholic emphasis on the social and political nature of the human person who can never be reduced merely to an isolated individual. In the Catholic approach, the state and political society are natural, necessary, and limited. First, the natural and necessary aspects of the political order come from an anthropology that sees persons as social and political beings. We are called to live in various communities—one of which is the political community of the state. The Catholic tradition believes that God made us as social beings. Our approach to education well illustrates the social and communitarian nature of human existence. Young adults go to a place called a college—note the communitarian term itself. And schools frequently refer to themselves as communities. Could not an adult learn as much (and save money) by going to the library and reading books on one's own? We believe that knowing takes place much better in a community where even the teachers can and should learn from one another and from their students. As colleges claim to be true learning communities, so the Catholic tradition sees the political community or state in an analogous manner. It is natural and necessary for human beings to live in political community, and this comes from the Creator as manifested in the communitarian nature of human beings.[44]

Such an understanding of political society contrasts with other theological and philosophical approaches to the state. The Lutheran tradition sees the state primarily in terms of the Noachic covenant— the promise God made to Noah to never again destroy the world. The state or political order is the order of preservation that God uses to prevent sinful human beings from killing and destroying one another. The state is a dike against the power of sin and not something natural and necessary for human beings because God made them as social creatures.[45] The traditional Catholic notion of the state is more positive than the traditional Lutheran. However, in the light of our stance, Catholics must recognize that certain aspects of the state are due to human sinfulness and not simply to the social nature of individuals.

The major non-Catholic philosophical approach to understanding the state is the contract theory that is generally accepted in the United States. Human beings are by nature individuals who come together with others to establish a political order. In the process one tries to give up as little to the state as necessary. Again, the Catholic understanding is much more positive about the political order and does not oppose the state to the individual as the contract theory tends to do.[46]

In the Catholic tradition the state seeks not just the good of individuals but the common good. The common good "embraces the sum of those conditions of social life by which individuals, families, and groups can achieve their own fulfillment in a relatively thorough and ready way."[47] Note how the individual needs the state and the political order for one's own good and fulfillment. In and through the state individuals can do what they could never do if they existed merely as individuals. The state strives to achieve the common good which then redounds to the good of the individual. The analogy from athletics is helpful here. A basketball team is more than the five individuals who make it up. You could have the five best individual basketball players in the world, and still not have the best team. All individuals must be prepared from time to time to subordinate themselves to the team. However, the good of the team redounds to the good of the individual. Even in the midst of the American cult of the individual and the astronomical salaries of individual athletes, one still hears the echo of communitarianism in the often heard remark of players who would rather win a championship for their team than be the most valuable players in the league.

The Catholic understanding of the state with its goal of pursuing the common good avoids the extremes of individualism and collectivism. The individualistic view sees the state only in terms of pursuing one's own good. The collectivist view sees the state as promoting the collectivity even if individuals suffer. The common good is common to all and thus redounds back to the good of the individual even though it is greater than the good of individuals.[48]

The proper role of the state in the Catholic tradition is construed as a middle way between individualism and collectivism. Extreme individualism insists that the role of the state be as minimal as possible. Extreme collectivism gives a maximum role to the state at the expense of individual initiative. The Catholic understanding of the role of the state is based on the principle of subsidiarity in tension with the principle of socialization. The principle of subsidiarity recognizes many different levels and groups in society. Very schematically, the different levels start with the individual, then the family, then neighborhood, racial and ethnic groupings and move on through many voluntary associations (e.g. labor unions, chambers of commerce, groups committed to a particular cause) and institutions such as the press, religion, education to different forms of government, local, state, and federal. All of these individuals, organisms, associations, institutions, and levels of government have a proper role to play in the good society. Government should support all the lower levels and help (the Latin word *subsidium* means help) them do all that they can, with as little intervention as possible. However, as John XXIII pointed out, in our modern world with its increased complexity and socialization, the government will have to intervene more often because only the government is big enough to deal with issues that touch so many.[49] Take the question of care for the poor. Government should help institutions, churches, voluntary associations, and others help the poor, but the problem is so vast that government must also intervene to do what the others cannot do. Governmental intervention is absolutely necessary for the common good, but such intervention must respect and promote the roles of individuals and small groups in our society. Thus, the Catholic tradition argues against the extremes of as little government as possible and as much government as possible.

The Catholic understanding of the state and its role in the United States will likely be critical of the more individualistic aspects of current theory and practice. The Catholic bishops in their pastoral letter on the economy (1986) insisted on the need for the principle of subsidiarity but noted that this principle rejects the axiom that the government that governs least governs best.[50] The letter developed the bishops' idea of the proper government involvement in selected economic issues: employment, poverty, food and agriculture, and relationships with developing nations. The final chapter of the letter, "A New American Experiment: Partnership for the Public Good," calls for economic planning involving the government and other interested parties "to expand economic participation, broaden the sharing of economic power, and make economic decisions more acceptable to the common good."[51] The bishops are very conscious that in our culture the mere mention of economic planning is likely to produce a strong negative reaction.[52]

The criticisms made by the bishops of economic life in this country practically all concern the individualism embedded in our society and its lack of concern for the common good and others, especially the poor.[53]

The Catholic social teaching tradition is critical of individualism, but it is also true that this tradition historically has often failed to value the individual person in the church and the larger society. Ever since the seventeenth century, the Catholic Church has been in dialogue with liberalism and the Enlightenment concerning their emphasis on individual human beings and their rights. This dialogue has brought about some significant changes in the Catholic approach, leading it to assign a greater importance to individuals while still accepting the importance of human solidarity and community.[54]

Historically the Catholic understanding of society and the state favored an organic approach using the metaphor of the body. There are different parts each with its own role to play under the guidance of the head—the ruler. This organic metaphor tends to see the parts primarily in terms of the whole body—effacing, to an extent, the individuality of each person. Society is static; people do not change their roles.[55]

From this perspective Catholic thought in general rejected the individualism of the Enlightenment as seen in religion, philosophy, politics, and economics. Religious liberalism, in the view shared by many Catholic thinkers, began when Luther separated the conscience of the individual person from the church. Philosophical liberalism exalted human reason (which was now cut off from its relationship to God's law), and political liberalism made the will of the majority the ultimate arbiter of what is right or wrong—again denying any role to God's will and law. Economic liberalism maintained that the individual could pursue as much profit as possible without regard for workers and others.[56] However, in the twentieth century a new dialogue partner (or "enemy" to use the nondialogical language of the times) appeared on the scene: totalitarianism, and especially totalitarianism from the left (i.e., communism). Catholic thought gradually gave more importance to freedom and the rights of the person in its opposition to communism.[57]

This change shows up especially in the difference between Leo XIII's approach at the very end of the nineteenth century and the contemporary hierarchical social teaching on the issues of freedom, equality, and participation in the life of society. Leo XIII condemned modern liberties. Freedom of worship, for example, goes against the chief and holiest human duty. He also opposed freedom of speech and freedom of conscience and taught that the only true meaning of the freedom of conscience is to follow the will of God. At best, society tolerates what is opposed to truth and justice for the sake of avoiding greater evils or preserving some greater good.[58] In fact, Leo stressed that natural inequalities, which bring about social inequalities, are essential for the good functioning of society.[59] With such a hierarchical view of an organic society, Leo saw no need for the active participation of all citizens. Citizens are the untutored or ignorant multitude that must be led by the ruler.[60]

Even Leo XIII, however, gave some indications of a different approach,[61] and a greater appreciation of human freedom, equality, and participation in the life of society began to surface as the twentieth century developed. In the 1940s in opposition to communism, Pius XII recognized that many people see political democracy as a demand of human reason.[62] And in 1965, Vatican II finally accepted religious liberty.[63] Perhaps the best single statement of this change comes from Paul VI's 1971 *Octogesima adveniens*: "[T]wo aspirations persistently make themselves felt in these new contexts, and they grow stronger to the extent that he [sic] becomes better informed and better educated: the aspiration to equality and the aspiration to participation, two forms of man's [sic] dignity and freedom."[64]

The evolution in official Catholic approaches to political freedom, equality, and participation is the best indication that living traditions can learn from others and change. Catholics, however, remain critical of one-sided individualisms that fail to recognize human solidarity and human community.

This chapter has discussed the person as a moral subject and agent in relational terms. The fundamental relationship with God includes relationships with neighbor, world, and self. The relational understanding grounds the need for the different communities in which the person lives. The primary community is the church, but the Christian lives in many other communities, institutions, and associations each of which has its own "autonomous" structures. These communities include especially the family and the state. Note that "community" in the Catholic tradition is an analogous term, and the family and state have some significant differences between them. The basic orientation of the Christian person and one's relational existence in various communities, natural institutions, and associations, form the context in which the virtues of the Christian person can shape one's moral character and dispose her to act in virtuous ways.

NOTES

1. For the position of the Council of Trent, see Henricus Denzinger et al., eds., *Enchiridion symbolorum definitionum et declarationum de rebus fidei et morum*, 32nd ed. (Barcelona: Herder, 1963), nn. 1520–83, pp. 369–81.

2. Romanus Cessario, *The Moral Virtues and Theological Ethics* (Notre Dame, Ind.: University of Notre Dame Press, 1991).

3. Saint Teresa of Avila, *The Way of Perfection* (New York: Image, 1991); John of the Cross, *Ascent of Mt. Carmel*, 3rd ed. (Garden City, N.Y.: Image, 1958).

4. E. E. Larkin, "Ways, the Three Spriritual," in *New Catholic Encyclopedia*, 14, pp. 835–36.

5. See, for example, the work of Paul J. Philibert, "Kohlberg and Fowler Revisited: An Interim Report on Moral Structuralism: A Review Essay," *Living Light* 24 (1988): 162–71; Philibert, "Addressing the Crisis in Moral Theory: Clues from Aquinas and Gilligan," *Theology Digest* 34 (1987): 103–13.

6. For the historical development of the question, see Vereecke, *Ockham à Saint Alphonse*, pp. 555–60; James Keenan, "Can a Wrong Action be Good? The Development of Theological Opinion on Erroneous Conscience," *Église et théologie* 24 (1993): 205–19; Josef Fuchs, *Christian Morality: The Word Becomes Flesh* (Washington, D.C.: Georgetown University Press, 1987), pp. 106–09. Fuchs presents this distinction between the person as subject and as agent better than any other contemporary Catholic moral theologian. Nevertheless, I have proposed a different understanding of the person as subject in this book. For Fuchs's latest collection of essays in English, see his *Moral Demands and Personal Obligations* (Washington, D.C.: Georgetown University Press, 1993).

7. Pope John Paul II, *Veritatis splendor*, n. 63, *Origins* 23 (1993): 316; Brian V. Johnstone, "Erroneous Conscience in *Veritatis splendor* and the Theological Tradition," in *The Splendor of Accuracy: An Examination of the Assertions Made by Veritatis splendor*, ed. Joseph A. Selling and Jan Jans (Grand Rapids, Mich.: William B. Eerdmans, 1995), pp. 114–35.

8. The following paragraphs depend heavily on Francis Schüssler Fiorenza, *Foundational Theology: Jesus and the Church* (New York: Crossroad, 1984), pp. 135–56.

9. Roger Haight, "Sin and Grace," in *Systematic Theology*, 2, ed. Fiorenza and Galvin, pp. 75–141.

10. Elizabeth A. Johnson, *Consider Jesus: Waves of Renewal in Christology* (New York: Crossroad, 1990).

11. Gustavo Gutiérrez, *A Theology of Liberation: History, Politics, and Salvation* (Maryknoll, N.Y.: Orbis, 1973), pp. 21–42.

12. Karl Rahner, *The Trinity* (New York: Herder and Herder, 1970). A new printing was published by Crossroad in 1997.

13. LaCugna, *God for Us.*

14. For a good overview of spirituality today, see Michael Downey, *Understanding Christian Spirituality* (New York: Paulist, 1997); for a fine study of the relationship between moral and spiritual theology, see Mark O'Keefe, *Becoming Good, Becoming Holy: On the Relationship of Christian Ethics and Spirituality* (New York: Paulist, 1995). The following pages often depend on these authors.

15. Dogmatic Constitution on the Church, nn. 39–42, in *Vatican Council II,* ed. Flannery, pp. 396–402.

16. Pastoral Constitution on the Church in the Modern World, in *Vatican Council II,* ed. Flannery, pp. 903–1001.

17. *Justitia in mundo,* in *Catholic Social Thought,* ed. O'Brien and Shannon, p. 289.

18. Gustavo Gutiérrez, *We Drink from Our Own Wells: The Spiritual Journey of a People* (Maryknoll, N.Y.: Orbis, 1984); see also Donal Dorr, *Spirituality and Justice* (Maryknoll, N.Y.: Orbis, 1984).

19. Charles Cummings, *Eco-Spirituality: Toward a Reverent Life* (New York: Paulist, 1991).

20. Judith Plaskow and Carol P. Christ, eds., *Weaving the Visions: New Patterns in Feminist Spirituality* (San Francisco: Harper, 1989); Sandra Marie Schneiders, *Women and the Word: The Gender of God in the New Testament and the Spirituality of Women* (New York: Paulist, 1986).

21. Richard Rohr, *The Wild Man's Journey: Reflections on Male Spirituality* (Cincinnati, Ohio: St. Anthony Messenger, 1992).

22. Downey, *Understanding Christian Spirituality,* pp. 137–39.

23. Mary E. Slamps, ed., *To Do Justice and Right Upon the Earth: Papers from the Virgil Michel Syposium on Liturgy and Social Justice* (Collegeville, Minn.: Liturgical, 1993).

24. Lawrence E. Mick, *Liturgy and Ecology in Dialogue* (Collegeville, Minn.: Liturgical, 1997).

25. B. Häring, "La conversion," in *Pastorale du péché,* ed. Ph. Delhaye (Tournai, Belgium: Desclée and Cie, 1961), pp. 65–145.

26. Häring, *Free and Faithful in Christ,* 1, pp. 168–81.

27. Bernard Lonergan, *Method in Theology* (New York: Herder and Herder, 1972), especially pp. 237–44.

28. Walter E. Conn, *Christian Conversion: A Developmental Interpretation of Autonomy and Surrender* (New York: Paulist, 1986).

29. Stephen Happel and James J. Walter, *Conversion and Discipleship: A Christian Foundation for Ethics and Doctrine* (Philadelphia: Fortress, 1986).

30. Brian V. Johnstone, "The Dynamics of Conversion," in *Spirituality and Morality: Integrating Prayer and Action,* ed. Dennis J. Billy and Donna L. Orsutu (New York: Paulist, 1996), pp. 32–48.

31. Fuchs has never systematically developed his moral theology. For the most significant essays dealing with fundamental option, see Josef Fuchs, *Human Values and Christian Morality* (Dublin: Gill and Macmillan, 1970), pp. 92–111; Fuchs, *Christian Morality: The Word Becomes Flesh* (Washington, D.C.: Georgetown University Press, 1987), pp. 3–133.

32. Timothy E. O'Connell, *Principles for a Catholic Morality*, rev. ed. (San Francisco: Harper, 1990), pp. 51–102.

33. Titus F. Guenther, *Ruhner and Metz: Transcendental Theology as Political Theology* (Lanham, Md.: University Press of America, 1994).

34. Karl Rahner, "Reflections on the Unity of the Love of Neighbor and the Love of God," in *Theological Investigations*, vol. 6, tr. Karl-H and Boniface Kruger (Baltimore, Md.: Helicon, 1969), pp. 231–49.

35. Pope John Paul II, *Veritatis splendor*, n. 67, *Origins* 23 (1993): 317.

36. For a similar criticism, see Josef Fuchs, "Good Acts and Good Persons," in *Understanding Veritatis Splendor*, ed. John Wilkins (London: SPCK, 1994), pp. 21–26.

37. Joseph A. Varacalli, *Toward the Establishment of Liberal Catholicism in America* (Washington, D.C.: University Press of America, 1983), pp. 27–31. I disagree with Veracalli's somewhat negative evaluation of this project.

38. Aristotle, *Nicomachean Ethics*, tr. Martin Ostwald (Indianapolis, Ind.: Bobbs-Merrill, 1983), n. 1169, p. 264; for an analysis of Aristotle's *Politics*, see C.C.W. Taylor, "Politics," in *The Cambridge Companion to Aristotle*, ed. Jonathan Barnes (New York: Cambridge University Press, 1995), pp. 233–58.

39. Aquinas, *Ia*, q.96, a.4.

40. Zalba, *Theologiae moralis summa*, 2, p. 199.

41. Ibid, pp. 199–229. The manuals of moral theology discussed the family under the fourth commandment.

42. Donald A. Miller, *Concepts of Family Life and Modern Catholic Theology: From Vatican II through "Christifideles Laici"* (San Francisco: International Scholars, 1996).

43. Christine E. Gudorf, "Encountering the Other: The Modern Papacy on Women," in *Feminist Ethics and the Catholic Moral Tradition*, ed. Curran, Farley, and McCormick, pp. 66–89.

44. For a classical Catholic understanding of the state, see Heinrich A. Rommen, *The State in Catholic Thought: A Treatise in Political Philosophy* (St. Louis, Mo.: B. Herder, 1945).

45. Helmut Thielicke, *Theological Ethics*, vol. 2, *Politics*, ed. William H. Lazareth (Philadelphia: Fortress, 1969), pp. 235–55.

46. For the difference between the Catholic perspective and individualistic and contract theories of the state, see Johannes Messner, *Social Ethics: Natural Law in the Western World*, rev. ed., tr. J.J. Doherty (St. Louis, Mo.: B. Herder, 1965), pp. 541–73.

47. Pastoral Constitution on the Church in the Modern World, n. 74, in *Catholic Social Thought*, ed. O'Brien and Shannon, p. 216. For some contemporary Catholic discussions of the common good, see James Donahue and Mary Theresa Moser, eds., *Religion, Ethics, and the Common Good*, vol. 41 of *The Annual Publication of the College Theology Society* (Mystic, Conn.: Twenty-Third, 1997).

48. John A. Coleman, "Neither Liberal nor Socialist: The Originality of Catholic Social Teaching," in *One Hundred Years of Catholic Social Thought: Celebration and Challenge*, ed. John A. Coleman (Maryknoll, N.Y.: Orbis, 1991), pp. 25–42.

49. Pope John XXIII, *Mater et magistra*, nn. 52–58, in *Catholic Social Thought*, ed. O'Brien and Shannon, pp. 92–93.

50. Catholic Bishops, *Economic Justice for All*, n. 124, p. 62.

51. Ibid., n. 297, pp. 146–47.

52. Ibid., n. 316, pp. 156–57.

53. Thomas M. Gannon, ed., *The Catholic Challenge to the American Economy: Reflections on the U.S. Bishops' Pastoral Letter on Catholic Social Teaching and the U.S. Economy* (New York: Macmillan, 1987).

54. Douglass and Hollenbach, eds., *Catholicism and Liberalism*.

55. Messner, *Social Ethics*, pp. 119–21.

56. William J. Engelen, "Social Observations IV: A Lesson in Social History," *Central-Blatt and Social Justice* 14 (January 1922): 321–23.

57. For a fuller discussion of this change, see Charles E. Curran, *Directions in Catholic Social Ethics* (Notre Dame, Ind.: University of Notre Dame Press, 1985), pp. 5–42.

58. Pope Leo XIII, *Libertas praestantissimum*, nn. 19–37, in *The Church Speaks to the Modern World: The Social Teachings of Leo XIII*, ed. Etienne Gilson (Garden City, N.Y.: Doubleday Image, 1954), pp. 70–79; see also Leo XIII, *Immortale Dei*, nn. 31–42, in *Social Teachings of Leo XIII*, ed. Gilson, pp. 174–80.

59. Leo XIII, *Humanum genus*, n. 26, in *Social Teachings of Leo XIII*, ed. Gilson, p. 130, and *Rerum novarum*, nn. 18–19, in *Social Teachings of Leo XIII*, pp. 214–15.

60. *Libertas praestantissimum*, n. 23, in *Social Teachings of Leo XIII*, p. 72.

61. *Rerum novarum*, nn. 6–12, in *Social Teachings of Leo XIII*, pp. 208–11.

62. Paul E. Sigmund, "Catholicism and Liberal Democracy," in *Catholicism and Liberalism*, ed. Douglass and Hollenbach, p. 226.

63. Declaration on Religious Liberty, in *Vatican Council II*, ed. Flannery, pp. 792–812.

64. Pope Paul VI, *Octogesima adveniens*, n. 22, in *Catholic Social Thought*, ed. O'Brien and Shannon, p. 273.

5

Virtues

That virtue has played an important role in Catholic moral theology is exemplified in the work of Thomas Aquinas. Here virtue is understood as a good habit or stable disposition inclining the person toward the good.[1] The manuals of moral theology, however, with their narrow focus paid basically no attention to virtue.

In the past decades philosophical ethics have paid more attention to virtue. Many have realized there is more to ethics than quandary ethics—the discussion on whether particular acts are right or wrong. In philosophical ethics the dissatisfaction with the unencumbered self of much contemporary thinking has occasioned a return by some to the tradition of Aristotle and the virtues.[2]

Protestant ethics tends to be suspicious of a virtue ethics approach because of its concept of justification and its reluctance to base any ethic on the principle of human flourishing and striving for perfection. Protestantism has generally insisted on God's gracious gift and feared the latent pelagianism (we are saved by our own efforts) in Catholic understandings of salvation and morality. However, in this country Stanley Hauerwas, while recognizing traditional Protestant problems with virtues, has proposed an approach to character and virtue that has sparked great interest.[3] Recall that Hauerwas's emphasis on narrative theology and virtue comes within the context of a morality based primarily on what is required for life in the church and does not directly address life for the world at large. Gilbert Meilander, writing from a Lutheran perspective, has problems with the eudaimonistic aspect of virtue ethics and the emphasis on human flourishing, which seem to detract from the role of God's gift of salvation. Meilander's virtue ethics seeks to maintain the tensions between the self-mastery of moral virtue and the self that is passive before God, between virtue as a possession and as continually reestablished by divine grace, and between a self that sees itself only partially and a self that is whole before God.[4] These examples show that Protestants today accept the role and importance of virtue and character in the moral life, even though they may have significant differences with the Catholic approaches.

VIRTUE IN THE CATHOLIC TRADITION

The Catholic tradition has generally seen virtue as a part of human flourishing and the call of God to strive for perfection in response to God's gift. The Catholic tradition has always insisted on a proper love of the self and the importance of happiness and self-fulfillment, not with the individual as absolute and the ultimate, but as a part of God's gracious reign and love. Love of God, love of neighbor, and love of self ultimately fit together. The Christian brings the human to its greatest perfection. The virtues are seen in this context of this theologically grounded vision of human flourishing and happiness.

There is a persistent tension between Aristotle and Christianity (especially as interpreted by Augustine) and between philosophy and theology in the writings and legacy of Thomas Aquinas that comes through in recent interpretations of the Thomistic approach to virtue. Jean Porter's *The Recovery of Virtue* deals only with the philosophical aspect of Aquinas and brackets the theological,[5] and in his *Moral Virtues and Theological Ethics*, Romanus Cessario insists on the theological aspects of Aquinas's approach by developing the Thomistic notion that the Christian moral virtues are infused and not acquired.[6] Likewise, Thomas O'Meara has strongly maintained that the Dominican tradition of Thomism (the theory espoused by members of the Order of Friars Preachers) is theological with regard to the virtues; that is, the virtues must be rooted in grace with emphasis on the infused virtues and not the acquired virtues. Just as grace changes the basic being of the individual person, the infused virtues affect and change the powers or faculties of the person.[7]

Contemporary Catholic debates about the virtues have historical precedents that began in Aquinas's day. Medieval theologians after Aquinas did not always accept his position on the infused virtues. Some medieval theologians accepted the acquired moral virtues but only as under the influence and direction of the theological virtues.[8] Such debates illustrate that the tension between the role of God's gift and human response will always remain in theological ethics. The danger in the Catholic tradition is the tendency toward pelagianism— overemphasis on the human response. This same tension affects our understanding of the virtues. Here too, we see the need for both God's gift and human response, but the Catholic tradition is not as paradoxical as the Lutheran in its manner of holding on to these two aspects. For the Catholic tradition, grace is a true possession of the believer as a result of God's gracious gift. Lutheran thought tends to see grace as imputed to the believer but not as intrinsically transforming the person.

The realities of historical consciousness, social location, diversity, pluralism, and individual vocations must also influence our interpretation of the virtues. Is it possible to propose that the virtues can still characterize Christian life in the midst of such diversity and pluralism? Here again is the tension between the particular and the universal. The unique individual has a particular character depending on the way different virtues are configured. Everyone creates her own personal synthesis. In addition, as we pointed out in the first chapter, within the Christian community, some individuals are called to bear witness to specific attitudes or virtues to the exclusion of others. Some are called to be pacifists; others are called to embrace celibacy, and still others, to accept voluntary poverty. Much individual diversity exists, but there remains a minimal understanding of those virtues that inform every Christian life. One can spell out the virtues of the Christian life common to all Christians but only in the sense of a loosely arranged minimum common to all.[9]

Other aspects of the Thomistic approach may not be so appropriate today. Thomas carried on the tradition by speaking about the cardinal virtues—prudence, justice, fortitude, and temperance. Cardinal, in this context, refers to logical primacy. The cardinal virtues are the hinges (in Latin, *cardo*) on which all other virtues can build and cluster in a logical way. They are logically prior but not existentially more important.[10] Thus, for example, justice is a cardinal virtue, and religion fits under justice. Most people would admit that religion, which attempts to give God that which is due to God, is more important than justice which deals with one's neighbors. However, justice fits perfectly the logical requirements of giving everyone what is due to them. Religion does not fulfill this criterion perfectly because we can never give God what is due to God. Since religion lacks the logical perfection of justice, it cannot be a cardinal virtue.[11]

Thomas Aquinas, with his emphasis on hierarchical ordering, maintained that the cardinal virtues could not be in competition with one another. Ultimately justice was the supreme arbiter and no real conflicts could exist.[12] Today we are much more conscious of tensions among the virtues. The tension between forgiveness and justice comes to the fore in many aspects of public life but also at times in private life.[13] Fidelity and truthfulness seem to conflict in some situations. The fact of such conflicts does not, however, detract from the role and importance of the virtues. It simply reminds us that tensions and conflicts based on human finitude and sinfulness are part of human and Christian experience.

How should we understand and develop the role of the virtues? Thomas Aquinas distinguished between the theological and the moral virtues. The theological virtues, faith, hope, and charity, which are gifts from God and infused, have God as their immediate object. The moral virtues, which are also gifts of God and infused, do not have God as their immediate object but rather human beings. In Aquinas the moral virtues are developed on the basis of the four cardinal virtues in a twofold way. The first way grounds the virtues in the four different faculties or powers that they modify. Many today reject such a Thomistic "faculty" psychology. But for Aquinas, the cardinal virtues of prudence, justice, fortitude, and temperance and the virtues related to them refer to the four faculties of intellect, will, irascible appetite (i.e., the faculty to overcome obstacles in the way of the good) and the concupiscible appetite (i.e., the faculty of desiring what is pleasing). A second approach in Aquinas is based on the relation between the person and the goods of value. The first relationship is the practical knowledge of the good to which the cardinal virtue of prudence belongs. Fortitude and temperance govern the relationship with oneself and justice directs the relationship with others through external actions.[14] Here, then, are traces of a relational model in Aquinas's theology.

The relationality-responsibility model influences how one understands the virtues—both the general virtues that affect our basic orientation and all our relationships and the particular virtues that modify our particular relationships with God, neighbor, world, or self.

GENERAL VIRTUES

The traditional theological virtues of faith, hope, and love, although generally described as gifts of God having God as their immediate object, basically modify the fundamental orientation of the person which includes in an implicit way the fundamental relationships described in the model. Consider, for example, the theological virtue of charity. In the Catholic tradition the theological virtue of charity refers to the love that we give in response to God's gracious gift of love to us. The biblical approaches to love recognize that the love of God is intimately connected in many ways with love of neighbor, world, and self, though individual biblical authors often emphasize different aspects of love.

Thomas Aquinas's approach to charity also includes the four fundamental relationships described in the model. Charity is primarily friendship with God—the love of God for God's own sake brought about by the Holy Spirit working in us. The first and formal object of charity is God, but love also reaches to others including enemies because they are loved for God's sake. In the same way, Aquinas recognizes that a person can love oneself in charity. Aquinas does, however, distinguish between rational and irrational creatures. Since love of God is friendship, we cannot love or have friendship with irrational creatures. However, irrational creatures (his term) can be loved with charity insofar as through charity we wish them to be conserved for the honor of God and the usefulness of human beings.[15] Today we recognize the material part of creation as more directly related to charity, but at least Thomas Aquinas recognized that the love of God includes neighbors, self, and, in some way, material creation. In keeping with the tradition of his day, Thomas was perhaps too anthropocentric to highlight the importance of the material world itself but this necessity can now be remedied. As already pointed out the exact meaning of love in the Christian tradition has been constantly debated. Amid these debates the Catholic tradition with its emphasis on inclusiveness, as illustrated by Thomas, sees love as affecting all our relationships.

Faith involves our fundamental recognition of God in Jesus and through the Spirit as our Creator, Redeemer, and Sanctifier.[16] Faith primarily involves a personal relationship with God. In Scripture faith is a surrender to and a total commitment to God which, however, affects the person in all other aspects of life. The Thomistic tradition with its faculty psychology tied faith to the intellect, but faith affects the total person. Whereas the Catholic approach at times has overstressed the intellectual aspect of faith and the truths to which the mind assents or believes, faith does involve an intellectual aspect and truths of faith. But faith is more than an intellectual assent to truth; it also involves our relationship with God and affects the totality of our being. The prayer for the liturgy of the twentieth Sunday in Ordinary Time speaks of God as present in and beyond all things. Such a perspective is the fruit of faith.

Faith also reminds us that we are not self-sufficient monads. We surrender ourselves to the gracious God but this act involves more than a passive response; it is our commitment to live out our existence as God's people. The Catholic's faith in God includes membership in the church, the community of faith, and our relationships with other believers, nonbelievers, and the whole world that God has made. In the world we journey together by faith which gives direction and intentionality to all we do as believers.

In the contemporary world the virtue of hope has come to the fore, for this virtue deals with the meaningfulness of human existence in this world.[17] Do we really live in a vale of tears? Is there any meaning in a world filled with problems and atrocities? For believers, the relationship between faith in God and life in the world becomes most significant. What is the meaning of existence in this world? In this vein, John Courtney Murray once asked if life in this world is simply like basket weaving which does not have any real inherent meaning.[18]

Hope as a theological virtue is based on the power and promise of God to bring us to the fullness of life.[19] Hope was central to the life of God's covenant people in the Hebrew Bible. Yahweh made a promise to the people, and Yahweh was faithful to that promise to safeguard and protect them and bring them forth from bondage in Egypt.

In the Christian tradition Augustine developed an understanding of hope that primarily emphasized the individual's hope for eternal life after death. On the other hand, Joachim of Fiore in the fourteenth century emphasized the effect of hope on human history and pointed out different stages of development in human history. In the modern era, scientific progress, Enlightenment thinking, the theory of evolution, and an emphasis on progress encouraged a belief in evolution and progress in history. Contemporary liberation theologies concerned with the poor, the racially oppressed, and women are rooted in the effect of eschatology on history and the need to develop and change history more in accord with the reign of God. But for Christian theology hope cannot be reduced to a secular ideal of progressive development.

Hope influences the personal and social life of the Christian. In personal life the believer hopes that death is not the end, but God's all enduring love will change death into life. Suffering is a fact of life in our world. Even in the midst of sorrow and suffering the Christian person lives in the hope of the Resurrection. In personal suffering the Christian participates in the paschal mystery of Jesus with its dying and rising. In social life our relationship to the world is not just a time of passive endurance but a vocation to make the reign of God more present in our world. The most significant question for theology today concerns the relationship between hope and history, between the eschatological future and contemporary historical realities. Our stance sheds considerable light on this question. Creation is good and God's redemption is already present and working in our world, but sin remains and the fullness of the reign of God will come only at the end of time. Our stance avoids the extreme dangers of either putting the reign of God completely into the future with nothing in the present, or putting the fullness of the reign of God into history with nothing more for the future. Christians are called to strive to bring about greater justice, freedom, and peace in this world and to recognize that the fullness of justice and peace will only come at the end of time and history. In all our relationships, despite the frustrations and negative aspects, we strive to grow and develop.

In personal and social life the Christian struggles to make the reign of God more present. However, it always remains a struggle. The Christian approach avoids both naive optimism and pervasive pessimism. We are called to grow in all our relationships, but growth will always be difficult, suffer reverses, and never be ultimately successful. Earlier in this century people were too optimistic—all over the world but especially in the United States. People often thought that change and progress could come quickly, easily, and without great problems. Today, in the world and in the United States, a greater pessimism reigns. The problems are manifold, answers are hard to come by, and people often retreat into their own private lives in light of the seemingly insoluble problems with which they live. Christian hope supplies the motivation and the energy to work for a better world with the knowledge that change will never be easy and that the fullness of the reign of God will only come as God's gracious gift on the other side of time and history. The Christian continues to struggle even when there are no accomplishments but only problems. Hope ultimately does not depend on tangible and visible results but on our trust in the promise of God who can turn sorrow into joy and death into life. The Christian struggling for justice in all aspects of life bears witness to the promise of God that can never be totally verified in human history. Only Christian hope enables believers to carry on the struggle in the absence of visible signs of success.

With regard to the life of the church pre-Vatican II Catholicism was rightly accused of triumphalism based on a practical tendency to equate the church with the reign of God.[20] Vatican II insists on a pilgrim church that is not the reign of God but at best the sacrament and witness to the reign of God. This pilgrim church is also a sinful church which is always in need of reform and renovation.[21] Today many progressive Catholics have been greatly frustrated by the problems of the institutional church and its failure to change. One often hears the question: Is there any hope for the church? In a sense such a question betrays a poor notion of hope. Hope does not depend ultimately on human accomplishments or works but on the promise and presence of God. There is always hope, but we have to struggle to bring about change and make the church a better witness to the reign of God.

The Aristotelian-Thomistic tradition sees virtue in the middle between the opposite extremes. Thus generosity stands between the extremes of prodigality and miserliness. The extremes of hope are presumption (excessive hope) and despair (defective hope). The manuals of moral theology developed these extremes as the two primary sins against hope.[22] The notion of virtue as a middle between extremes continues to have some meaning for us today. We may, for example, find hope between the opposites of an easy optimism and a negative pessimism. Hope thus affects the Christian person in all one's relationships and is very often a distinguishing feature of Christian life in this world. The Christian hopes in good times and in bad, in life and in death, in joy and in suffering.

Other general virtues also affect all our relationships. Creativity, for example, plays a very important role in Christian life, as we try to find ways to improve, deepen, widen, and develop our multiple relationships. The *kairos,* in biblical understanding, is a special time given by God—the opportune moment.[23] The Christian person takes advantage of the kairos to grow in relationships. The emphasis on historicity, growth, and development in the moral life underscores our need for creativity. But note how this concept compares with the legal model's stress on obedience. In the context of law, obedience becomes the primary and, seemingly, the only virtue; in the relationality-responsibility model, creativity becomes the more important virtue.

The emphasis on the subject in contemporary thought makes us rethink the virtues and stress the need for the virtue of creativity. We no longer have a single model of character or template of the virtues that everyone must follow. Each individual is unique. Again there are many common elements in the Christian moral life, but each individual puts them together in a unique way. As a result, the creativity of the individual assumes an even greater role in one's development, and some contemporary moral theologians insist on the important role of imagination.[24]

Creativity exists in tension with the need for fidelity. We are not free to do anything we please. Our existing relationships are to be strengthened and deepened not abandoned and overturned. Fidelity plays a significant role in the covenantal relationship between God and us, and it must also be present in all our relationships. Only recently with the advent of historical consciousness, has the Catholic tradition acknowledged the importance of creativity. But virtue is still the mean: we cannot absolutize creativity because we must remain conscious of our limitations and our involvement with others. Thus, the inclusive Catholic approach today once again insists on a "both-and" approach. Bernard Häring perceptively entitled his second three volumes on moral theology *Free and Faithful in Christ*.[25]

From an ethical perspective the insistence on both creativity and fidelity avoids the dangers of either a one-sided consequentialism or a one-sided deontology. Creativity or freedom is often associated with doing good or achieving good consequences. But we are limited human beings and exist in multiple relationships that direct our creativity. The Catholic tradition has recognized that one cannot directly kill innocent civilians in the course of war no matter how much good one wants to accomplish.[26] On the other hand, fidelity has never been proposed as an absolute. Vows, for example, which are promises made to God, can be broken if the matter of the vow or the persons involved have substantially changed. The Catholic Church has always given dispensations from some religious vows or promises.[27] Thus, both creativity and fidelity characterize all our different relationships. Other general virtues affecting all our relationships include truthfulness and honesty. However, my purpose here is not to present all the virtues but to illustrate the most significant virtues and how they shape the Christian person as both subject and agent.

PARTICULAR VIRTUES

In addition to the general virtues that affect the total person and all her relationships, there are particular virtues affecting particular relationships. A brief sketch of some of these virtues follows.

RELATIONSHIP TO GOD. The Christian accepts life and reality as a gift from God: God gives, we receive; God calls, we respond. The Christian's fundamental disposition with regard to God is openness and readiness to receive the gift. The believer must constantly be open to recognize, receive, and respond to the gift of God's gracious love in all its dimensions. The significant biblical figures are those who were open to hear and respond to the call of God—Abraham and Sarah, Moses, the Prophets, and in the New Testament, Mary. Mary is the model of all believers since she was most open to the Word of God and totally responded to it—"be it done unto me according to your word" (Luke 1:38), and Jesus has the same openness in relation to his heavenly Father (John 17). Membership in the community of disciples entails this fundamental openness to God's life-giving words and deeds. The Gospels frequently insist on the need to be open and ready or "vigilant and watchful" when God comes (Mark 13:32–35, Matt 25:1–13, Luke 12:35–48).

Openness is a virtue that many Americans are glad to accept. We talk about the importance of being open and the danger of being closed. However, being open is more challenging than it seems. Being open to God (and others) stands in opposition to self-centeredness and self-sufficiency. The person who is closed in on oneself can never hear the promptings of the Spirit. This fundamental openness to God opposes the self-sufficiency and absolute individualism that is so pervasive today.

Openness to God and the need for vigilance continue throughout our life. God is constantly coming to us. The Spirit is always prompting us. The danger is that we become so preoccupied with self in our daily concerns that we are deaf and blind to the call and sight of God. As mentioned before, Christian theology speaks about the *kairos*—the time or the moment in which God comes to us (Eph 5:16, Col 4:5). The Christian has to be open to hear the call of God and seize the opportunity in the midst of all the duties, obligations, and distractions of our lives. True openness thus calls for a contemplative aspect to our being that we may truly discern the call of God amid the din and cacophony of many voices. God comes to us not only in the depths of our heart but also in the circumstances and relationships of our daily lives and especially in the needs of others. The spiritual tradition often recommends time for contemplation and retreat precisely to dispose one to hear and heed the call of God in daily life.[28]

The first beatitude is this: "blessed are the poor in spirit for theirs is the kingdom of God" (Matt 5:3). The notion of being poor in spirit underscores the emphasis on openness. The poor in spirit recognize their dependence on God for all things and by their posture of open arms signify their watchfulness and need to receive from God. Both the materially poor and the poor in spirit are important biblical concepts, but the danger exists among affluent Christians of overemphasizing the poor in spirit at the expense of the materially poor. Nevertheless, there always remains an important role in the Christian life for the poor in spirit.[29]

Thankfulness or gratitude is another important virtue in our relationship with God that stems from God's initiating gracious act. Whatever we have, we have received as God's gift. Praise and thanks are fundamental Christian attitudes. The centrality of liturgy in the Catholic tradition illustrates the emphasis on praise. The eucharist is at the heart and center of Catholic life; the word "eucharist" is from the Greek and means thanksgiving. According to the beginning of the eucharistic prayer, we do well always and everywhere to give thanks but especially in this eucharist.[30]

At times even in Catholic tradition, the praise aspect of the sacraments has been diminished or forgotten. As we noted earlier, the older format and name of the sacrament of reconciliation was confession— the confession of sins according to number and species to the priest. The experience of the sacrament involved little or no praise or thanksgiving. But the primary reality of every sacrament is the worship and praise of God for mercy and forgiveness. The Catholic tendency toward pelagianism has in instances such as this downplayed the aspect of God's gracious initiative to which our first response is gratitude. Ironically, the Latin word for confession actually means to give praise and thanks. The *Confessions* of Augustine are not the memoirs in which he tells all the experiences of his early life but a book of praise and thanks to God. Penance celebrates the reconciling mercy and forgiveness of God and praises God for these gifts.[31]

RELATIONSHIP TO OTHERS. Since justice in the Catholic tradition has been the most significant virtue involving our relationships with others, this section will concentrate on justice. Modern papal social teaching, beginning with Leo XIII's encyclical *Rerum novarum* in 1891, used the Thomistic understanding of justice to develop the official teaching.[32] Subsequent hierarchical teaching has followed the same approach as exemplified in the pastoral letter of the U.S. bishops on the economy. The recent documents as illustrated by this pastoral letter continue to see this Thomistic approach as consonant with, and a good way of organizing, the different aspects of justice found in Scripture.[33]

Justice in this tradition involves giving the person that which is due. The ultimate question concerns the meaning and reality of what is due. The basic reality of justice is itself complex precisely because it is undergirded by an anthropology that emphasizes the social nature of human beings. Justice involves three types of relationships—individual to another individual, society (or the state) to the individual, and the individual to society (or the state). Each of these relationships brings into play a different type of justice. Notice how the Catholic recognition of the social and political nature of human beings emphasizes that the individual is not an isolated monad but a being living in relationship to others in the general society and political order of the state.[34]

Commutative justice governs the relationship of one individual to another, but this individual can also be a "moral person" or corporation. Thus commutative justice involves all sorts of contracts, agreements, or relationships involving a one to one relationship. Commutative justice has two distinctive characteristics—arithmetical equality and blindness; it is not a respecter of persons. This type of justice is concerned only with the reality or thing itself, not the person. Sears must charge the same price for a refrigerator whether you buy it or the richest person in the world buys it. The price is the same for all. In this approach justice is blind because it pays no attention to the condition of the person. Commutative justice covers all contracts and relations of individuals or corporations to each other. What is due in this case depends on reality independently of the nature of the persons involved.[35]

Distributive justice involves the relationship between society or the state and the individual. An important difference exists between society and the state. Society is the broader reality referring to all aspects of social life, whereas the state is the strictly political order that wields the power of coercive law. The state as a lesser part of society embodies the fundamental principle of a limited constitutional government. The government does not control all aspects of life in society but its powers are limited. However, government exists to promote the public good of society and not just to protect and promote individual goods.[36] For our limited purposes we cannot delve into the different ramifications of the role of the state and society with regard to justice.

Society basically has two realities to distribute—goods and burdens. With regard to the distribution of goods one important aspect is the distribution of material goods or wealth. What is a just distribution of such goods? The Catholic tradition, continuing the biblical and Aristotelian-Thomistic approaches, insists on the fundamental importance of human need but also recognizes other criteria of just distribution. John A. Ryan, the most significant figure in Catholic social ethics in the United States in the first half of the twentieth century, defended every person's right to a minimum of goods necessary to satisfy basic human needs. He also recognized other canons of distribution such as equality, effort, sacrifice, productivity, and security.[37]

Ryan's ideas underscored what is a significant aspect in Catholic social teaching: the right of every human being to a minimally decent human existence. The Pastoral Constitution on the Church in the Modern World states: "(T)he right to have a share of earthly goods sufficient for oneself and one's family belongs to everyone."[38] The pastoral letter of the U.S. bishops on the economy maintains: "Distributive justice requires that the allocation of income, wealth, and power in society be evaluated in the light of its effects on persons whose basic material needs are unmet."[39] John Paul II in his 1991 social encyclical *Centesimus annus*, insists: "It is a strict duty of justice and truth not to allow fundamental human needs to remain unsatisfied."[40]

The right of human beings to a minimally decent human existence and the obligation of society to meet these fundamental needs is grounded in the realization that the goods of creation exist primarily to serve the needs of all. All other rights whatsoever, including private property rights and free commerce, are to be subordinated to this social destination of the goods of creation. The doctrine of creation recognizes that God made the world and material creation to serve the needs of all God's people not just a few. (Furthermore, the goods of creation and ecological realities [natural resources] have some meaning in themselves apart from human needs.) Such an approach does not deny the right to private property, but this right to private property is meant to order the destination of the goods of creation to serve the needs of all.[41]

Another basis for the fundamental importance of human need in distributing material goods comes from the traditional Christian emphasis on helping those in need. Christianity often sees our relationship to others in terms of God's relationship to us. Our needs, not our merits or accomplishments, are the basis for God's gracious gift to us, and, therefore, we should respond to the needs of others in the same way. Paul VI's *Populorum progressio* quotes St. Ambrose to the effect that, in giving what you possess to the poor, you are really handing over what is theirs.[42] Peter the Lombard, who wrote the text for theology in the Middle Ages, defined justice as coming to the assistance of the poor.[43] To this day Catholics remain divided over the nature of the obligation of almsgiving. Because he worked in Aristotelian categories, many theologians maintain that Thomas Aquinas saw this obligation in terms of charity and not strict justice.[44] Some commentators, however, relate Aquinas's teaching on almsgiving to justice.[45] Others accept Peter the Lombard's position, namely, that we are obliged in justice to help the poor.[46]

Contemporary liberation theology has developed the notion of a preferential option for the poor. Throughout the Hebrew Bible and Christian Scripture, God is portrayed as the protector and defender of the poor. Liberation theology begins with this approach and develops an epistemology coherent with this preference as opposed to a neutral, universal, value-free perspective of the human knower. Yet this preferential option for the poor wants to avoid an exclusivity that understands God as loving only the poor. The preferential option for the poor grounds the need to provide all human beings with the material goods necessary for a minimally decent human existence.[47]

Need is a fundamental canon of just distribution but not the only canon. Ryan also mentions effort, sacrifice, productivity, and scarcity.[48] This perspective has guided the Catholic approach to political and economic ethics to develop a position between the extremes of individualistic capitalism and collectivistic communism. The Catholic position calls for a basic and decent human minimum for all but allows for differences in material goods based on the other canons of distribution. Effort, productivity, risk, and scarcity may justify greater material goods for certain people. Thus, the Catholic tradition does not require an absolute equality for all, or allow the free market to determine how goods are distributed. Extreme inequality in wealth and income threatens the solidarity of the human community. Society and the state have an obligation to make sure that all individuals have this basic minimum and that extreme inequalities do not exist.[49] The individual Christian person with the virtue of distributive justice is inclined toward working in this direction.

Society distributes not only goods but also burdens to its members. What is the just distribution of these burdens? Perhaps the most significant burden in political society is taxation. Here the Catholic tradition has insisted on the need for progressive taxation. Those who have more should pay not only arithmetically more but proportionately more taxes.[50]

The virtue of distributive justice is ultimately rooted in an anthropology that recognizes the relational social nature of human beings. We are not isolated monads, but we are members of the human community with responsibilities for one another precisely because we are all children of a gracious and loving God. Distributive justice, precisely because it takes into consideration the social aspect of human beings, differs by definition from commutative justice. Whereas commutative justice is blind, no respecter of persons, and deals with arithmetical equality; distributive justice is not blind, definitely considers the person involved, and insists on proportionate equality. Thus, for example, if one were to consider the obligation of paying taxes solely on the basis of some type of contract by which we pay society for what it provides for us, then the criteria of commutative justice come into play. But taxation involves distributive justice precisely because it is part of our obligation to the total society in which we live and is not merely a tax we pay for services provided for us.[51]

The 1986 pastoral letter of the U.S. Catholic bishops on the economy caused quite a stir in this country because of its negative critique of the American economy. The bishops elaborated and developed the requirements of distributive justice for our society. The letter did not call for the abolition of capitalism but for limits on the free market to insure the requirements of distributive justice for all citizens. The precise challenge facing this country today is to secure economic rights for all just as it earlier faced the challenge to secure political rights for all.[52] Distributive justice further reminds us of the danger in the narrow individualism that is so often prevalent in our society. The Catholic approach stresses the solidarity of all in the human family and the need to be concerned for others especially the poor and the needy.

Legal justice, also known as social or contributive justice, guides the relationship of the individual to society and the state. In the past, the primary consideration in this category involved obedience to just laws made for the common good of society. Today the emphasis is on the need for individuals to participate and contribute to the life of society—hence, the name contributive justice. All others have an obligation to make sure that every individual is able to participate fully in the life of the total society.[53]

In sum, justice in the Catholic tradition is a complex reality which, as a virtue, disposes the individual person to act in accord with the demands of the three types of justice outlined here. Many other virtues such as compassion and care also guide and direct our relationships to other human beings, but justice remains a very significant virtue with important ramifications especially for our relationships in society.

Our relationships to others are not always to others as particular individuals but to others as members of different organisms, institutions, or social communities. In the classical tradition piety is the virtue that disposes children to act properly toward their parents and family, and individuals to act properly toward their country.[54] Today it seems more accurate to speak of patriotism as the virtue directing one's love of country. Once again this virtue is in the middle. The defect comes from a lack of appreciation and respect for one's country. More often than not problems arise from an exaggerated and absolutized love and reverence for one's country. Every state or country is limited and subject to being wrong. The Christian tradition has always recognized that our obligation to God limits and directs our obligation to Caesar (Matt 22:21). To absolutize one's own country is epitomized in the line—"my country right or wrong." Patriotism calls for a critical love of one's country and a recognition that individual states and countries have an obligation to the whole world. Our global existence today relativizes every country, race, tribe, or ethnic group. The primary danger remains an absolutizing or idolizing tendency to substitute a part for the whole.

RELATIONSHIP WITH THE WORLD. Our relationship with the world calls for care, concern, reverence, and solidarity with our environment. We might call this virtue ecological stewardship. Stewardship is the name of the virtue that Christians have traditionally used to describe our relationship with the earth and the environment. However, in the past there have been some difficulties in the Christian and Catholic tradition, and we have not recognized the importance of the natural environment. Some of the ecological neglect in the Christian tradition can be traced to the Genesis command to subdue the earth and have dominion over the fish of the sea, birds of the air, and every living thing that moves on the earth (Gen 1:26). Such a command has been interpreted to give human beings a right to interfere in the ecological world for their own purposes and needs. Moreover, a dualism of spirit and matter, which has been much stronger in certain periods of Christian history, tends to downplay all that is material including the world of nature. The Catholic tradition has often employed hierarchical perspectives for its understanding of human relationships and the dominion of humans over nature and creation. Christian theology, both Protestant and Catholic, has tended especially in the last centuries to be very anthropocentric in its approach. James M. Gustafson has insisted on a theocentric ethic in place of the anthropocentric ethic that is so characteristic of our times and, in the process gives much more significance to the patterns and processes of nature.[55] In the United States, an exaggerated emphasis on individualism has given free reign to individuals to do whatever they want with regard to nature and ecosystems. Modern technology, in the service of that individualism, has accepted no boundaries or limits in its quest to shape the world in accord with what human beings want.

We are, however, beginning to experience the need for ecological stewardship and awareness. We have a responsibility to the ecosystem and cannot see the earth merely as a means to fulfill our human wants. A Catholic perspective is here developing around an understanding of the earth's sacramentality. All of God's creation is a sacrament and sign of the presence of God. Thus creation itself has meaning and incorporates an aspect of reverence and awe because it makes God present to us.[56] In addition, ecofeminism links ecology and feminism on the basis of their common exploitation by powerful, mostly white males,[57] and Native Americans also have much to teach us about respect for the earth and all that is in it.[58]

Catholic moral theology is struggling to identify the exact relationship between human beings and the ecosystems of our world. Many people recognize that human beings are superior to animal and plant life. A human being has more importance than a dog, a cat, a tree, or a plant. Thus human beings can and should use the so-called lesser forms of life on our planet, especially when truly human needs are involved and not merely wants. But all of created reality and the environment and ecosystems in which we live are not simply means to be used by human beings. Creation and the environment have a value and meaning in themselves, and cannot be totally subordinated to human beings. The genetic makeup of human beings is very close to the genetic makeup of animals. As a result ecological stewardship calls for awe and reverence with regard to all God's creation though at times the lesser may serve the higher.[59] Ecological concern as a virtue produces an attitude of respect and reverence for all God's creation.

Stewardship is another virtue that guides our attitude toward the material goods of this world. Aristotle recognized that human happiness and well-being require a sufficiency of material goods such as food, clothing, shelter, but external goods are not the highest good or the basis for our happiness.[60] The Catholic tradition has built on this approach in the light of its own biblical origins. Material goods are necessary for human existence but they are not the most important or the most humanly satisfying goods. True human happiness and fulfillment can never consist merely in the accumulation of material goods. In fact the quest for material goods often becomes an obstacle to human fulfillment and Christian discipleship. Recall the biblical story of the rich young man who sadly refused the call of Jesus because he had many possessions (Matt 19:16–30). The problems of consumerism and materialism abound in our contemporary society. The Christian vision appreciates the need for material goods but recognizes their limits. Consumerism and materialism flourish in an ethos that stresses individual wants, but these wants and desires have to be moderated for truly human and Christian purposes. The emphasis on individualism grossly exaggerates the importance of material and consumer goods. The same basic attitudes contribute to the exploitation of earth and are the source of many ecological problems. Stewardship disposes the person to have a proper relationship to the world and to material goods.

RELATIONSHIP TO SELF. Other virtues modify the person as subject and agent in terms of the relationship with oneself. The Catholic tradition in theory, despite some practical contradictions, has insisted on a proper love for self.[61] All of us are made in the image and likeness of God, and God has called each of us by our own name. We can and should love ourselves, but again a proper self-love will avoid opposite extremes. An excessive or exaggerated love of self goes too far by making self the center of the world and failing to appreciate our dependence on God and our multiple relationships with others. Without doubt individualism and an inordinate love of self constitute very strong temptations in our world. But these problems do not diminish the importance of and need for a proper love of self. Failing to love one's self is often described in psychological terms as insecurity or a poor self-image. In religious language the person fears that she is evil or sinful and unworthy of God's love. The Christian understanding of a proper love of self overcomes and corrects this Christian, human, and psychological inability to truly appreciate one's own self. The Christian understands the self as a unique gift of God, an image of God called to become a child of God. The individual person is not the center of the world or the most important reality, but proper love of self recognizes one's relationship to and dependence on God and others.

Honesty and a self-critical attitude should mark the Christian's attitude to oneself. The virtue of honesty gives some direction to the proper love of self. Honesty and a self-critical attitude are necessary if we are to grow in our multiple relationships. From the Christian perspective, the call to conversion reminds us of the continuing need to overcome the sinful elements in our lives. There can be no growth unless we recognize the need to change. Catholic asceticism has long recognized this reality. The sacrament of reconciliation makes us conscious of our continuing sinfulness and the need for forgiveness and reconciliation in all our relationships. Every eucharistic assembly begins with calling to mind our sinfulness although the danger exists that this ritual can become a routine practice that does not meaningfully involve members of the assembly. The Catholic tradition has also recommended the need for a daily examination of conscience as a way to be critical and to be able to grow in our multiple relationships. Being self-critical does not involve denying the gifts we have received and our own personal talents. Here again one can see the stance at work. As human beings we experience the goodness of creation and the presence of God's redeeming love in us, but we are also conscious of our limitations, our finitude, our sinfulness, and our lack of eschatological fullness.

The danger of making oneself the center of the world and living in accord with such an inflated self-concept remains very strong. In this context the Kantian notion of universality can become a significant practical means of exercising a self-critical attitude. The Kantian categorical imperative insists that one can do a particular action only if one is willing to let other persons in similar situations do the same thing.[62] I have difficulty with the ultimate metaphysics and ethics of the Kantian approach because it tends to be purely formal or lacking in material content. However, the categorical imperative is a means to ensure that we continue to be self-critical. The great danger consists in our willingness to make exceptions for ourselves. Applying the Kantian principle of universalizability to our actions constitutes an excellent practical means of overcoming this danger.

Integrity is another important virtue for Christians and all human beings. Integrity calls for cohesiveness and coherence. All the aspects of our lives should fit together; especially our words and deeds. It is easy to talk a good game but not so easy to live in accord with what we say. Integrity is especially important for those in leadership and teaching roles—for example, parents with regard to their children. Integrity also argues against the importance of appearances and the desire to seem better or to have more than others. Especially in a consumer society that overvalues material possessions people are often tempted to give too much importance to appearances whether in terms of the size of one's home or the cost of one's automobile.

The virtue of temperance, which has traditionally been labeled one of the four cardinal virtues, regulates and moderates the "concupiscible appetites" or our desires for physical pleasures, such as food, drink, and sex. These appetites are common to human beings and other animals; we must, therefore, live with them in a truly human way.[63] The proper function of the virtue of temperance is to moderate and direct these appetites, not to deny, suppress, or annihilate them. Alcoholic beverages, for example, are not evil or bad. Like all other human realities involved with the concupiscible appetites, alcoholic beverages are limited goods that can be abused. I have always been intrigued by the fact that many of the world's best wines and liqueurs are named after monks! These monks apparently saw no incompatibility between their religious life and alcoholic beverages. But drink, food, and sex are limited human goods that can be abused. The virtues of sobriety and chastity recognize the good involved in these appetites but also the need to order them in a truly human way against the dangers of abuse.

Vices opposed to the virtue of temperance are usually vices of excess. Gluttony and drunkenness illustrate such abuses. Likewise, in sexuality the primary abuse comes from failing to see human sexuality in the context of loving human relationships. However, in the Catholic tradition (and in many other religious and Christian traditions), abuse often comes from a defect in the concupiscible appetites, especially sexuality. The fear and denial of sexuality have often fostered a repressive attitude toward sex. Many factors have influenced this negative attitude to sexuality in the past. The Greek philosophical background too often distinguished between the spirit which is good and matter which is evil; and though Paul the apostle speaks eloquently about a struggle between spirit and flesh, tradition has inaccurately restricted the term "flesh" to problems connected with sexuality. In reality, "spirit" for Paul means the whole person who is under the influence of the life-giving Spirit, whereas "flesh" refers to the whole person, body and soul, under the control of sin (Rom 8:4–20). Many Christian heresies from early Gnosticism to eighteenth-century Jansenism and down to the present day have denigrated the material aspect of human existence especially with regard to sexuality.[64] Undeniably, sexuality has often been abused, but the abuse does not negate the proper use. Thus, the virtue of chastity moderates but does not deny or repress human sexuality.

Christian asceticism has often been narrowly defined—or practiced—as control of the concupiscible appetites. These appetites do readily escape one's control and may need to be redirected. Thus we continue to uphold the importance of this exercise (asceticism means exercise) in our world today, but asceticism is always in the service of true human good, not repression or denial.

Both general and particular virtues modify the person as subject and agent. These dispositions truly constitute the character of the individual person. They make the individual a better person and dispose that person to act for the good. The virtues thus play a significant role in both human moral life and in theoretical reflection on that life. In Catholic tradition vice is the opposite of virtue. There is no need for a long separate discussion on vice or the habits that dispose a person to do evil. The extreme vices have already been mentioned in connection with individual virtues.

POWER

Virtue empowers an individual as agent to act in a particular way. In fact, power itself is a moral reality that affects persons and how they act. Agents can use power with regard to others or be the objects of others' use of power. Power's role in the social and political worlds in which we live is significant; it helps people and institutions achieve their purposes. Such uses of power can be morally right or wrong depending on the agent's purpose.

The Catholic tradition has seldom reflected on power. For example, *The New Dictionary of Catholic Social Thought* published in 1994 has no separate article on power. This volume contains over 1,000 pages, but discusses only "force," a class of terms that includes power, coercion, and manipulation in a single article of slightly more than one page.[65] Note how power in this sense has a pejorative connotation.

Why has Catholic tradition not discussed power in social and political life? Catholic social ethics traditionally proposed an organic understanding of society and the state. The analogy of the body was often employed to explain the political order. Each part of the body plays a role under the direction of the head. The classicist methodology stressed the unchanging roles of the various parts, while a hierarchical order determined the relationship among them. In the family, mother, father, and children had their appropriate roles under the leadership of the father. In political society the ruler directed people to the common good though such an approach was paternalistic at best and authoritarian at worst. Power existed in reality, but it was connected to roles and often called authority. The Catholic tradition heavily emphasized harmony and order with all parts working for the good of the whole under the direction of the legitimate authority. Likewise the tradition was rational rather than voluntaristic so that authority and law were ordered by reason for the common good. Protestant theologians often discussed power in the light of human sinfulness, but the Catholic natural law tradition downplayed and often underestimated the role of sin. Instead, Catholics insisted on stability, harmony, rationality, and hierarchy and overlooked the reality of power in social and political life.

With the shift from classicism to historical consciousness, a greater acceptance of the subject, and a heightened awareness of the Gospel's call for justice and more equitable social and political structures, the Catholic tradition has begun to recognize the role of power. Liberation theologies, especially, call attention to power and the need to empower the oppressed and transform unjust and oppressive structures. Thomas Schubeck, for example, devotes a chapter to power in his book on liberation ethics.[66] Feminists and black liberationists have also recognized the role of power. In practice the Campaign for Human Development sponsored by the American bishops strongly supports community organizations that empower poor and marginalized persons to come together to change their situation and their relationship with the holders of power in society.[67] Contemporary Catholic thought and practice have begun to grapple with power, but this discussion has not yet moved to the fore.

Christine Firer Hinze, on the basis of the literature in social and political theory and Christian social ethics, suggests that two different models of power have been proposed. The first and more prominent model involves an agent's "power over" another and can be understood in terms of superordination. The second model is an agent's "power to" exercise an effective capacity to transform both self and social structures.[68] In the U.S. Protestant tradition Reinhold Niebuhr understood "power over" in relationship to human sinfulness and the need to check and balance the adverse effects of the power of group egoism and domination. The Catholic philosopher Jacques Maritain also emphasized "power over" but bases it on creation rather than sin.[69] The differences between these two thinkers illustrate the different emphases of the Catholic and Protestant traditions. The Catholic approach is more positive about power,[70] but it has not given enough importance to sin and its effects.

The second model, which is more muted in the Christian tradition, involves the transforming aspect of power. It has been developed by

Paul Tillich, process theologians, and liberation theologians.[71] Hinze argues that a comprehensive understanding of power recognizes the role of both models.[72] This recognition of power as both dominative and transformative coheres with the stance. Direction and domination come from the finite, limited, and sinful aspects of human existence. Transformative power comes from the positive aspects of creation and redemption. Power is necessary to direct others, to check the effects of the will to power in individuals and in groups, and to transform both self and unjust social structures. These different aspects of power can be seen in the emphasis given today to structural sin. Sinful structures are supported by the dominant group's will to power; the same sinful structures can be transformed by the power of the poor and the oppressed working to transform structures.[73]

Perhaps the most significant ethical development in recent times involves the radical extension of human power. Our global society illustrates the enormous impact of power. Nuclear power is sufficiently deadly to destroy entire continents, economic power has worldwide effects, and what happens on Wall Street has repercussions in all parts of the world. Scientific and technological developments have given human beings enormous power with respect to life and death itself. In our society knowledge and skills constitute a great power and without these one is powerless and further marginalized. Power needs an ethical evaluation. The all-pervasive presence of power today and its possible use for good or for ill calls for an ethic of responsibility.[74] Power can be used for good or evil. Moral virtues, values, and principles must guide the proper use of power. From our relationality-responsibility perspective, power must be seen in terms of promoting the multiple relationships of persons and institutions in the light of the values and virtues that guide the moral life. Precisely because of the sheer availability of so much power today, human domination and oppression can be much more severe than in the past, but properly and responsibly used, this power can also be an instrument for good.

The last two chapters have dealt with the human person who is both subject and agent. Without doubt the human person constitutes the most important aspect in morality and in our systematic reflection on morality. The agent aspect of the person begins a shift to the object pole of morality. The just person is disposed to act justly. The hopeful person lives hopefully. The person as agent is much more significant than particular moral acts because the virtuous person is disposed to do many good acts. The object pole of morality includes the goods, the values, and all the realities existing in the world in which we live and act. Virtues play a very central role in guiding and directing the person who is acting. In addition to virtues, principles and norms serve to guide and direct human acts by protecting and promoting basic goods and values in our multiple relationships with God, neighbor, world, and self. The next chapter will consider principles and norms.

N O T E S

1. Aquinas, *IaIIae*, q.55–67.
2. Charles Taylor, *Sources of the Self: The Making of the Modern Identity* (Cambridge, Mass.: Harvard University Press, 1989).
3. Stanley Hauerwas, *Character and the Christian Life: A Study in Theological Ethics* (San Antonio, Tex.: Trinity University Press, 1975).
4. Gilbert C. Meilander, *The Theory and Practice of Virtue* (Notre Dame, Ind.: University of Notre Dame Press, 1984), p. 122.
5. Jean Porter, *The Recovery of Virtue: The Revelance of Aquinas for Christian Ethics* (Louisville, Ky.: Westminster/John Knox, 1990).
6. Romanus Cessario, *Moral Virtues and Theological Ethics* (Notre Dame, Ind.: University of Notre Dame Press, 1991).
7. Thomas F. O'Meara, "Virtues in the Theology of Thomas Aquinas," *Theological Studies* 58 (1997): 254–85.
8. Odon Lottin, *Morale fondamentale* (Tournai, Belgium: Desclée and Cie, 1954), pp. 467–70.
9. James F. Keenan, "Proposing Cardinal Virtues," *Theological Studies* 56 (1995): 711–15. Keenan does, however, propose his own list of cardinal virtues—prudence, justice, fidelity, and self-care.
10. George P. Klubertanz, *Habits and Virtues* (New York: Appleton-Century-Crofts, 1965), pp. 201–03.
11. Ibid., p. 241.
12. Keenan, *Theological Studies* 56 (1995): 718–19.
13. For example, Donald W. Shriver, *An Ethic for Enemies: Forgiveness in Politics* (New York: Oxford University Press, 1995).
14. Klubertanz, *Habits and Virtues*, pp. 202–03.
15. Thomas Aquinas, *IIaIIae*, q.23–25. For an overview of faith in Catholic systematic theology, see Avery Dulles, "Faith and Relevation," in *Systematic Theology*, ed. Fiorenza and Galvin, 1, pp. 92–128.
16. For the theological virtue of faith, see Romanus Cessario, *Christian Faith and the Theological Life* (Washington, D.C.: Catholic University of America Press, 1996).
17. For a contemporary Catholic understanding of hope, see Dermot A. Lane, *Keeping Hope Alive: Stirrings in Christian Thinking* (New York: Paulist, 1996).
18. John Courtney Murray, *We Hold These Truths: Catholic Reflections on the American Proposition* (Kansas City, Mo.: Sheed and Ward, 1960) pp. 175–96.

19. For an overview of the historical development in the theology of hope, see Michael Scanlon, "Hope," in *New Dictionary of Theology,* ed. Komonchak, Collins, and Lane, pp. 492–98.

20. For the famous intervention of Bishop de Smedt of Bruges on triumphalism at the first session of Vatican II, see Gérard Philips, "History of the Constitution," in *Commentary on the Documents of Vatican II,* ed. Herbert Vorgrimler, 5 vols. (New York: Herder and Herder, 1967), 1, p. 109.

21. Dogmatic Constitution on the Church, nn. 48–51, in *Vatican Council II,* ed. Flannery, pp. 407–13.

22. Zalba, *Theologiae moralis summa,* 1, pp. 731–33, 812–17.

23. Paul Nevenzeit, "Time," *Sacramentum Verbi: An Encyclopedia of Biblical Theology,* 3 vols., ed. Johannes B. Bauer (New York: Herder and Herder, 1970), 3, pp. 911–15.

24. Daniel C. Maguire, *The Moral Choice* (Garden City, N.Y.: Doubleday, 1978), pp. 189–217; Philip S. Keane, *Christian Ethics and Imagination: A Philosophical Inquiry* (New York: Paulist, 1984).

25. Bernard Häring, *Free and Faithful in Christ.*

26. Zalba, *Theologiae moralis summa,* 2, pp. 302–13.

27. Ibid., pp. 127–35.

28. Thomas Merton, *Contemplation in a World of Action* (Garden City, N.Y.: Doubleday Image, 1973).

29. Albert Gelin, *The Poor of Yahweh* (Collegeville, Minn.: Liturgical, 1964).

30. Leo C. Hay, *Eucharist: A Thanksgiving Celebration* (Wilmington, Del.: Michael Glazier, 1989).

31. For worship as a central aspect in the sacrament of reconciliation, see James Dallen, *The Reconciling Community: The Rite of Penance* (New York: Pueblo, 1986).

32. Paul Misner, *Social Catholicism in Europe: From the Onset of Industrialization to the First World War* (New York: Crossroad, 1991), pp. 213–20.

33. Catholic Bishops, *Economic Justice for All,* nn. 28–125, pp. 15–63.

34. For an overview of the Thomistic approach to justice, see Josef Pieper, *Justice* (New York: Pantheon, 1955), Daniel C. Maguire, "The Primacy of Justice in Moral Theology," *Horizons* 10 (1983): 72–85. Maguire has frequently emphasized the importance of justice in social ethics; see Daniel C. Maguire, *A New American Justice: Ending the White Male Monopoly* (Garden City, N.Y.: Doubleday, 1980), and his most recent work *The Moral Core of Judaism and Christianity: Reclaiming the Revolution* (Minneapolis, Minn.: Fortress, 1993). For my development and analysis of the Thomistic understanding of justice, see Charles E. Curran, *Tensions in Moral Theology* (Notre Dame, Ind.: University of Notre Dame Press, 1988), pp. 110–37. For a different reading of the Thomistic tradition which sees legal justice as a general virtue, see Jeremiah Newman, *Foundations of Justice* (Cork, Ireland: Cork University Press, 1954).

35. Catholic Bishops, *Economic Justice for All,* n. 69, pp. 35–36.

36. John Courtney Murray emphasized a distinction between society and the state in his theory of religious freedom; see John Courtney Murray, *The Problem of Religious Freedom* (Westminster, Md · Newman, 1965), pp. 28–31.

37. John A. Ryan, *Distributive Justice: The Right and Wrong of our Present Distribution of Wealth* (New York: Macmillan, 1916), pp. 243–53.

38. Pastoral Constitution on the Church in the Modern World, n. 69, in *Catholic Social Thought*, ed. O'Brien and Shannon, p. 213.

39. Catholic Bishops, *Economic Justice for All*, n. 70, p. 36.

40. *Centesimus annus*, n. 34, in *Catholic Social Thought*, ed. O'Brien and Shannon, p. 464.

41. *Populorum progressio*, n. 22, in *Catholic Social Thought*, ed. O'Brien and Shannon, p. 245.

42. Ibid., n. 23, p. 245.

43. Petrus Lombardus, *Sententiarum Libri IV* (Lyons, J. Sacon, 1515), lib. 3, dist. 33, cap. 1.

44. Aquinas, *IIaIIae*, q.32, a.1; see Odon Lottin "La nature du devoir de l'aumône chez les prédécesseurs de Saint Thomas d'Aquin," *Psychologie et morale au XIIᵉ et XIIIᵉ siècles* (Louvain, Belgium: Abbaye du Mont César, 1949), III–1, pp. 299–313.

45. L. Bouvier, *Le précepte del'aumône chez Saint Thomas d'Aquin* (Montreal: Immaculata Conceptio, 1935).

46. Hermenegildus Lio, *Estne obligatio justitiae subvenire miseris?* (Rome: Desclée, 1957).

47. Donal Dorr, *Option for the Poor: A Hundred Years of Vatican Social Teaching*, rev. ed. (Maryknoll, N.Y.: Orbis, 1992).

48. Ryan, *Distributive Justice*, pp. 243–53.

49. Catholic Bishops, *Economic Justice for All*, nn. 61–95, pp. 32–49.

50. Ibid., n. 76, pp. 38–39.

51. For my in-depth defense of progressive taxation, see Charles E. Curran, *Toward an American Catholic Moral Theology*, (Notre Dame, Ind.: University of Notre Dame Press, 1987), pp. 93–118.

52. Catholic Bishops, *Economic Justice for All*, p. 49.

53. Ibid., n. 71, pp. 36–37.

54. Aquinas, *IIaIIae*, q.101.

55. James M. Gustafson, *Intersections: Science, Theology, and Ethics* (Cleveland, Ohio: Pilgrim, 1996).

56. Kevin W. Irwin, "The Sacramentality of Creation and the Role of Creation in Liturgy and Sacraments," in *Preserving the Creation: Environmental Theology and Ethics*, ed. Kevin W. Irwin and Edmund D. Pellegrino (Washington, D.C.: Georgetown University Press, 1994), pp. 67–111.

57. Elizabeth A. Johnson, *Women, Earth, and Creator Sprit* (New York: Paulist, 1993).

58. Jana Stone, *Every Part of This Earth Is Sacred: Native American Voices in Praise of Nature* (San Francisco, Calif.: Harper, 1993).

59. For a similar position taken by the bishops in the United States, see U.S. Catholic Conference, "Renewing the Earth: An Invitation to Reflection and Action on the Environment in the Light of Catholic Social Teaching," *Origins* 21 (1991): 425–32; also Daniel M. Cowdin, "Toward an Environmental Ethic," in *Preserving the Creation*, ed. Irwin and Pellegrino, pp. 112–47; Charles M. Murphy, *At Home on Earth: Foundations for a Catholic Ethic of the Environment* (New York: Crossroad, 1989); Drew Christiansen and Walter Grazen, eds., *And God Saw That It Was Good: Catholic Theology and Ecology* (Washington, D.C.: U.S. Catholic Conference, 1996). For a more radical approach, see Thomas Berry,

The Dream of the Earth (San Francisco, Calif.: Sierra Club, 1988). For developments away from anthropocentricism in the teaching of John Paul II, see Daniel M. Cowdin, "John Paul II and Environmental Concern: Problems and Possibilities," *Living Light* 28 (1991): 44–52.

60. Aristotle, *Nicomachean Ethics*, nn. 1097–98, pp. 13–20.

61. Aquinas, *IIaIIae* q.26, a.3–5.

62. Sullivan, *An Introduction to Kant's Ethics*, pp. 28–45.

63. Josef Pieper, *The Four Cardinal Virtues: Prudence, Justice, Fortitude, and Temperance* (Notre Dame, Ind.: University of Notre Dame Press, 1966), pp. 145–206.

64. For my evaluation of the Catholic sexual tradition, see Charles E. Curran, *A Living Tradition of Catholic Moral Theology* (Notre Dame, Ind.: University of Notre Dame Press, 1992), pp. 27–57; see also Christine Gudorf, *Body, Sex, and Pleasure: Reconstructing Christian Sexual Ethics* (Cleveland, Ohio: Pilgrim, 1994); Gareth Moore, *The Body in Context: Sex and Catholicism* (London: SCM, 1992).

65. Judith A. Dwyer, ed., *The New Dictionary of Catholic Social Thought* (Collegeville, Minn.: Liturgical, 1994), pp. 398–400. Johannes Messner, *Social Ethics* (p. 547), recognizes the role of power in the state and that power always appears in a partially perverted form. He points out that Christian natural law in particular must remember that the power instinct is not exempt from the perversion to which the instincts of our actual human nature are subject.

66. Thomas L. Schubeck, *Liberation Ethics: Sources, Models, and Norms* (Minneapolis, Minn.: Fortress, 1993), pp. 203–29.

67. Campaign for Human Development, *Empowerment and Hope.*

68. Christine Firer Hinze, *Comprehending Power in Christian Social Ethics* (Atlanta, Ga.: Scholars, 1995).

69. Ibid., pp. 63–105.

70. For example, Marie Egan, "Power and Its Use in the Writings of John Coleman Bennett: A Theological-Ethical Critique" (S.T.D. Diss., Catholic University of America, 1976).

71. Hinze, *Comprehending Power*, pp. 181–265.

72. Ibid., pp. 267–90.

73. Mark O'Keefe, *What Are They Saying about Social Sin?* (New York: Paulist, 1990).

74. Schweiker, *Responsibility and Christian Ethics*, pp. 24–28 and passim.

6

Principles

We turn now to the object pole of morality—the world in which we live. Principles, together with the related concept of casuistry, guide human moral actions in this world. Two questions concerning principles are frequently proposed today. First, are there moral principles that can guide actions for all human beings? Given our insistence on particularity and diversity, some exclusive communitarians deny the existence of universal principles and insist that morality is tradition and community dependent. Particular moral approaches make sense to them within a community, but cannot influence actions that transpire in other communities. Likewise, some postmodern approaches reject the possibility of universal principles. The second question, presupposing a positive answer to the first, concerns how principles are arrived at. A further introductory question concerns the exact meaning of principles. Principles are generally understood to be more general than rules which are more specific. Rules often serve as specific determinations of broader principles. Thus, for example, the principle that life is to be respected is a basis for the rule that capital punishment is wrong. A discussion of principles will by definition include the question of rules as more specific and concrete guides for action.

No doubt exists about where the Catholic tradition stands on principles and rules. The legal model of the manuals obviously gave great importance to principles and rules; so, too, the teleological method of Aquinas. The Catholic moral tradition has employed principles and rules, insisted on universal and immutable principles and rules, and established such principles and rules primarily on the basis of the natural law theory.

Within the Catholic tradition one distinguishes two important aspects of the natural law tradition—the theological and the philosophical. The theological aspect recognizes that Christians share much moral wisdom and knowledge with other human beings. Human reason and human experience constitute true and legitimate sources of Christian moral wisdom and knowledge. The problem with this approach before Vatican II was its tendency to see morality primarily and almost exclusively in just these terms; that is, its failure to recognize the role of faith, grace, Jesus Christ, and Scripture and its tendency to downplay the role of sin. The task now is to incorporate the basic thrust of the natural law tradition into the total Christian horizon, which in turn incorporates our stance—the fivefold Christian mysteries of creation, sin, incarnation, redemption, and resurrection destiny.[1]

The philosophical aspect of natural law deals with the meaning of human reason and human nature. As will become clearer later, one cannot claim there is only one approach to natural law. The theory has been employed by different people in different ways.[2] Here too it is important to reflect on how theories or systems develop. Today one has the impression that ethical theories are abiding realities that are simply applied to particular issues and questions as they arise. However, in my judgment ethical theories do not come first. Rather, theories are used to explain in a coherent, consistent, and systematic way positions on particular issues and aspects that are already accepted on other grounds. In other words, even before the acceptance of historical consciousness ethical theories did not arrive full-blown, delivered by the hand of an angel, but were developed to explain systematically, consistently, and comprehensively how particular issues and aspects of morality fit together. The movement is not only from theory to particular application, but also from positions on particular issues to a broader theory. Theories thus originate with the implicit help of a more inductive approach. Today we are more conscious of the need for an ongoing dialogue between the theoretical and practical aspects of moral norms and judgments. And the dialogue needs to move in both directions—from the general to the particular, and the particular to the general.

THE APPROACH OF THE HIERARCHICAL MAGISTERIUM

The Roman Catholic approach as exemplified in John Paul II's encyclical *Veritatis splendor* follows the natural law theory of Thomas Aquinas,[3] but even here there is no monolithic Thomistic theory available for the pope to follow. The approach used by John Paul II claims to be Thomistic, but others can and do disagree with it even on Thomistic grounds.[4] Thomistic natural law approaches all belong to the same family, so to speak, but great differences exist even within families.[5]

NATURAL LAW. More often than not, documents of the hierarchical magisterium appeal to natural law but do not develop the theory in any detail. In *Veritatis splendor* John Paul II gives a more developed exposition of his natural law approach since he is dealing with the question of moral theory. However, even John Paul II cannot develop his understanding of natural law in a totally systematic and complete way given the limitations of his format and his attention to the particular aspects of morality that he thinks are threatened by recent developments within Catholicism. In this document he passes very quickly over the matter of principles to deal with his primary concerns: norms that are always obliging and, especially, intrinsically evil actions.

The pope strongly affirms the Thomistic understanding in which natural law is seen as participating in the eternal law which is nothing other than the divine wisdom itself.[6] John Paul II cites Vatican Council II to show that the supreme rule of life is the divine law—the eternal, objective, and universal law by which an all-wise God arranges, directs, and governs the world. In this context the pope quotes Aquinas's identification of the eternal law with divine wisdom moving all things to their proper end. The human being shares in divine providence in an excellent way above all inanimate creation through human reason by which the person is called to provide for oneself and all others. The natural law is the participation of the eternal law in the rational creature.[7]

Notice here the traditional Catholic and Thomistic insistence on mediation or participation. God, the all-wise and directing Creator, gave reason to human beings which, reflecting on human nature and the creation God has made, can help us arrive at the eternal law or how God wants us to act. Yes, the natural law is based on human reason, but this reason ultimately discovers the eternal law of God. John Paul II recognizes that the Catholic approach to natural law avoids the extremes of autonomy and heteronomy. Autonomy makes the individual person absolute without any relationship to God. Heteronomy puts the human being under the control and rule of another. John Paul II describes his Thomistic approach as theonomy or participated theonomy. By our free obedience to God's law as known in and through the natural law, we participate in God's wisdom and providence. This law is the rightful autonomy of the person by which the individual comes to know truth and one's true good and fulfillment. Thus, human flourishing and fulfillment are not in opposition to the eternal law of God.[8]

Throughout *Veritatis splendor* the pope, in keeping with many others in the Catholic tradition, uses a legal model. As in the parable of the rich young man (Matt 19), we come to Jesus and now to the church to learn the commandments we must obey to have eternal life.[9] The primary thrust of the whole encyclical is God's law. But the pope —with the best of Catholic tradition—does not see God's law as a heteronomic command imposed on us from the outside. The very title of the encyclical insists that truth ultimately leads us to our own goodness and flourishing. Such an understanding serves as a basis for the papal insistence that there can be no genuine conflict between freedom and nature or between freedom and truth.[10]

Although emphasizing a legal model *Veritatis splendor* also acknowledges the teleological aspects in the natural law approach of Aquinas.[11] Here, the encyclical points out the natural inclinations of the individual to the good.[12] Thomas developed his understanding of moral principles and the good on the basis of these natural inclinations because reason apprehends those things to which we are naturally inclined as good and consequently as something to be pursued.[13] Building, then, on this foundation in Aquinas, John Paul II begins to develop his notion of the basic goods or general principles for guiding human actions.

The pope mentions general goods and more general principles in the context of the universality and immutability of natural law. Since the natural law is inscribed in the nature of the person, it is known by all those endowed with reason and living in history. To perfect oneself, "the person must do good and avoid evil, be concerned for the transmission and preservation of life, refine and develop the riches of the material world, cultivate social life, seek truth, practice good, and contemplate beauty."[14] The footnote in *Veritatis splendor* refers to Aquinas.[15] Note how general these goods are.

The encyclical points to universal norms, for example, to serve God, to render God worship, and to honor one's parents as they deserve.[16] Again, note the general nature of such norms. They do not tell us what the worship of God involves or how to respect our parents. The pope points out that by overemphasizing historicity some call into question the immutability of the natural law itself. However, while strongly defending the universality and immutability of natural law, John Paul II recognizes our need to seek the most adequate formulation for universal and permanent moral norms in different cultural contexts. The norms expressing the truth of the moral law remain valid in their substance; but the church's magisterium must specify and determine that they retain the same sense and meaning in different historical circumstances.[17] The encyclical is dealing here with the general goods or principles known by natural law.

UNIVERSAL AND IMMUTABLE NORMS. The pope, however, goes beyond general precepts to defend the universal and permanent validity of concrete norms taught by the church and specific precepts prohibiting intrinsically evil acts.[18] Precepts prohibiting intrinsically evil moral acts such as contraception are examples of such universal and unchanging moral norms.[19] John Paul II notes that the commandments of the second table of the decalogue which constitute the indispensable rules for all social life are formulated in general terms, but they can be specified and made more explicit in a detailed code of behavior.[20] The emphasis of the encyclical is on these more specific norms. According to the pope "the central theme" of this encyclical, restated with the authority of St. Peter, is "the reaffirmation of the universality and immutability of the moral commandments, particularly those which prohibit always and without exception intrinsically evil acts."[21]

Veritatis splendor's theoretical defense of universal and immutable moral commandments prepared the way for John Paul II's 1995 encyclical *Evangelium vitae.* Here the pope deals with specific norms and commandments regarding life issues especially killing, abortion, and euthanasia, and quite solemnly invokes the authority that Christ conferred on Peter and his successors. Then, in communion with the bishops of the church, he proclaims very specific and concrete negative precepts regarding killing,[22] abortion,[23] and euthanasia[24] that are based on natural law, the word of God, and the teaching of the magisterium of the church.

Note how specific the norm is in the case of abortion. "I declare that direct abortion, that is, abortion willed as an end or as a means, always constitutes a grave moral disorder. . . . No circumstance, no purpose, no law whatsoever can make an act licit which is intrinsically illicit, since it is contrary to the law of God that is written in every human heart, knowable by reason itself, and proclaimed by the church."[25] This norm is much more specific than simply respect the life of the unborn child. In accord with the Catholic moral tradition this specific formulation of the immutable law recognizes the possibility of some conflict situations and thus forbids only direct abortions that are defined very specifically. These negative precepts of the natural law oblige always and at all times without exception. On the other hand, the fact that these negative commandments oblige always and under all circumstances does not mean that these negative commandments are more important than positive commandments. Negative commandments or norms establish the level beneath which the command is broken.[26]

The papal teaching on sexuality has been the source of much discussion within and outside the Catholic Church.[27] The hierarchical teaching office employs a natural law methodology to justify its teachings in this area. The "Declaration on Sexual Ethics" issued by the Congregation for the Doctrine of the Faith in 1975 insists that the essential order of human nature must be respected. Concrete human conditions and needs change historically, "but all evolution of morals and every type of life must be kept within the limits imposed by the immutable principles based upon every person's constitutive elements and essential relations—elements and relations that transcend historical contingency. The basic principles in question can be grasped by man's reason. They are contained in 'the divine law—eternal, objective, and universal—whereby God orders, directs, and governs the entire universe'."[28] We can also find absolute and immutable norms for particular actions in human nature. The declaration distinguishes between principles and norms but claims immutability for both.[29] The document then goes on to defend the well known Catholic positions on sexual morality.

Humanae vitae, the 1968 encyclical condemning artificial contraception for spouses, proposes as a basic principle a statement in the Pastoral Constitution on the Church in the Modern World—spouses "must conform their activity to the creative intention of God, expressed in the very nature of marriage and of its acts. . . ."[30] *Humanae vitae* clearly spells out the twofold finality of the sexual faculty and the sexual act—the unitive meaning and the procreative meaning. Since each and every act must remain open to the procreation of life, artificial contraception is wrong.[31] The Declaration on Sexual Ethics uses the same moves to go from the general principle to the finality of the sexual faculty and act. And it, too, makes specific conclusions.[32]

Some have erroneously maintained that the Catholic teaching against artificial contraception comes from a pronatalist position. But such is not the case. Hierarchical Catholic teaching has also opposed artificial insemination and in vitro fertilization based on the nature and finality of the sexual faculty and act. Each and every sexual act must be both open to procreation and expressive of love union. These two ends of the sexual faculty and the marriage act can never be dissociated or separated. "Contraception deliberately deprives the conjugal act of its openness to procreation and in this way brings about a voluntary dissociation of the ends of marriage. Homologous artificial insemination, in seeking a procreation which is not the fruit of a specific act of conjugal union, objectively effects an analogous separation between the goods and meanings of marriage."[33] The very nature of the marital act means that it must always be both open to procreation and expressive of love. This criterion of the nature of the sexual act thus serves as the basis for the Catholic Church's condemnation of masturbation, contraception, homosexual acts, and artificial insemination.

How does this teaching move from the principle or nature of the sexual or marriage act to the criterion that every such act must be open to procreation and expressive of love union? No appeal or mention is made in these official documents to human experience. Rather, these norms are apparently deduced by human reason from the nature of the sexual faculty and act. Indeed, "The Instruction on Respect for Human Life in Its Origin and the Dignity of Procreation" issued by the Congregation for the Doctrine of the Faith in 1987, describes the move from the first principles as deductions.[34] The hierarchical teaching on sexuality moves deductively from the general principle of the nature of the marital act based on its twofold finality to specific norms condemning contraception, masturbation, artificial insemination, and homosexual acts.

Intrinsically Evil Acts. John Paul II insists in *Veritatis splendor* on the existence of intrinsically evil actions. What criterion should be used to determine the moral assessment of free human acts? Again, the pope appeals to the traditional and Thomistic teaching on the sources of morality—object, end (intention), and circumstances.[35] The existence of intrinsically evil acts rests on the recognition that some acts tend toward objects that are always and everywhere wrong. "The primary and decisive element for moral judgment is the object of the human act, which establishes whether it is capable of being ordered to the good and to the ultimate end, which is God."[36] The natural law points to goods or objects that serve the good of the person. Reason also recognizes goods that are incapable of being ordered to God because they radically contradict the intrinsic good of the person made in God's image. Such goods lead to actions that the church's moral tradition has called intrinsically evil. They are always evil per se and cannot be justified by any evolution or circumstance. A good intention or circumstances may diminish the evil of these actions, but they remain irremediably evil acts because they cannot be ordered to God and to the good of the person. An intention is good when it aims at the true good of the person in the light of her ultimate end. But if the object of the act cannot be ordered to God and the good of the person, its intention cannot be good.[37] In the process of defending acts that are intrinsically evil by reason of their object, the pope disagrees with teleological, consequentialist, and proportionalist approaches to moral acts which would deny the existence of intrinsically evil acts based on the object or species of the act.[38]

The pope does not give a detailed list of intrinsically evil acts but cites the Pastoral Constitution on the Church in the Modern World which does list a number of such acts. Whatever is hostile to life itself or a violation of human integrity falls under the criterion of intrinsically evil acts. But in reality the examples given in the Pastoral Constitution on the Church in the Modern World include homicide, abortion, mutilation, and other acts that the Catholic tradition has seen as good in some circumstances. Thus the examples given by Vatican II are problematic because they are not intrinsically evil actions.[39] However, anyone familiar with the debate in contemporary Catholic moral theology knows that the debate includes direct killing, direct abortion, euthanasia, homosexual acts, masturbation, contraception, and artificial insemination. The primary purpose of *Veritatis splendor* is to defend these particular moral teachings of the church on the basis of a natural law theory.

CRITICISMS OF THE HIERARCHICAL APPROACH

This section draws on contemporary sources and on the history of the Catholic tradition itself to criticize the natural law approach found in papal moral teaching as illustrated in the encyclical *Veritatis splendor* and other hierarchical documents.

A MORE PERSONALIST APPROACH. Papal teachings on sexuality are grounded in the nature of the sexual faculty and its act. Papal social teaching, on the other hand, gives much greater emphasis to the person than does papal sexual teaching. A shift has occurred in papal social teaching that has not occurred in papal sexual teaching. The earlier papal social encyclicals beginning with Leo XIII's *Rerum novarum* in 1891 emphasized human nature, order, the need for inequalities in society, and obedience to legitimate civil authorities. But developments over the last hundred years have emphasized the human person and its demands for freedom, equality, and active participation in the life of society.

Leo XIII's encyclicals, including *Rerum novarum* (1891), stressed order and social cohesiveness rather than freedom. During his time, the Enlightenment was the church's primary opponent with its emphasis on human freedom and individuality. As the twentieth century developed, however, totalitarianism emerged as the primary threat. As a result Catholic social teaching began to stress the freedom and dignity of the person.[40] In 1961 John XXIII maintained that the ideal social order rests on the values of truth, justice, and love,[41] but in 1963 in *Pacem in terris*, the pope added a fourth element—freedom—to the original triad.[42] The greater emphasis on the person as subject came to the fore in the Declaration on Religious Liberty at Vatican II. This document finally accepted religious freedom into the Catholic tradition and based it "on the very dignity of the human person as known through the revealed word of God and by reason itself."[43]

Paul VI opened a large section of *Octogesima adveniens* (1971) by pointing out that "two aspirations make themselves felt in these new contexts, and they grow stronger to the extent that he [sic] becomes better informed and better educated: the aspiration to equality and the aspiration to participation, two forms of man's [sic] dignity and freedom."[44] A decade later, in *Laborem exercens* (1981), John Paul II recognizes that the person as the subjective aspect of work is more important than the object or what is done. The personal aspect grounds the priority of labor over capital.[45] The emphasis has shifted from human nature to the human person, from passive obedience to active participation, and from inequality to equality.

In sexual ethics, however, the emphasis remains on the nature of the sexual faculty and act and its immutable ordering. Nevertheless, the principle for sexual norms formulated in the Pastoral Constitution on the Church in the Modern World is somewhat new because the Council wanted to stress a personalist perspective. Sexual norms must be based on the nature of the person and of his [sic] acts.[46] Compare this criterion with the understanding of Marcellino Zalba, the author of a manual written in the 1950s, who defined impurity as the abuse of the sexual faculty.[47] Vatican II wanted to emphasize the personalist perspective but it did not consider contraception because Pope Paul VI had reserved this issue to himself.[48] The 1975 "Declaration on Sexual Ethics" also cites the more personalist criterion or principle—"the nature of the human person and of his acts."[49] More personalist language also appears in other official documents such as the 1986 "Letter to the Bishops of the Catholic Church on the Pastoral Care of Homosexual Persons." But this document insists that the use of the sexual faculty can only be good within marriage.[50] In short, papal teaching on sexuality has recently employed more personalistic terminology, but the present papal sexual teaching is still grounded in the nature of the sexual faculty and its act.[51]

The criterion of the nature of the person and of the person's acts should logically lead to a different conclusion and norm with regard to artificial contraception. The sexual faculty must be seen in its relationship to the person and the person's relationship to others. For the good of the person or the marital relationship, a case can be made that one can and should at times interfere with the physical purpose of the faculty. The sexual faculty cannot be absolutized but must always be subordinated to the person. The same holds true for artificial insemination with the husband's semen. Likewise the sexual orientation of the person and not just the nature of the sexual faculty should enter into the discussion of homosexuality. A more personalist approach grounds the position of many who criticize and disagree with the hierarchical teaching on masturbation, contraception, and homosexual acts.

A RELATIONALITY-RESPONSIBILITY MODEL. Chapter three argued for a relationality-responsibility model of ethics rather than a teleological or deontological model. However, hierarchical sexual teaching and recent papal encyclicals on moral theory are still using a deontological model.

Without doubt, the latest encyclicals of John Paul II stress the legal model. In these encyclicals the pope is primarily dealing with questions of laws that are always and everywhere true, so obviously invoking the legal model is reasonable. However, the impression persists that it is the ideal model for Catholic moral theology—notwithstanding that official hierarchical social teaching has definitely moved from a legal model to a relationality-responsibility model. No doubt the legal model and its emphasis on natural purposes and the finalities of sexual faculties cohere very well with particular positions taken by the papal magisterium on issues such as masturbation, homosexual acts, artificial contraception, and artificial insemination. A relationality-responsibility model, however, could readily lead to different approaches to these issues.

HISTORICAL CONSCIOUSNESS AND INDUCTION. Papal teachings on sexual and medical ethics and the encyclicals *Veritatis splendor* and *Evangelium vitae*, which deal primarily with the existence of immutable and universal laws in these areas, generally cling to a classicist understanding of reality with its emphasis on that which is eternal and unchanging and a corresponding deductive approach with little or no room for induction. Papal documents from *Humanae vitae* in 1968 to *Veritatis splendor* in 1993 defend the existing church teachings in the area of sexual and medical ethics and, therefore, downplay any significant role given to historical and cultural development. *Humanae vitae* insists that the natural law is "inscribed in the very being of man and woman."[52] *Veritatis splendor* recognizes the

> great concern of our contemporaries for historicity and culture which has led some to call into question the immutability of the natural law itself and thus the existence of "objective norms of morality" valid for all people.... (T)here is something in man which transcends those cultures. This "something" is precisely human nature. This nature is itself the measure of culture.... To call into question the permanent structural elements of man which are connected with his own bodily dimension would not only conflict with common experience, but would render meaningless Jesus' reference to the "beginning," precisely where the social and cultural context of the time had distorted the primordial meaning and role of certain moral norms (cf. Matt 19:1–9).[53]

This method proposed in *Veritatis splendor* is congruent with the defense of traditional Catholic norms and invokes Jesus' teaching on divorce to show how history and culture can corrupt what is true from the beginning.

Earlier chapters have pointed out the need to accept a more historically conscious approach and to include a greater emphasis on induction. Here again official papal social teaching has already made such a change. In his 1931 encyclical *Quadragesimo anno*, Pius XI proposed his plan for a reconstruction of the social order. His position has been called a moderate corporatism or solidarism. This plan understands society as an organism with all its parts working together for the good of the whole. In moderate corporatism labor, capital, and consumers all work together in one group to control what happens in a particular industry. This group would set wages, prices, and determine the amount of goods to be produced. Groups on a higher level and the state would coordinate and direct individual industries and professions.[54]

Pius XI believed that other short-term remedies that he had mentioned earlier in the encyclical should be adopted, but he presented this plan as the goal that should ultimately be achieved. It was a proposal for reconstruction that was applicable to the whole world, though of course for Pius and his contemporaries, the world was basically Eurocentric. The deductive method is obvious. The plan for a reconstruction of the social order is based on "the principles of sound philosophy and the sublime precepts of the Gospel."[55] In reality the plan had little chance of succeeding precisely because its deductive and ahistorical basis did not correspond to existing realities. Pius XII, the successor of Pius XI, spoke less and less about this plan of reconstruction as his pontificate continued, and John XXIII basically ignored the proposal.[56]

All recognize that significant changes occurred in hierarchical Catholic social teaching in the twentieth century. As pointed out earlier nineteenth-century papal teaching strongly condemned individualistic liberalism, the Enlightenment, and democracy. However, the growth of totalitarianism on the right and especially on the left inclined papal teaching to defend the dignity, freedom, and rights of the individual without totally accepting the individualism of the Enlightenment.[57] But it was only in the 1940s that Pius XII recognized democracy as the best form of government;[58] only in 1963 that John XXIII in *Pacem in terris* began to develop a systematic Catholic approach to human rights;[59] and only in 1965 that Vatican II accepted religious liberty.

Since Catholic social teaching changed on many specific issues, its methodology had to be more historically conscious and inductive, although John XXIII's *Pacem in terris* still basically followed a somewhat deductive approach based on the laws governing how individuals and states should act. For John, these laws, which are to be sought in human nature where the Father of all things wrote them, teach human beings how to live together in society.[60] However, each chapter of the encyclical ends with a short section on the signs of the times—the special characteristics of the present day.[61] Two years later the Pastoral Constitution on the Church in the Modern World gave a much greater emphasis to historical consciousness and embraced a more inductive approach. The five chapters in its second part deal with specific areas of concern (e.g., marriage and family, political life, cultural life) and each begins with signs of the times rather than the laws inscribed in human nature.

Paul VI's *Octogesima adveniens* (1971) also reflects a heightened awareness of historical consciousness and the need for a more inductive approach. Paul insisted that it was neither his ambition nor his mission in the face of widely varying situations to put forward solutions capable of universal validity. "It is up to the Christian communities to analyze with objectivity the situation which is proper to their own country, to shed on it the light of the Gospel's unalterable words, and to draw principles of reflection, norms of judgment, and directives for action from the social teaching of the church."[62]

John Paul II, as his first social encyclical *Laborem exercens* illustrates, has not always adopted a historically conscious approach. However, even John Paul II recognizes the need for such an approach in some of his social teachings. Consider, for example, his 1995 address to the United Nations. Here John Paul recognized the tension between universality and particularity and sees moral truth emerging through dialogue. "The human condition thus finds itself between these two poles—universality and particularity—with a vital tension between them; an inevitable tension, but singularly fruitful if they are lived in a calm and balanced way."[63] He mentions the universal values of peace, solidarity, justice, and liberty but insists no social model is sufficient for the whole world.[64] "To cut oneself off from the reality of difference— or worse, to attempt to stamp out that difference—is to cut oneself off from the possibility of sounding the depths of the mystery of human life. The truth about man is the unchangeable standard by which all cultures are judged; but every culture has something to teach us about one or other dimension of that complex truth. Thus the "difference" which some find so threatening can, through respectful dialogue, become the source of a deeper understanding of the mystery of human existence."[65] How different is the search for moral truth portrayed in this address from the approach taken in *Veritatis splendor*. Once again, papal social teaching has been willing to adopt a more historically conscious approach with a greater emphasis on induction. Such an approach would have significant ramifications if used in sexual ethics.

CERTITUDE. There can be no doubt that the legal model emphasizes a classicist and deductive approach that can arrive at greater certitude about its conclusions than a relationality-responsibility model employing a more historically conscious and inductive approach. The syllogism is the characteristic mode of reasoning in a deductive approach. The syllogism consists of a major premise, a minor premise, and a conclusion. The major and minor premises express truths already known. The conclusion is the new truth that the mind deduces from the two premises. For example: All things composed of matter are corruptible (in the sense of subject to decay and death). But all human beings are composed of matter. Therefore, all human beings are corruptible. In a syllogism the conclusion is just as certain as the premises provided the logic is correct. The syllogism aims at certitude.

Recent papal encyclicals and teachings on morality, especially in the area of sexual and some aspects of medical ethics, claim to arrive at certain, immutable, and universal norms of acting that are quite specific. The whole thrust of *Veritatis splendor* is to defend such norms. The specific norms solemnly declared by John Paul II in *Evangelium vitae* well illustrate this approach. "I confirm that direct and voluntary killing of an innocent human being is always gravely immoral."[66] Note how specific the norm is because of the concept of "direct," which modifies the way the killing is done, and "innocent" human being, which recognizes that some killings are not always wrong. In practice Catholic teaching claims to know with certitude what is a direct killing and who is innocent. Over the years the Holy Office, now called the Congregation for the Doctrine of the Faith, has intervened to settle these particular questions. The specific norms proposed in *Humanae vitae* and in the "Declaration on Sexual Ethics" also claim to be certain in their condemnation of artificial contraception, masturbation, homosexual acts, artificial insemination, and other sexual acts.

In the cases of killing or abortion the hierarchical Catholic teaching recognizes some conflict situations. Not all killing of human beings is wrong. Only the direct killing of innocent human beings and direct abortion are wrong. What is the difference between direct and indirect actions and how does it function? The solemn papal condemnation of direct abortion in *Evangelium vitae* spells out to a degree the meaning of direct—"direct abortion, that is abortion willed as an end or as a means."[67] The more precise description of direct is that which by the agent's intention or the nature of the act itself aims at evil either as a means or as an end.[68] Those familiar with the Catholic tradition recognize two classical examples of indirect abortion. If the pregnant woman has a cancerous uterus, one can directly remove the uterus though it unfortunately contains a fetus. The physical causality of the act directly touches or is aimed at the cancerous uterus and not at the fetus.[69] In ectopic pregnancies, after much discussion, the Holy Office maintained that it is an indirect abortion to remove a fallopian tube that has become infected from carrying the fetus. The physical structure of the act directly attacks the infected tube and not directly the fetus as a means for saving the mother. It would, however, be a direct abortion and morally wrong if the fetus were merely taken out of the tube and the tube left in place. One cannot remove a fetus from the mother—even one that in the best medical understanding, can never come to term and which now threatens the life of the mother.[70] Can one claim certitude with regard to a philosophical distinction used to solve complex conflictual situations?

The claim for certitude on specific moral norms goes against the understanding proposed by Thomas Aquinas but never mentioned in the official documents cited here. Aquinas points out that the natural law includes everything to which the human being is naturally inclined, including the inclination to act according to reason. Reason moves from the general to the more particular or specific. However, there is a difference between speculative reason and practical reason governing morality. Speculative reason deals with those things that are necessary and cannot possibly be anything else. Thus, for instance, all triangles must have 180 degrees. But someone might be deceived and not realize that a particular figure is a triangle with 180 degrees. The more specific conclusions of speculative reason (this "thing" is a triangle) are always true, but they might not be known as such by every human knower because of a defect in intelligence.

Practical reason deals with contingent things among which are human acts. The more one descends to the specific, the greater the possibility of contingent circumstances entering into the picture. Thus, for example, the general principle to act according to reason is always and everywhere true. The example that Aquinas gives of a more specific conclusion of the natural law is that deposits should always be returned. A deposit is something given to another with the obligation to give it back when the owner asks for it. However, circumstances could arise in which the deposit should not be returned to the owner because the owner is intending to use it to bring some harm to another. With regard to the more specific conclusions of the natural law, moral truth and obligation generally exist but not in all circumstances. In some cases it could happen that it would be harmful and consequently immoral to hand the deposit over to the owner. Aquinas thus accepts as a general principle that the more one descends from the general to the specific, the greater the possibility of exceptions in moral truth and obligation. The word that Aquinas uses is "defect" rather than "exception."[71]

Catholic hierarchical teaching does not recognize the Thomistic principle that the more specific conclusions of secondary principles are not always and everywhere obliging. A more historically conscious and inductive methodology more easily recognizes the difficulty of arriving at certitude on specific moral principles and norms. By its very nature such an approach is tentative and more open to revision in the light of change and development.

The American Catholic bishops in their pastoral letters on peace and the economy clearly distinguish between principles that are certain and the application of principles to concrete issues which cannot claim to have moral certitude.[72] Their recognition that certitude can be lacking in the application of principles to particular issues is consistent with the Thomistic understanding that the more specific one becomes the harder it is to achieve certitude. But for Aquinas not only the application of principles but even some principles and norms or laws cannot always claim certitude and must admit some exceptions.

PHYSICALISM. The natural law approach developed by Aquinas and continued in the manuals of moral theology and contemporary hierarchical teaching is guilty at times of physicalism. Physicalism refers to the a priori identification of the human moral act with the physical or biological aspects of the act.

To understand the criticism of physicalism being made against papal and hierarchical teaching, one needs to move from the theoretical to the practical realm. *Veritatis splendor* deals with the crisis in Catholic moral theology caused by theologians' dissent from specific moral teachings of the church. However, these dissents and disagreements are comparatively few. Major areas of disagreement center on questions of sexuality, such as contraception, masturbation, homosexual acts, divorce, and artificial insemination. In addition, abortion and euthanasia have been disputed but with nowhere near the disagreement expressed over contraception. Dissent and disagreement also exist on how the Catholic tradition has tried to resolve conflicts on the basis of the distinction between direct and indirect actions. All would agree that these are the major moral issues in contention in the Catholic Church today.

Many of these issues are affected by physicalism insofar as the traditional teaching identifies the human moral act with its physical aspect. For the most part, the Catholic moral tradition has not identified the moral with the physical. Killing is a physical act, but not every killing is wrong. Murder is always wrong, but murder is a moral act. Mutilation of the body is a physical term. Not every mutilation is wrong. The manuals recognize that mutilation of one's own body, if done out of necessity or to help the total individual preserve health and life, is morally good. Abortion itself is a physical term, and the Catholic tradition has not said that all abortions are wrong—only direct abortion. Thus, the Catholic tradition in most areas does not equate the physical and moral aspects of the act. However, at times the physical and moral aspects do coincide. The moral and human person are the same as the physical person. We die when the physical body dies. We cannot merely assume that the physical is the same as the totally human and moral, but we have to provide reasons for it.

As already pointed out the traditional Catholic condemnation of contraception is ultimately based on the physical or biological finality of the sexual faculty and act. This twofold finality of love union and openness to procreation must be present in every marital sexual act. The physical purpose and finality of the sexual faculty and act serve as the basis for condemning masturbation, homosexual acts, and contraception.

From a different perspective the physical sexual act is always wrong if the partners are not married. Nonmarried people may share very intimate and personal exchanges, but this physical act is always wrong. All Catholic moralists recognize that adultery is wrong, but note all the different reasons that are opposed to adultery—injury to the spouse, the violation of one's own commitment, and harm to other people especially to children. There is, however, some discussion today among Catholic moral theologians about premarital sexuality. Full sexual expression calls for a personal relationship and commitment between two persons, but some question whether the full commitment of marriage is always needed.[73]

The same basic identification of the human with the physical is at work in the controversy over abortion. The primary question concerns the exact status of the fertilized ovum, zygote, and fetus. Contemporary proponents of the traditional Catholic approach appeal to the laws of biology and genetics which recognize that the genetic makeup of the human being is already there in the fertilized ovum. Opponents point out that in the early stages it is hard to claim that the fertilized ovum or zygote is a truly individual human being or a human person. Being an individual human is more than just the genetic blueprint or the biological aspect. However, defenders point out that the

accepted criterion for declaring death is based on physical criteria—
for example, no heartbeat or no brain waves. As already pointed out
the concept of "direct" is based on the physical causality and structure
of the act as illustrated in the two acceptable instances of indirect
abortion and the moral condemnation of abortion done to save the life
of the mother. One cannot go into detail on all these issues, but the
point is raised to show that differences and debates in Catholic moral
theology often occur in those areas in which the physical aspect of the
act is identified with the human and moral aspect. In my understanding
physicalism is the a priori identification of the human or moral aspect
with the physical, natural, or biological aspect. I again emphasize that
at times the physical and the moral or the human are the same.

The problem of physicalism has roots in Aquinas's natural law
theory itself. The natural law is primarily an ordering of reason not
nature. However, Aquinas sees these inclinations of the sexual faculty
and sexual act as normative. At times Aquinas even accepts the definition of natural law proposed by Ulpian, a Roman lawyer who died in
228. For Ulpian, the natural law is what nature teaches all the animals
including humans. This natural law is distinct from the *ius gentium*
which is proper to human beings and identified with reason.[74] Note
the tension in Aquinas who at times identifies the natural law with
what nature teaches as distinguished from reason. The manuals of
moral theology following Aquinas have distinguished two kinds of
sexual sins. Sins against nature are those that go against the natural
act of depositing male semen in the vagina of the female (e.g., masturbation, sodomy, bestiality, and artificial contraception). Sins according to
nature are those in which the physical biological structure of the sexual
act is present, but the human aspect is missing (e.g., fornication, adultery, and rape). Note that we have sins according to as well as against
nature! In the sexual area in the Catholic tradition, the natural refers
only to the physical and biological as distinguished from the rational.[75]
The charge of physicalism is the claim that in the realm of sexual ethics,
the Catholic tradition has too readily identified the physical or natural
with the fully human.

Veritatis splendor attempts to refute the critics of physicalism or
naturalism. According to the encyclical these critics embrace an opposing position that "ends up treating the human body as a raw datum
devoid of any meaning and moral value until freedom has shaped it
in accord with its design Consequently, human nature and the body
appear . . . extrinsic to the person, the subject, and the human acts. . . .

(T)he finalities of these inclinations would be merely 'physical' goods, called by some *premoral*."[76] Such charges against the critics of physicalism are not accurate. The physical is not devoid of meaning and not extrinsic to the person. The physical is part of the human but only one part, and the total human can never be reduced only to the physical. The human is made up of many dimensions—for example, the physical, the psychological, and the sociological. In the above citation, the pope contradicts himself because he refers to "physical goods," thus recognizing that they are not extrinsic but are part of the human. In fact, those who criticize physicalism in Catholic teaching take seriously Pius XII's statement dealing with the prolongation of life: the physical and the bodily exist to serve the higher spiritual good of the person.[77]

THE OBJECT OF THE ACT AND INTRINSICALLY EVIL ACTS. One of the most significant aspects of *Veritatis splendor* is its insistence that some actions are intrinsically evil and can never be justified no matter what the intention and the circumstances. Here the pope appeals to the traditional three sources of morality—object, end or intention, and circumstances. A good intention is never enough to justify an act. The pope staunchly defends the existence of intrinsically evil acts based on the object of the act independent of the intention and circumstances. Certain species or objects are always and everywhere wrong. The pope accuses revisionist Catholic moral theologians of denying this.[78]

The precise problem in this case is how to define and describe the species or object of the act. Here again the problem of physicalism comes to the fore. The object of the act is the moral object. By definition understanding the moral object of the act involves moral deliberation and judgment and cannot be based on just the physical structure itself. In other words, the moral object of the act cannot be determined by a mere snapshot of the event. Murder is always wrong but killing is not always wrong. Causing pain to another might be the moral act of torture or the moral act of medical intervention to save a life. Thus, a "snapshot" description of someone inflicting pain on another could be illustrating a morally good act or a morally bad one. Jean Porter has shown how *Veritatis splendor* diverges from Aquinas on this point.[79]

PROPORTIONALISM. The theory of proportionalism has been proposed by many Catholic theologians to deal with conflict situations. This approach often disagrees with the position of the hierarchical magisterium, but on comparatively few issues and in specific circumstances.

The pope correctly recognizes this fact, but he caricatures the approach of proportionalism. "Such theories, however, are not faithful to the church's teaching when they believe they can justify as morally good deliberate choices of kinds of behavior contrary to the commandments of the divine and natural law."[80] Later the pope states: "If acts are intrinsically evil, a good intention or particular circumstances can diminish their evil but they cannot remove it."[81] But proportionalism does not claim to justify morally wrong actions by a good intention. Proportionalists maintain, if the moral object is wrong (e.g., torture), no intention or circumstance can justify it. But if the object is described in physical terms and not moral terms (e.g., inflicting pain), these can be justified, for instance, by the good intention of surgically removing a cancerous organ.

Proportionalists, properly insist on certain physical, or premoral goods or values. Premoral goods are those values we pursue in human action such as life, health, procreation. But these values often can and do conflict with other premoral values. Moral values, on the other hand, are realities such as justice and integrity that correspond to what we earlier called the moral object of the act. Justice, however, is quite generic and doubt often exists whether a particular act is just or not. By the very nature of human existence, premoral values can never be absolutized because they always exist in connection with other premoral goods in our world. Life is certainly the most fundamental and basic premoral good, but all human beings and the Catholic tradition have recognized that life can on occasion be taken as in the case of self-defense.[82]

The premoral goods are often described in terms of behavioral norms or physical acts, such as no killing, no mutilating, no taking other people's property, no false speech. But the Catholic tradition recognizes that these so-called behavioral norms or premoral goods may be gone against if there is a proportionate reason. Chapter three pointed out the distinction between falsehood and lying. If the neighbor does not have the right to truth, then the physical or behavioral reality of falsehood is not the moral reality of lying.[83]

Proportionate reason discerns whether there is sufficient reason to justify the premoral evil. Thus, killing an unjust aggressor is justified by the right to self-defense if one has no other way to save one's life. Likewise one may directly abort a fetus in order to save the life of the mother. Revisionist Catholic moral theologians have used proportionalism or similar approaches to argue against papal positions on contraception, masturbation, artificial insemination, homosexual acts, and the concept of direct and indirect effect. That is, for a proportional reason one can justify contraception or homosexual acts. One problem I have with proportionalism is the tendency to identify as evil what may only be a matter of finitude. Take the example of contraception. The integrity of the physical aspect of the marital act is one aspect. Other aspects include the psychological, the sociological, the aesthetic, and the economic. No one human act is ever perfect from every dimension. But the inability to be perfect comes from finitude, and not from evil.

Recognizing the distinction between moral evil and premoral evil, a theory of proportionalism could be developed along general lines. To intend premoral evil as an end is always wrong. You cannot inflict pain on another human being as an end in itself. Intending premoral evil as a means is morally acceptable if there is a proportionate reason. Thus, to inflict pain that is necessary to cure an illness would be acceptable.

In general proportionalists rank themselves between the two extremes of total consequentialism and the physicalism of the Catholic tradition. Morality cannot be reduced only to consequences or only to the physical structure of the act. The theory has often been developed in discussion of particular cases that have been proposed in the Catholic and the broader philosophical literature. For example, proportionalists in general reject the evil of directly killing noncombatants no matter what the good to be obtained. Likewise they generally oppose judicial murder cases in which an innocent person is killed to save others. Thus a dialogue exists between theory and the solution to particular cases in attempting to spell out and develop the theory of proportionalism.

There is general agreement on the criterion that a proportion is needed between the premoral evil of the means and the end. It is, for example, a principle of good medicine and of medical ethics that one do as little harm to the patient as possible in trying to cure her. In addition, the premoral evil in the means should not undermine the good of the end even in the long run. The possible harm that might come to the forest in the midst of a drought from one campfire, lit and tended by very conscientious girl scouts, would not seem to harm the forest. But by allowing all to build fires, one could very well endanger the good of the forest. The literature contains further criteria for determining proportionate reasons but they are too detailed and complex for the purposes of this book.[84]

Some opponents of proportionalism (e.g., Germain Grisez, John Finnis) have maintained that one cannot use proportionalism because it does not and cannot provide an exact method of comparing different values.[85] How do you compare life and freedom or life and friendship? It is like comparing apples and oranges. But a moment's reflection reminds us that we often have to make such judgments in human life. No one can give a mathematical value to each good and then weigh them to arrive at a mathematical certainty. But in human existence we often have to make such comparisons. Think of judgments about the burden and benefit of certain acts at the end of life. Is it necessary to continue the respirator to preserve human life at all costs? One cannot expect criteria of proportionate reason to do away with all gray areas, but we must continue to strive toward more adequate criteria of proportionate reason.

A DIFFERENT METHODOLOGICAL DEFENSE OF HIERARCHICAL TEACHINGS. In Catholic moral theology at the present time a school associated primarily with Germain Grisez and John Finnis strongly rejects proportionalism and staunchly defends the negative moral absolutes proposed by the hierarchical magisterium (e.g., prohibitions of contraception, homosexual acts, and artificial insemination), but reinterprets or even rejects the natural law theory of Aquinas and the papal documents. I will discuss this theory primarily as it is developed by Germain Grisez.

Grisez does not accept what he calls the scholastic natural law theory. Nature has no normative character. One cannot go from "is" to "ought." The argument against contraception based on violating the God-given procreative purpose of the faculty of sexuality is not valid. Many times we do go against the purpose of a faculty; for example, we hold our nose to avoid breathing in a bad odor.[86] However, proportionalism is also unacceptable. The primary negative argument against proportionalism consists in the impossibility of making a judgment about the greater good because diverse values cannot be compared. Moral situations do not have fixed borders, and we can never know all that might be involved in a situation and its consequences. Further, there is no common denominator for judging what is the greater good. Ultimately, basic human goods are incommensurate.[87]

Grisez acknowledges that his theory is not really Thomistic, as do others,[88] and Grisez and Finnis admit that their theory is neither teleological nor deontological.[89] Aquinas begins with the teleology of the ultimate end and recognizes inclinations in nature that have moral content. For Grisez, Aquinas's first principle of practical reason—"good is to be done and pursued, and evil is to be avoided"—is not itself a moral precept.

The basic principle of morality for Grisez is "In voluntarily acting for human goods and avoiding what is opposed to them, one ought to choose and otherwise will those and only those possibilities whose willing is compatible with a will toward integral human fulfillment."[90] Intermediate principles or modes of responsibility, which are of a somewhat formal nature involving not moral actions but ways of choosing and acting, spell out this first principle. The first mode of responsibility maintains that one should not be deterred by inertia from acting for intelligible goods.[91] The eighth mode of responsibility maintains that one should not be so moved by desire for one instance of an intelligible good that one chooses to destroy, damage, or impede some other instance of an intelligible good to obtain it, whether that same one or another.[92]

Grisez proposes eight basic human goods that are self-evident. They are not a priori, not deduced from any first principle, and not derived from any metaphysical understanding of human nature. These goods are self-evident to us—we know them just by knowing the meaning of their terms.[93] Grisez distinguishes four existential goods (self-integration; practical reasonableness or authenticity; friendship and justice; and religion or holiness) and three substantive goods (life and bodily well-being; knowledge of truth and appreciation of beauty; and skillful performance and play). The eighth good is the complex good of marriage and family.[94] In the light of the eight modes of responsibility which develop the first moral principle, one can move to more specific norms. Some negative norms are absolute because they concern actions of such a kind that willingness to perform them per se violates a mode of responsibility. No change of circumstances or additional information can change that. You cannot go directly against another basic good. Contraception is wrong because it is a choice to prevent the handing on of human life. Deliberate contraception involves a direct attack on the basic good of life.[95]

Grisez has proposed a very complex and tightly reasoned theory. *Veritatis splendor*, although it invokes a Thomistic natural law approach, also at times employs Grisez's approach to basic human goods.[96] I disagree with the theory and with some of its applications as illustrated by the case of contraception. Most people would agree that life is a very basic human good. But the distance between accepting life as a basic good to claiming that one act of contraception in marriage goes directly against it is very great and contraception remains far removed from the basic good of life itself. Would someone who did not begin with a conviction that contraception and masturbation are intrinsically evil acts ever claim that one deliberate act of contraception or masturbation involves an attack on the basic good of life?

More theoretically, I think that on occasion one can go against a basic human good. The relational model recognizes the relational character of all reality so that one cannot absolutize basic goods. Sometimes the goods of friendship and life come into conflict. In addition the Catholic tradition recognizes a very significant hierarchical ordering with regard to various goods as is evident from discussions about the ultimate good or the ultimate end to which everything else is directed. Pius XII pointed out that bodily goods exist to serve the higher spiritual good of the person. However, Grisez does not want to accept such ordering.

This chapter has discussed the role of principles and norms in moral theology primarily through a criticism of the hierarchical magisterium's approach to these matters in questions of sexual and some medical ethics as well as in the two recent encyclicals *Veritatis splendor* and *Evangelium vitae*. I do not agree with the methodological approaches taken in these documents in general. Note, however, that the Roman Catholic tradition itself has identified the basis for this criticism. Papal social teaching follows a very different methodology from that of papal sexual and medical ethics. The shifts from classicism to historical consciousness, from nature to the person or subject, and from a legal model to a relationality-responsibility model have already occurred in papal social teaching. Such an approach in sexual and medical ethics would call for different positions on the comparatively few issues in which Catholic theologians frequently dissent from the teachings of the hierarchical magisterium. In addition Thomas Aquinas has recognized that practical and specific moral reasoning cannot claim to have the universality and immutability of general principles. Papal sexual teaching generally ignores this approach.

ROLE OF PRINCIPLES AND NORMS

A brief sketch will show positively my approach to the question of principles and norms in moral theology. These questions involve very complex and controversial issues of epistemology and moral truth. The Catholic tradition by definition claims to be universal—to be open to all and appealing to all despite its great diversity of cultures, ethnicity, history, and geography. For that reason, as pointed out in chapter one, the Catholic approach to morality cannot accept a total relativism or subjectivism. Likewise the Catholic moral approach cannot accept the claim that morality is so tradition bound that no common human morality exists for all traditions and cultures. On the other hand, one who writes as a Catholic must constantly remember not to so stress universality that not enough importance is paid to individuality, particularity, and diversity.

One approach to universality in contemporary philosophical ethics employs what has been called a "thin concept of the good." These approaches often stress the formal aspects and not the material or substantive goods that people hold in common. Various conversation theories illustrate this more formal approach.[97] The theory of John Rawls exemplifies a method based on a thin concept of the good. The good and the just derive from what rational people behind the veil of ignorance choose as being just and good for a society. There is no prior substantive agreement on what is the good and the just.[98]

The Catholic tradition has traditionally insisted on a "thick" or substantive concept of the good but has claimed at times a greater and more specific universality than could be justified. Catholic social ethics, to this day, insists on the common good of society. There are some goods that all in society can and should agree on. Thus, for example, papal social teaching since *Pacem in terris* insists on four very significant values: justice, truth, charity, and freedom,[99] and Pope John Paul II has made the concept of solidarity a very significant guiding principle in his social teaching.[100] The basis for this solidarity or recognition of the social reality of human beings is grounded in theological and philosophical concerns. Behind the doctrine of creation lies the fact that all human beings are brothers and sisters of one another related to God as our common parent. One can also support the social nature of human beings and human solidarity on a philosophical basis by recognizing the relationality-responsibility model that unites us in various ways with all other human beings and the world in which we live.[101]

My own approach has been heavily influenced by my having been brought up in the Catholic tradition, and today tends to be a chastened Aristotelian-Thomistic approach. There are certain moral values and basic goods that all human beings can know and agree on. Other approaches to universality may be compatible with the Catholic theological emphasis, but a chastened epistemological realism and universality is very much in keeping with the Catholic tradition's emphasis on the existence of substantive goods or values that can be recognized by all. Thus, for example, all can agree on the fundamental and basic importance of human life and the need to respect human life. However, even this general value or principle includes significant differences about its practical meaning. Both proponents and opponents of abortion claim to respect human life.

An earlier chapter has developed the virtue of justice, which can also be seen from the object pole of morality as the principle of justice that should guide and direct human activity in this world. The three basic understandings of justice proposed earlier correspond to the different types of relationships in which human beings find themselves. The emphasis here on the social nature of the person and the person's relationship to society and society's to the person must be assimilated into our understanding of justice. I agree with the Catholic social tradition's claim that all human beings can recognize the broad reality and significance of the three types of justice—commutative, distributive, and social.

These very basic and general human goods and values are part of our reality as human persons, and they are illuminated for us in our own experience. As we deal with somewhat more specific goods, we know them again through reason and experience. The four sources of morality—Scripture, tradition, reason, and experience—all contribute to our knowledge and acceptance of these basic moral goods. But I insist that the basic goods found in Scripture are also in principle open to verification by human reason and human experience.

Although the Ten Commandments should not be seen as the central and controlling aspect of Christian morality, they have obviously played a very significant role in Christian and human moral life. Did God hand these commandments down from on high in a special revelation? I tend to agree with the biblical scholars who see the second tablet of the decalogue as originally arising from the experience of the tribe and the community.[102] Some moral standards are necessary for the proper functioning of individuals and society as a whole. "Honor thy father and thy mother" regulates moral relationships and responsibilities within the family, the basic unit of society. Note again how generic and broad is the commandment. There may have been and still are many disagreements about what honor for parents calls for in particular circumstances. The life of any tribe or community requires that the people respect others and refrain from killing. The sixth commandment refers to the need to regulate sexual relations for the good of both individuals and society as a whole. Stealing, bearing false witness, and coveting neighbors' goods are also detrimental to the good of individuals and society. Thus, the second tablet of the Ten Commandments come from the experience of the tribe; it codifies what is minimally necessary. Human experience can agree on these basic human goods.

CHANGES IN SPECIFIC NORMS. All recognize that significant changes have occurred on the level of official Catholic teaching with regard to particular moral issues such as usury, slavery, torture, human rights, and religious liberty. A critical analysis of how these changes occurred throws light on the role of principles, norms, and concrete issues and their mutual relationships.[103] The norms governing the proper use of human sexuality have also changed dramatically over time. In the early church, the intention to procreate within marriage was required to justify sexual relations. As time went on the intention of procreation was no longer necessary for a married couple to justify their marital relations, and by officially accepting rhythm, now better called natural family planning, Pius XII recognized that not only did spouses not have to intend procreation in every marital act; they could even intend not to procreate![104] What has taken place in this dramatic change? In the light of a very negative view of sexuality as being close to sin, the intention of procreation to continue the species was required to justify marital acts. All recognize some relationship between sexuality and procreation. However, by 1960, while still rejecting contraception, papal teaching recognized that spouses could justifiably intend not to procreate in their marital act.

One of the more significant changes at Vatican II involved religious liberty.[105] In the nineteenth century, Gregory XVI and Pius IX wrote encyclical letters referring to freedom of worship as a madness, and official Catholic teaching did not accept the fundamental right to religious liberty until Vatican II. At best, the Catholic position tolerated religious freedom as a lesser evil in some situations such as where Catholics were not a majority. The older teaching rejecting religious liberty and the separation of church and state was based on two principles—error has no rights and the state has a paternalistic role in promoting the religious good of individuals (insofar as this good is interpreted by the church). As the twentieth century developed, both these principles were substantially modified. The emphasis was no longer on abstract, objective truth but on the dignity of the human person which became the basis for religious freedom. In addition the principle determining the role of government changed. The limited constitutional understanding of government no longer involved government directly in promoting religious truth. Here again, as newer principles came to the fore (the dignity of the human person), the concrete norm changed.

A closer examination of these and other instances in which Catholic moral teaching has changed shows that the relationship among specific principles, concrete norms, and specific issues is not merely a one way street from the principle to the norm to the case. Within the Christian community certain concrete norms are no longer confirmed by the experience of people. Ecclesiologists refer to this confirmation as the reception of hierarchical teaching by the church community.[106] The experience of the community rejects the norm which then calls for a change in the principle or the addition of another principle to govern the situation.

CASUISTRY. The movement from the specific moral judgment to a change of the norm and modification of the principle can also be illustrated in the understanding of casuistry.[107] Casuistry is a very significant method within moral theology but one that is complementary to and not entirely different from the role of principles.[108] A more static approach to casuistry found in the manuals of moral theology gave the impression that casuistry involved the application of the principle or norm to the particular case under consideration. The very genre of the moral manual—its provision of answers to particular issues—reinforced this understanding. The resolution of cases came after the basic principles and norms were explained and applied.

A moment's reflection shows that ordinary Christians do not usually make decisions based on the application of a theory (e.g., proportionalism) to a particular issue. They are more likely to choose a more experiential and less discursive approach to decision making, and such is also the case even with professional ethicists and moral theologians. Moral theologians often begin with an experiential and somewhat intuitive judgment that a particular act, such as the direct killing of noncombatants or the sacrifice of an innocent human person to save others, is morally wrong or that the use of contraception by spouses can be good. They then construct a theory to explain this judgment and other more specific judgments in a consistent and coherent manner. One thus moves from practice to theory and from individual moral judgments to norms and principles, not just from principles to particular cases.

Casuistry plays a very significant role in this dialogue and two-way street between concrete issues, norms, and principles. Casuistry is not the same as "deductive applied ethics." Casuistry employs the proper description of the issues and then works through paradigmatic cases and analogies. The general principle "thou shalt not kill" is confronted by the particular case of killing an unjust aggressor to save one's life. In the light of this exception, the general principle must be refined. Other analogous conflict situations are also considered. What about killing an unjust attacker of material goods, of moral virtue, of reputation? Through moral experience and casuistry the more specific principle can be fine-tuned and even corrected as we know from the specific issues on which official Catholic teaching has changed. In the Catholic tradition the general principle of not killing was fine-tuned to read: The direct killing of the innocent on one's own authority is always wrong. This more specific principle was formulated to allow for a number of exceptions such as killing in self-defense, killing at the command of God, and killing in capital punishment on the part of the state.[109] Now the pope disagrees with capital punishment.[110] Consequently, it is necessary to revise or reinterpret the specific principle to reflect this new approach to capital punishment. Many Catholic theologians today disagree with the concept of "direct killing" and would further modify the specific principle.

The emphasis on the moral experience of the church community and of individual Christians raises the question of how one tests that experience. If moral decisions are reached apart from the application of norms, how exactly does it occur? Is there any way to examine the truth claims and validity of such judgments? Moral decision making obviously cannot be based on the purely subjective preferences of an individual; otherwise, there would be no possibility of criticizing moral judgments and no possibility of having a shared ethic. The next chapter will discuss the important issue of decision making in depth.

ABSOLUTE NORMS

This brief concluding section deals with the existence of so-called absolute norms or norms that are universally and always obliging. The existence of absolute norms follows logically from all that has been said in this chapter. Reasonable people recognize some norms or laws that are universally and always obliging. Discussions of absolute norms are too often restricted to individual norms in the area of sexuality. Absolute moral norms exist in both individual and social ethics. Very general principles or norms are always and everywhere obliging. Thus, murder and injustice are always wrong. The problem arises in determining what constitutes murder or injustice in a particular situation. Moreover, there are some acts that by reason of their moral object (not their physical object) are always wrong, such as adultery, lying (i.e., the violation of my neighbor's right to truth), rape, and torture. The Catholic tradition has recognized that many moral norms admit exceptions. Confidentiality is an important human obligation, but the Catholic tradition and many others recognize that it is not an absolute obligation. Sometimes confidentiality no longer obliges because of the good of another person or the good of society.[111] Notice how a relationality-responsibility model easily points out the impossibility of absolutizing confidentiality. Law, for example, often requires physicians to report gun shot wounds to civil authorities. However, all can agree that to break confidentiality to enrich one's self is always wrong. Thus norms that are qualified can be absolute.

To have a viable social morality, some universal norms are necessary; but, again, these norms are rather general and admit different interpretations of particular issues. A global ethic requires some universal principles and general norms.[112] The best example of these absolute norms are human rights that are common to all. Here I agree with the papal teaching that insists on two kinds of rights—political and civil rights such as religious freedom and freedom of speech, and social and economic rights such as the right to food, clothing, and shelter.[113]

Yes, absolute moral norms do exist. However, they cannot be based on the physical structure or object of the act. Likewise, as one becomes involved in more specific complex circumstances, the possibility of exceptions increases. Law can never be the primary model for moral theology, but a relationality-responsibility model can and should recognize the existence of some absolute norms. However, such norms are not the primary reality in moral theology, nor do they cover a very great part of the map of morality.

This chapter has explored the role of principles and norms in contemporary Catholic moral theology—an area of significant debate and disagreement. Both the importance and limitations of principles have been pointed out. The next chapter will discuss conscience and concrete decision making.

NOTES

1. Pope John Paul II, *Veritatis splendor*, nn. 46–53, 71 80, *Origins* 23 (1993): 311–14, 318–22.

2. For some contemporary discussions of natural law, see Charles E. Curran and Richard A. McCormick, eds., *Readings in Moral Theology No. 7: Natural Law and Theology* (New York: Paulist, 1991).

3. John Paul II, *Veritatis splendor,* n. 4, *Origins* 23 (1993): 311.

4. For example, Jean Porter, "The Moral Act in *Veritatis splendor* and in Aquinas' *Summa theologiae:* A Comparative Analysis," in *Veritatis splendor: American Responses,* ed. Michael E. Allsopp and John J. O'Keefe (Kansas City, Mo.: Sheed and Ward, 1995), pp. 278–95.

5. See, for example, Pamela M. Hall, *Narrative and the Natural Law: An Interpertation of Thomistic Ethics* (Notre Dame, Ind.: University of Notre Dame Press, 1994); Ralph McInerny, *Ethica Thomistica: The Moral Philosophy of Thomas Aquinas,* rev. ed. (Washington, D.C.: Catholic University of America Press, 1997); Jean Porter, *Moral Action and Christian Ethics* (Cambridge: Cambridge University Press, 1995).

6. John Paul II, *Veritatis splendor,* n. 40, *Origins* 23 (1993): 310.

7. Ibid., n. 43, p. 311.

8. Ibid., nn. 40–41, p. 310.

9. Ibid., nn. 25–27, pp. 306–7.

10. Ibid., n. 48, pp. 312–13.

11. Ibid., n. 73, p. 319.

12. Ibid., n. 50, p. 313; n. 47, p. 312.

13. Aquinas, *IaIIae,* q.94, a.2.

14. John Paul II, *Veritatis splendor,* n. 51, *Origins* 23 (1993): 313.

15. Ibid., fn. 93, p. 333.

16. Ibid., n. 52, p. 313.

17. Ibid., n. 53, p. 314.

18. Ibid., n. 96, p. 325.

19. Ibid., n. 80, p. 321.

20. Ibid., n. 97, pp. 325–26.

21. Ibid., n. 115, p. 330.

22. Pope John Paul II, *Evangelium vitae,* n. 57, *Origins* 24 (1995): 709.

23. Ibid., n. 62, p. 711.

24. Ibid., n. 65, p. 712.

25. Ibid., n. 62, p. 711.

26. John Paul II, *Veritatis splendor,* n. 52, *Origins* 23 (1993): 313–14.

27. See, for example, Charles E. Curran and Richard A. McCormick, eds., *Readings in Moral Theology No. 8: Dialogue about Catholic Sexual Teaching* (New York: Paulist, 1993).

28. Congregation for the Doctrine of the Faith, "Declaration on Some Questions of Sexual Ethics," n. 3, *The Pope Speaks* 21 (1976): 62.

29. Ibid., nn. 4–5, pp. 62–64.

30. Pope Paul VI, *On the Regulation of Birth: Humanae vitae* (Washington, D.C.: U.S. Catholic Conference, 1968), n. 10, p. 7.

31. Ibid., nn. 11–12, p. 7.

32. "Declaration on Sexual Ethics," n. 5, *The Pope Speaks* 21 (1976): 63–64.

33. Congregation for the Doctrine of the Faith, *Instruction on Respect for Human Life,* II, B, 4, p. 27.

34. Ibid., Introduction, n. 3, p. 8.

35. John Paul II, *Veritatis splendor,* n. 74, *Origins* 23 (1993): 319.

36. Ibid., n. 79, p. 321.

37. Ibid., nn. 80–82, pp. 321–22.

38. Ibid., nn. 71–78, pp. 318–20.

39. Ibid., n. 80, p. 321. Cf., Pastoral Constitution on the Church in the Modern World, n. 27, in *Catholic Social Thought,* ed. O'Brien and Shannon, p. 182. For a further discussion, see James Gaffney, "The Pope on Proportionalism," in *Veritatis splendor: American Responses,* ed. Allsopp and O'Keefe, pp. 63–65.

40. For my discussion of the change and development in papal social teaching, see Curran, *Tensions in Moral Theology,* pp. 87–109.

41. Pope John XXIII, *Mater et magistra,* n. 212, in *Catholic Social Thought,* ed. O'Brien and Shannon, p. 118.

42. Pope John XXIII, *Pacem in terris,* n. 35, in *Catholic Social Thought,* ed. O'Brien and Shannon, p. 136.

43. Declaration on Religious Liberty, n. 2, in *Vatican Council II,* ed. Flannery, p. 844.

44. Pope Paul VI, *Octogesima adveniens,* n. 22, in *Catholic Social Thought,* ed. O'Brien and Shannon, p. 273.

45. Pope John Paul II, *Laborem exercens,* n. 15, in *Catholic Social Teaching,* ed. O'Brien and Shannon, pp. 373–74.

46. Pastoral Constitution on the Church in the Modern World, n. 51, in *Vatican Council II,* ed. Flannery, p. 955.

47. Zalba, *Theologiae moralis summa,* 2, p. 323.

48. Bernard Häring, "Fostering the Nobility of Marriage and the Family," in *Commentary on the Documents of Vatican II,* vol. 5, *Pastoral Constitution on the Church in the Modern World,* ed. Vorgrimler, p. 243.

49. "Declaration on Sexual Ethics," n. 5, *Pope Speaks* 21 (1976): 63.

50. Congregation for the Doctrine of the Faith, "Letter to the Bishops of the Catholic Church on the Pastoral Care of Homosexual Persons," n. 7, *Origins* 16 (1986).

51. Scholars have pointed out some significant differences between the Pastoral Constitution on the Church in the Modern World and later papal sexual teaching beginning with *Humanae vitae.* See, Ph. Delhaye, "L'encyclique *Humanae vitae* et l'enseignement de Vatican II sur le mariage et la famille (*Gaudium et spes*)," *Bijdragen* 29 (1968): 351–68; Joseph A. Selling, "Magisterial Teaching on Marriage, 1880–1968: Historical Constancy or Radical Development?" in *Historia: Memoria futuri: Mélanges Louis Vereecke,* ed. Réal Tremblay and Dennis J. Billy (Rome: Editiones Academiae Alphonsianae, 1991), pp. 351–402.

52. Paul VI, *Humanae vitae,* n. 12, pp. 7–8.

53. John Paul II, *Veritatis splendor,* n. 53, *Origins* 23 (1993): 314.

54. Pope Pius XI, *Quadragesimo anno,* nn. 76–98, in *Catholic Social Teaching,* ed. O'Brien and Shannon, pp. 54–64.

55. Ibid., n. 76, p. 59.

56. Richard L. Camp, *The Papal Ideology of Social Reform: A Study in Historical Development, 1878–1967* (Leiden: E. J. Brill, 1969), pp. 128–35; John F. Cronin, "Forty Years Later: Reflections and Reminiscences," *American Ecclesiastical Review* 164 (1971): 310–18.

57. See, for example, Douglass and Hollenbach, eds. *Catholicism and Liberalism.*

58. Paul E. Sigmund, "Catholicism and Liberal Democracy," in *Catholicism and Liberalism*, ed. Douglass and Hollenbach, pp. 217–41.

59. John XXIII, *Pacem in terris*, nn. 11–27, in *Catholic Social Thought*, ed. O'Brien and Shannon, pp. 132–35.

60. Ibid., nn. 6–7, p. 133.

61. Ibid., nn. 39–45, 75–79, 126–29, 142–45, pp. 137–38, 143–44, 151, 154.

62. Paul VI, *Octogesima adveniens*, n. 4, in *Catholic Social Thought*, ed. O'Brien and Shannon, p. 266.

63. Pope John Paul II, "United Nations Address: The Fabric of Relations among People," n. 7, *Origins* 25 (1995): 296.

64. Ibid., n. 18, p. 299.

65. Ibid., n. 10, p. 297

66. John Paul II, *Evangelium vitae*, n. 57, *Origins* 24 (1995): 709.

67. Ibid., n. 62, p. 711.

68. The distinction between direct and indirect is intimately associated with the principle of the double effect. The famous third condition states that the good effect cannot be produced by means of the evil effect. In other words the evil effect must be equally immediate causally with the good effect.

69. Zalba, *Theologiae moralis summa*, 2, p. 295.

70. T. Lincoln Bouscaren, *Ethics of Ectopic Operations*, rev. ed. (Milwaukee, Wis.: Bruce, 1944).

71. Aquinas, *IaIIae*, q.94, a.4.

72. Catholic Bishops, "The Challenge of Peace," nn. 9–10, in *Catholic Social Teaching*, ed. O'Brien and Shannon, p. 494; "Economic Justice for All," n. 135, in *Catholic Social Thought*, ed. O'Brien and Shannon, p. 610.

73. For an overview of contemporary discussions about sexuality in the Catholic tradition, see Curran and McCormick, eds., *Readings in Moral Theology No. 8*.

74. Aquinas, *IaIIae*, q.90, a.1, ob.3; q.95, a.4; q.96, a.5, ob.3; q.97, a.2; *IIaIIae*, q.57, a.3. For my fuller discussion of Aquinas and Aquinas's use of Ulpian, see Charles E. Curran, *Directions in Fundamental Moral Theology* (Notre Dame, Ind.: University of Notre Dame Press, 1985), pp. 127–32.

75. Aquinas, *IIaIIae*, q.154, a.1; Zalba, *Theologiae moralis summa*, 2, pp. 350–380.

76. John Paul II, *Veritatis splendor*, n. 48, *Origins* 23 (1993): 312.

77. Pope Pius XII, "The Prolongation of Life," (November 24, 1957), in *Medical Ethics: Sources of Catholic Teachings*, ed. Kevin D. O'Rourke and Philip Boyle (St. Louis, Mo.: Catholic Health Association, 1989), p. 207.

78. John Paul II, *Veritatis splendor*, nn. 71–83, *Origins* 23 (1993): 318–22.

79. Porter, in *Veritatis splendor: American Responses*, ed. Allsopp and O'Keefe, pp. 278–95.

80. John Paul II, *Veritatis splendor*, n. 76, *Origins* 23 (1993): 320.

81. Ibid., n. 8, p. 321–22.

82. Richard A. McCormick has developed a theory of proportionalism more than any other Catholic moral theologian in the United States. For an overview of his position, see Paulinus Ikechukwu Odozor, *Richard A. McCormick and the Renewal of Moral Theology* (Notre Dame, Ind.: University of Notre Dame

Press, 1995); James J. Walter, "The Foundation and Formulation of Norms," in *Moral Theology: Challenges for the Future: Essays in Honor of Richard A. McCormick*, ed. Charles E. Curran (New York: Paulist, 1990), pp. 125–54.

83. Dorszynski, *Catholic Teaching about the Morality of Falsehood.*

84. In addition to McCormick and Walter (note 82), see, for example, John Langan, "Direct and Indirect—Some Recent Exchanges Between Paul Ramsey and Richard McCormick," *Religious Studies Review* 5 (1979): 95–101; Bernard House, *Proportionalism: The American Debate and Its European Roots* (Washington, D.C.: Georgetown University Press, 1987).

85. Germain Grisez is a prolific scholar. He is now writing a multivolume systematic moral theology—Germain Grisez, *The Way of the Lord Jesus*, vol. 1, *Christian Moral Principles* (Chicago: Franciscan Herald, 1983), vol. 2, *Living a Christian Life* (Quincy, Ill.: Franciscan, 1993), vol. 3, *Difficult Moral Questions* (Quincy, Ill.: Franciscan, 1997). For a succinct but accurate summary of his basic theory, see Germain Grisez and Russell Shaw, *Fulfillment in Christ: A Summary of Christian Moral Principles* (Notre Dame, Ind.: University of Notre Dame Press, 1991). In the following section, I will refer primarily to this work.

86. Grisez and Shaw, *Fulfillment in Christ*, pp. 44–48.

87. Ibid., pp. 66–71.

88. Hall, *Narrative and Natural Law*, pp. 16–19.

89. John Finnis, Germain Grisez, and Joseph Boyle, "Practical Principles, Moral Truth, and Ultimate Ends," *American Journal of Jurisprudence* 32 (1987): 101.

90. Grisez and Shaw, *Fulfillment in Christ*, p. 80.

91. Ibid., p. 86.

92. Ibid., p. 93.

93. Finnis, Grisez, and Boyle, *American Journal of Jurisprudence* 32 (1987): 106.

94. Grisez and Shaw, *Fulfillment in Christ*, p. 56.

95. Ibid., pp. 113–18.

96. John Paul II, *Veritatis splendor*, nn. 46–53, *Origins* 23 (1993): 311–14.

97. Jürgen Habermas, "On Hermenutics Claim to Universality," in *The Hermeneutic Reader: Texts of the German Tradition from the Enlightenment to the Present*, ed. Kurt Mueller-Volmer (New York: Continuum, 1985), pp. 294–319.

98. John Rawls, *A Theory of Justice* (Cambridge, Mass.: Belknap Press of Harvard University Press, 1971). For a Catholic appreciation and use of Rawls, see Leslie Griffin, "Good Catholics Should Be Rawlsian Liberals," *Southern California Interdisciplinary Law Journal* 5, n. 3 (1997): 297–373.

99. John XXIII, *Pacem in terris*, n. 35, in *Catholic Social Thought*, ed. O'Brien and Shannon, p. 136.

100. For example, Pope John Paul II, *Sollicitudo socialis*, nn. 35–44, in *Catholic Social Teaching*, ed. O'Brien and Shannon, pp. 419–24.

101. Pope John Paul II, *Centesimus annus*, n. 54, in *Catholic Social Thought*, ed. O'Brien and Shannon, pp. 479–80.

102. Johann Jakob Stamm with Maurice Edward Andrew, *The Ten Commandments in Recent Research* Studies In Biblical Theology, Second Series, n. 5 (Naperville, Ill.: Alec R. Allenson, 1968), pp. 66–75; A.D.H. Mayes, "The Decalogue of Moses: An Enduring Ethical Programme?" in *Ethics and the Christian,* ed. Sean Freyne (Dublin: Columba, 1991), pp. 25–40.

103. For an enlightening discussion and analysis of some of these issues, see John T. Noonan Jr., "Development in Moral Doctrine," *Theological Studies* 54 (1993): 662–77.

104. For the details of this development, see Noonan, *Contraception.*

105. Noonan, *Theological Studies* 54 (1993): 667–77; J. Robert Dionne, *The Papacy and the Church: A Study of Praxis and Reception in Ecumenical Perspective* (New York: Philosophical Library, 1987), pp. 147–94.

106. Dionne, *The Papacy and the Church.*

107. Three important studies on casuistry are Albert R. Jonsen and Stephen Toulmin, *The Abuse of Casuistry: A History of Moral Reasoning* (Berkeley: University of California Press, 1988); James F. Keenan and Thomas A. Shannon, eds., *The Context of Casuistry* (Washington D.C.: Georgetown University Press, 1995); Richard B. Miller, *Casuistry and Modern Ethics: A Poetics of Practical Reasoning* (Chicago: University of Chicago Press, 1996).

108. Albert R. Jonsen, "Casuistry: An Alternative or Complement to Principles," *Kennedy Institute of Ethics Journal* 5 (1995): 237–51.

109. Zalba, *Theologiae moralis summa*, 2, pp. 270–86.

110. John Paul II, *Evangelium vitae*, n. 56, *Origins* 24 (1995): 709.

111. Zalba, *Theologiae moralis summa*, 2, pp. 1040–49.

112. Hans Küng, *Global Responsibility: In Search of a New World Ethic* (New York: Crossroad, 1991).

113. John XXIII, *Pacem in terris*, nn. 11–27, in *Catholic Social Thought*, ed. O'Brien and Shannon, pp. 132–35.

7

Conscience

Conscience is generally understood as a judgment about the morality of an act to be done or omitted or already done or omitted by the person. All human beings have to deal with this issue of decision making which from the perspective of moral theology concerns the morality of our actions. The previous chapter discussed principles and norms which form part of the decision-making process. The historical role of the Ten Commandments in Jewish and Christian history illustrates the value tradition puts on principles and norms in Christian decision making. Social ethics also acknowledges the role of principles and norms in determining justice in individual societies and throughout the world. However, principles and norms do not cover much of the area of human and Christian decision making. No principle or norm (I hope) is the reason one decides to marry. In addition specific principles and norms change over times. The last chapter referred to the moral experience of the individual and the community in bringing about these changes. Although principles and norms have some role to play in conscience and decision making, the reality of conscience relies on many features besides principles and norms.

PRELIMINARY CONSIDERATIONS

Earlier chapters discussed the subject and the object poles of human and Christian morality. These two aspects come together in the matter of conscience and greatly add to the complexity of moral decision making. In every moral act I contribute to making myself the kind of person I am, but I also do a particular act that affects myself, others, and the world in which we live. The complex nature of the human act involves this twofold aspect. In every act I must be properly related to myself as the moral person who is subject and agent, and also properly related to the reality of the objective situation itself.

In its long history the Catholic moral tradition has dealt to some extent with this twofold aspect of conscience. The manualist tradition has recognized two important distinctions with regard to conscience although the terminology has varied at times. Conscience, understood as a judgment about the morality of an act to be done, is true or erroneous depending on whether the judgment of conscience is in conformity with objective reality. Conscience is sincere (often called right) or insincere depending on its relationship to the person placing the act. A sincere conscience is in accord with my sincerely held convictions. The insincere conscience, which is patently wrong, was never discussed.[1]

In the light of these distinctions, four logical possibilities exist. The ideal is the conscience that is both sincere and true. Both the subjective and the objective aspects are what they should be. Thus, I give alms to a needy person because I want to help that person. The exact opposite is the insincere and erroneous conscience which is out of kilter in both ways. I give alms to a person who is a fake, and I do it because I want to appear generous before others. In such a case conscience is both insincere and erroneous. The third possibility is the insincere and true conscience. I give alms to a person who is truly needy, but I do it in order to give the appearance of being a generous person. Here I am not sincere with my better moral self, and my act itself is bad even though the objective act of giving money to someone who needs it is good. Note here how the Catholic tradition gives some primacy to the subjective aspect of conscience over the objective.

The other conflict situation involves a conscience that is sincere but erroneous. After examining a patient, the doctor believes that the patient does not have AIDS. In reality, however, the patient does have AIDS. The doctor's erroneous judgment is in accord with her sincerely held conviction. Here a further distinction has been made between vincible and invincible ignorance. If the ignorance is your fault, your conscience is vincibly erroneous. A doctor who did not diagnose AIDS in 1970 was invincibly erroneous. She had no idea what AIDS was and did not know what symptoms to look for. However, today the diagnosis of AIDS is well known, and a doctor who does not know the symptoms of AIDS is derelict in her duty as a doctor and vincibly erroneous. A conscience that is sincere but invincibly erroneous can and should be followed without any guilt on the agent's part. Historically, there has been a significant development in the Catholic approach especially as illustrated by Alphonsus Liguori (1787) and many of the manualists who actually went beyond the teaching of Thomas Aquinas. Aquinas held that the act of such a conscience is not wrong. Alphonsus maintained that such an act is not only not wrong but it is also good and even meritorious.[2] Notice here the primacy that even the Catholic manualist tradition accords to the subjective aspect of conscience.

These distinctions help illustrate the complex reality of conscience and how it should operate. Even in the development of the Catholic tradition the subjective aspect of conscience has some priority over its objective aspect. Such a priority existed even when the Catholic tradition gave less emphasis to the dignity and role of the person. The primacy of the subjective aspect together with the need for the true objective conscience sheds some light on how we are to understand conscience and how it works, as will become evident in the following pages. At the same time this understanding makes clear the great dilemma of conscience for Christians and others. Simply stated the dilemma is this: I must follow my conscience, but my conscience may be wrong. The appeal to the subjective aspect does not do away with the objective aspect. Many evils have been perpetrated in the name of conscience, yet we cannot deny some primacy of the subjective aspect. Such a complex approach highlights the need for a well-formed conscience. This chapter develops that need from the Christian and Catholic perspective.

THE CATHOLIC MORAL TRADITION

A brief overview of the Catholic tradition helps illuminate the meaning of conscience. The moral conscience (*syneidesis*) was introduced into Scripture by Paul.[3] Although the Hebrew Bible does not use the word conscience or anything similar to it, the reality of conscience is not missing from its pages. The people of the covenant were called to hear and respond to the word of God. The "heart" often refers to the total person who hears the word of God and responds to it. Paul found the word *syneidesis* in the Greek world especially in the ordinary usage of the time. Conscience here generally refers to what was later called consequent and negative conscience—the remorse one feels after having done a bad action. We are all familiar with the remorse of conscience.

Protestants such as C.A. Pierce stress the aspect of consequent conscience in Paul and see no presence of the so-called antecedent or legislative (as opposed to judicial or consequent) conscience which serves as a guide for what the person should do.[4] On the other hand,

Catholic scholars generally interpret Paul as having given a greater role to the antecedent and legislative aspect of conscience.[5] This difference in interpretation illustrates how often we approach Scripture with our own presuppositions. The negative consequent conscience fits the classical Protestant notion of salvation coming to the sinner who is conscious of sin and in need of a saving God. The antecedent conscience fits the Catholic stress on works and their proper role and importance. There can be no doubt, however, that Paul, at the very minimum, downplays the antecedent conscience. However, the Christian tradition over the centuries has assigned an important role to conscience as a director and guide of actions.

Catholic scholastic theology in the twelfth and thirteenth centuries systematically addressed the antecedent conscience in addition to the consequent conscience.[6] The medieval theologians distinguished between two Greek words—*syneidesis* and *synderesis*. The distinction was found in a famous text from Saint Jerome known to the medievalists through the *Glossa ordinaria*. Peter the Lombard accepted the distinction between these two realities and set the direction for further development in the Middle Ages and subsequently. Apparently, however, *synderesis* was a scribal mistake (perhaps the monk had too much wine with dinner) and not really Jerome's idea.[7] Nevertheless, subsequent theologians had to deal with two different concepts. *Syneidesis* is what is meant by conscience or the judgment act; *Synderesis*, in the text from Jerome, is an element of the soul that makes us feel our sinfulness and corrects the other elements when they err. In the light of different positions Thomas Aquinas understood *synderesis* as the habit of practical reason by which one knows the first principles of the natural law— do good and avoid evil, act according to right reason. Conscience is then the act of applying the first principles known in *synderesis* to conduct.

The most extensive development in the understanding of conscience in the Catholic tradition came in the context of the manuals of moral theology that emerged at the end of the sixteenth century and continued until Vatican II. Chapter three has traced the history of the manuals showing how the controversies of the seventeenth and eighteenth centuries intensified the legal model. Law was the remote, objective, and extrinsic rule or norm of human actions, and conscience was the proximate, subjective, and intrinsic rule of actions.

The manuals of moral theology followed a legal model which emphasized the extrinsic character of law. Three aspects of their treatment contributed to this emphasis on the heteronomic understanding of law despite the fact that the manuals also claim to follow the natural law which is intrinsic. In the intrinsic approach, something is commanded because it is good, but the manualists definitely give the impression that something is good because it is a matter of law. First, the probabilism controversy resulted in seeing in theory an opposition between law and freedom so that the law had to be certain to take away my freedom. The best of the natural law tradition sees law as the proper ordering and fulfillment of human nature ultimately bringing human beings to their true happiness. Second, in practice the primary determination of probability came from the opinions of experts. The intrinsic reasons for probability tended to fade into the background. Third, the papal teaching office frequently intervened—using authority to solve the particular issues that were being debated by moral theologians. In such a context obligation was felt as something imposed on the freedom of the individual by an outside authority often claiming to speak in the name of God.

The manuals emphasized the legal model in their understanding of how conscience works. However, in their comparatively short explanation of theory, the manuals understood conscience to operate in a deductive way. Conscience proceeds by way of a syllogism. In keeping with the Thomistic understanding, the manuals very briefly mention that *synderesis* is a property of the intellect by which the human being knows the most general principles of the natural law—good is to be done, the Supreme Being is to be worshiped, promises are to be kept. Moral science deduces other truths and principles from these more general principles using a syllogism. Evil is to be avoided; adultery is evil; therefore, adultery is to be avoided. These deductive truths or principles constitute moral science. The more general principles known by *synderesis* and the principles of moral science are universal. The dictate of conscience, however, is a particular judgment that is immediately deduced from the principles of moral science and mediately deduced from the more general principles known by *synderesis*. The dictate of conscience is virtually equivalent to the conclusion of a syllogism. The major expresses the moral law; the minor is the act here and now to be done to which the law is applied; the conclusion states whether the action comes under the moral law. Thus, for example: theft is wrong; this action is a theft; therefore this action is wrong.[8] Thus the very brief theory about conscience in the practical manuals of moral theology understood the reasoning of conscience to be the deductive syllogism.

Although conscience is depicted as virtually and for all practical purposes moving deductively through a syllogism, some manuals hinted at another way in which conscience might work. Zalba, for example, understands conscience as a virtual conclusion from more general principles which is reached through a strict deductive reasoning process or from a certain sense or intuition of probity.[9] Zalba footnotes this latter phrase referring to two citations from the *Summa* of Aquinas. Both citations refer to connatural knowledge—the first is related to prudence and the second to wisdom.[10] The manuals thus contain hints that conscience can operate in another way than deduction, but they never develop such an approach. In addition, as Zalba illustrates, this other way could never go against what was known from deduction. A later section will develop this connatural way of knowing.

OTHER WAYS OF DECISION MAKING

The manuals do not exhaust the understanding of moral decision making in the Catholic tradition. Catholic spiritual theology has developed a very important concept of discernment which has a long history in the Christian tradition and Scripture.[11] In the Hebrew Bible the influence of the spirit of God is contrasted with the influence of the evil spirit in the life of Saul (1 Sam 16:14–23). The spirit of Yahweh plays a very significant role in the Hebrew Bible. It is the force that inspires prophecy, and in the messianic era, this spirit will give all Israel prophetic insight (Joel 3:1–2). The spirit plays many other roles, but its relationship to prophecy and to knowing God's will are connected to our question of knowing how God wants us to act.

In the New Testament, the Holy Spirit plays a very significant role with regard to helping us know what God asks of us. In addition there are other spirits both good and bad. In Matthew's Gospel, Jesus is led by the good spirit into the desert where he is tempted by the evil spirits (Matt 4:1–11). The First Letter of John cautions the early disciples of Jesus to test the spirits to see whether they are of God because there are many false spirits. John even begins the long Christian tradition of trying to develop some criteria for discerning the good spirits from the bad spirits. His criteria, however, are very broad and obvious. Every spirit which confesses that Jesus has come in the flesh is of God, while every spirit which does not confess Jesus is not from God. (1 John 4:1–6) In First Corinthians 12:10 Paul lists the ability to distinguish between the spirits as a gift of the Spirit.

The early monks, whether alone in the desert or later in communities, developed the notion of the discernment of spirits. The Middle Ages continued their interest in the subject. Acknowledged masters of the spiritual life, for example, Ignatius of Loyola and Francis de Sales, emphasized the importance of the discernment of spirits for the spiritual life. It is both necessary and difficult for a person to know the origin and nature of the inspirations and intuitions that come to the soul. Earlier generations gave much more importance to the role that good spirits and evil spirits play in our lives. These spirits were believed to directly affect the human person. Today we are more likely to emphasize the role of natural causes, for example, our own inspirations and feelings. The question of discernment can include both these realities.[12] The discernment of spirits is a narrower concept than the discernment of God's will and was treated differently even by authors as late as Ignatius of Loyola in the sixteenth century.[13] However, the two are closely related, and what is said about discerning the spirits can also be applied to discerning God's will in a somewhat broader way.

The classical treatises on the discernment of spirits usually deal with three phenomena—revelations and visions that come from outside the person, internal enlightenment or impulses concerning a determinate object of choice, and general states of consolation or desolation that the soul experiences. These realities can arise from either a good spirit or an evil spirit. The possibility of illusion and deception is ever present so it is important to discern the source of these realities to know whether we should follow them or not. Two ways of discerning spirits have been developed. The first is the God-given gift or charism of discerning spirits—a notion first mentioned by Paul (1 Cor 12:10). The second way is through the rules that test the origins and good or bad nature of these phenomena. There is, of course, no infallible way to test these spirits. Generally speaking these rules are based on a single principle: by their fruits you will know them. The fruits of these phenomena occur in the individual person and are also tested in the life, actions, and teaching of the church. Good spirits, for example, produce humility, trust in God, patience, true freedom, and charity. Heavy emphasis is also placed on obedience to lawful authority.[14]

Interior peace is one of the most important and significant signs for discerning spirits and the will of God. Both Ignatius of Loyola and Francis de Sales emphasize the role of interior peace. God's action results in peace; the devil disquiets the soul. Good inspirations and thoughts bring tranquillity and peace. However, there is also a false peace that can arise. At times it can be rather difficult to discern what is true peace.[15] This emphasis on interior peace as a primary way of discerning spirits and the will of God coheres with a broad human experience of the peace of conscience. Especially in considering the consequent conscience, the remorse of a bad conscience is contrasted with the peace of a good conscience.

The Catholic philosophical tradition also embraces approaches to conscience that differ from the primary emphasis on a deductive syllogistic reasoning process. Jacques Maritain, the foremost Thomist in the twentieth century, saw conscience as working through knowledge by inclination or connaturality. Maritain, in fact, maintains that this approach is the proper interpretation of Aquinas.[16]

In his discussion of natural law the French philosopher distinguishes two aspects—the ontological and the gnoseological aspects of natural law. The ontological aspect is the human essence with its unchangeable structure and intellectual necessities. The nature of a reality determines how it should properly function. A plant, a dog, or a horse has its own natural law by reason of its own specific structure. Human beings likewise have a normality of functioning grounded in the human essence. This essence is the ontological aspect of natural law.

The gnoseological aspect of natural law involves how we know the ontological aspect. Practical human reason comes to know the natural law though it is unwritten. Our knowledge of the natural law is imperfect and will continue to develop and become more refined as long as humanity exists. How precisely do we know the natural law? We know the natural law not through a conceptual exercise of the intellect or by way of rational knowledge but through the guidance of the inclinations of human nature. This knowledge is not clear knowledge through concepts and conceptual judgments. It is obscure, unsystematic, vital knowledge by connaturality or congeniality. The intellect in making its judgment consults and listens to the inner melody that the vibrating strings of abiding tendencies make present in the subject.

In proposing this approach as the correct interpretation of Aquinas, Maritain points to the famous question 94 on natural law in the *Prima secundae* to substantiate his interpretation: All things to which a human being has a natural inclination are naturally apprehended by reason as good (a. 2). Many people fail to recognize the role of knowledge by inclination in Aquinas because he speaks of the specific principles of the natural law somewhat like conclusions from the first principle. In the speculative realm truths are deduced from the first principles. But this is not so in the realm of practical reason. These specific precepts of the natural law function in the practical realm as conclusions do in the speculative realm. Thus, Maritain emphasizes the difference between speculative reason and practical reason in Aquinas.

Another more philosophical approach to decision making in the Catholic tradition stresses the virtue of prudence and its role (see chapter 5). Prudence in the Thomistic tradition is the virtue associated with practical reason.[17] Recall Aquinas's distinction between speculative reason which deals with necessary and universal things and practical reason which deals with contingent and particular realities. Prudence for Aquinas is associated with art, not science. Art is the right reason of things to be made, whereas prudence is the right reason of things to be done. Prudence is analogous to art. The artist does not work by deduction. The imagination, the ability to discern what is appropriate, the feeling for the most expressive, and a sense of harmony among all the parts help make a good artist. Think of a great painter, or poet, or even a chef! Prudence for Aquinas has none of the cautious, wary, conservative approach often associated with prudence in contemporary language and thought, but it is obtained and perfected through practice in deliberation and action. It does not reason in a syllogistic manner but practices the art of discernment and deliberation. Choosing the fitting means to the end is the function of prudence. According to Etienne Gilson, a renowned twentieth century neo-Thomist, reason, foresight, and circumspection are essential aspects of prudence; without these there is no real prudence.[18]

In Aquinas's approach prudence is the first cardinal virtue and the one virtue that affects all the others. This virtue deals with the acts of all the other virtues. Josef Pieper explains that prudence is the cause, root, mother, measure, precept, guide, and prototype of all the moral virtues. Prudence is active in all the other virtues, perfecting them to their true nature. All the other virtues participate in prudence and become virtues through their participation in prudence.[19] Any approach to the concept of the virtues as found in Aristotle and Aquinas must give great importance to the virtue of prudence and its role of discerning, deliberating, and choosing well—especially of the means to the end.

Although the Catholic tradition, as exemplified in the manuals of moral theology and recent papal teaching, highlighted the legal and deductive approaches to moral decision making, we recognize other strands in the Catholic tradition that propose a more inductive approach and even provide some nonrational aspects that must be considered. The next section will sketch out a more systematic understanding of the process of moral decision making and conscience.

A CONSTRUCTIVE THEORY OF
CONSCIENCE AND DECISION MAKING

Before attempting to develop a more systematic understanding of conscience and decision making, it is important to understand more precisely the role of moral theology as it relates to the moral life in general and to conscience in particular. Moral theology studies the Christian moral life in a systematic, reflexive, and critical manner. Moral theology is second-order discourse that stands back and tries to understand in a thematic way what takes place in moral decision making. Moral theologians are not necessarily better persons or better decision makers than those who have never studied the discipline.

Perhaps an analogy with the role of psychiatrists can help illustrate the role of moral theology and its relationship to daily moral life. Psychiatrists study psychological and emotional human behavior. As a discipline analogous to moral theology psychiatry also involves second-order discourse in which it stands back from lived human reality to study it in a reflexive, critical, and scientific way. The aim of the discipline of psychiatry, like moral theology, is primarily in the realm of intellectual understanding. Are psychiatrists the most emotionally mature, well-balanced human beings in the world? The answer is obviously no.

On the other hand, there are individuals who are extremely well-balanced and psychologically mature who have never studied Freud or any other psychoanalytical theory. The vast number of people live a mature life without ever consciously reflecting thematically and systematically on what they are doing. However, an intellectual search for knowledge impels some people to study the reality in a more reflexive and scientific manner. Their reflexive and scientific knowledge can then be used to help people existentially. That is why people who are experiencing problems and difficulties consult a psychiatrist. Moral theology performs an analogous role for the moral life. It is primarily an intellectual discipline that stands back to understand thematically and scientifically how people make decisions of conscience. At times it can make a contribution to individual persons in their conscience decisions, but one does not have to be a moral theologian to be a good person, a good Christian, or a good decision maker. In short, one should not exaggerate the role and importance of moral theology in the lives of most Christians.

In reality we are shaped and formed by the circumstances in which we live, the traditions out of which we come, the communities which nurture us, and the experiences of our lives. Our moral attitudes or virtues, values or ideals, and principles and norms usually come from these sources. How do all these aspects comes together in conscience and decision making? This section will now develop a more systematic and thematic view of conscience.

A HOLISTIC UNDERSTANDING OF CONSCIENCE.   Both the subject and object poles of morality come together in the judgment of conscience. First, consider the subject pole, the person trying to make the proper judgment or decision. Much has been mentioned earlier in this book to contribute to a proper understanding of the Christian as a subject and agent. One is called to be an authentic Christian and human being. The call to discipleship involves a continuing conversion or change of heart. The relationality-responsibility model sees this call to holiness in light of the multiple relationships in which we live—with God, our neighbors, ourselves, and the world. The Christian person strives to live virtuously as a disciple in the community of Jesus.

The Catholic tradition recognizes that grace does not destroy the human aspects of persons but brings them to perfection. Our striving to be a good human being and a good Christian should not be seen in opposition but as closely related. In addition Christian and human decision making involves much more than the cognitive aspect. The affective aspects and the emotions are important parts of Christian and human existence and also play a significant role in the judgment of conscience. The person, moreover, is never merely an isolated monad but part of the Christian and human communities—including natural communities such as the family, neighborhoods, civic organizations and the many other voluntary communities with which one chooses to be associated. These community relationships affect the person as subject.

The object pole deals precisely with the concrete reality involved in the decision-making process. The Catholic moral tradition, as exemplified in both the Thomistic and manualistic traditions, has understood the objective reality of acts to embrace the moral object, the end, and the circumstances. The manual tradition generally acknowledges seven circumstances—who, what, where, by what means, why, how, and when.[20] These various aspects help one discover the objective reality under discussion. Daniel C. Maguire has developed these seven "reality revealing questions" and added an important new question—viable alternatives. This question fits with his emphasis on the creative moral imagination. The creative moral imagination sees and discerns possibilities in the present to bring about changes and make possible what does not readily appear on the surface.[21]

In moral decision making the subject and object poles come together, but the subject makes decisions in many ways depending on how reason, grace, emotion, and one's intuitions are involved in the judgments of conscience. In making conscience judgments individuals will at times apply principles or norms to particular questions. In this context, reason functions in a discursive way. Maritain has emphasized knowledge by connaturality. In addition there is always an important role for prudence. What means should be taken to achieve this end? What career should I choose? What volunteer projects should I engage in? Should I break my promise in this case? Should the nation resort to violence in this extreme situation?

Prudence needs to be rooted in the total person and modified by all the virtues of the good Christian. However, the art of prudential decision making can be developed and perfected over time like any virtue or art. The drama aficionado and I can go to the same play. The odds are that the aficionado will discern more going on in the particular play than I will. She will have a much better understanding of plot, characterization, staging, and lighting, for example, than I who have never studied drama. However, there can also be significant differences of discernment between two people who have doctorates in drama. Discerning what is going on in a play brings out a person's creative and imaginative abilities. The playwright, like the critic, depends heavily on the creative imagination. Discernment, likewise, involves more than intellectual knowledge. Some people have developed a better facility in discernment than others. The prudent person will discern moral matters using creativity, sensitivity, and imagination, and will continue to develop this art of properly discerning the morally fitting thing to do in each situation.

Conscience thus employs human reason in at least three different ways—a discursive deductive way; a connatural way; and a discerning and prudential way. However, reason acting in these ways is always informed by faith.[22] Faith and grace are mediated in and through human reason and discernment in keeping with the Catholic insistence on mediation. Christians have also recognized the role of the Holy Spirit in guiding Christian choices. Liturgical and private prayer are ways to ask the Holy Spirit to enlighten our hearts and minds. The Holy Spirit is especially connected with the gifts of wisdom and knowledge, but the Catholic tradition recognizes seven gifts of the Holy Spirit based on the Septuagint version of Isaiah 11:1–3—wisdom, understanding, counsel, fortitude, knowledge, piety, and fear of the Lord. These gifts of the Spirit play a significant role in the discernment of conscience.[23]

In addition to the role of grace and reason, a holistic understanding of conscience recognizes the role of the affective and emotional sides of the human.[24] We all experience revulsion at needless killing and violence. The American public changed its attitude to the Vietnam War not because of arguments alone but especially because of pictures portrayed on television and in newspapers. The old adage rightly points out that a picture is worth a thousand words. The picture, above all, appeals to our emotions—sympathy for those in need, anger at those who take advantage of the defenseless and the young, disgust with those who abuse positions of authority and trust. At times the affective can correct the errors of reason as illustrated by the change in U.S. public opinion on Vietnam precipitated by having the war in our living rooms for the first time in human history.

The Hebrew Bible uses the word "heart" to describe the reality that we refer to today as conscience. Such an approach recognizes the affective dimension and opposes any simplistic reduction of conscience to the cognitive. Again, as the axiom has it, the heart has its reasons.

Faith itself has a very significant affective side. Many people interpret the Christian moral message primarily in terms of love, which is more than an intellectual concept. The emphasis on narrative and telling the biblical story also recognizes the affective aspect of faith and conscience formation. In the Catholic tradition, the centrality of the liturgy and the eucharist accentuates this aspect of faith and its effect on the community. Formed by the liturgy and the story it tells, Catholic people strive to discern what it is that God is calling them to do. The traditional Catholic appreciation of the importance of art and statues as expressions of faith also underscores the importance given to the affective approach.

A holistic approach to conscience also recognizes an intuitive aspect. Intuitions arise unconsciously in us and spontaneously insert themselves into our understanding. There exists a dimension of the person and even a part of the mind that is unavailable to our reflex consciousness. Psychology has recognized this realm of the mind and with it the role of intuition.[25] Our own moral experience reminds us of the role of intuition. Often we have a hunch that this is the way to go. Sometimes I have the feeling that I should do something, but I cannot articulate the reasons supporting such a move. How many times when wrestling with a problem do we "sleep on it" in the hope that something may arise unconsciously over night? Intuitions can come from many different sources including grace, human nature, and our affective selves.

These four aspects—reason, grace, emotions, and intuition—involved in conscience could be wrong or at least erroneously interpreted, but many claim that emotion and intuition are especially open to error and misinterpretation. Many criticisms have been made against intuitionism in philosophy. The rational is often seen as the necessary guide for the emotions which tend to be suspect. Yet, here again, another axiom still holds—the possibility of abuse does not do away with the use. Intuitions and emotions may be wrong, but they play a significant role in decision making. Reason and our perception of grace can also be mistaken and can at times be corrected by intuitions and emotions.

The holistic understanding of conscience proposed here recognizes the complexity and manifold aspects of decision making. As significant differences also exist with regard to the object of our decision making, the process of decision making is somewhat different in different contexts. Judgments about a marriage partner, a vocation to be or do a certain thing, whether or not to move to another city or to take a difficult job, differ from judgments about whether the country should have an all-volunteer army or the feasibility of nuclear power plants. Personal decisions will obviously take into account the particularities of the person; decisions on social issues require a knowledge of all the data involved in community decisions and rely less on the particularity of the person. Thus, not all judgments of conscience proceed in the same way but are somewhat determined by the matter under consideration.

How Do I Know My Conscience Is True? The dilemma of conscience recognizes that I must follow my sincere conscience but my conscience can be wrong. How can I be sure that my conscience is not wrong? There are no criteria that can give an infallible answer to that question. The last few pages have insisted on a complex and holistic approach to conscience. Many different criteria have been proposed down through the years, but the most adequate criterion in my judgment is the peace and joy of a good conscience.

Many reasons support the primacy of this criterion. Both the theory and experience of consequent conscience emphasize the remorse of conscience as a sign of an erroneous conscience. Remorse is exactly the opposite of the joy and peace of a true conscience. Rules for the discernment of spirits also put heavy emphasis on the peace and joy of a good conscience. Conscience involves a moral judgment. What criteria do we employ to determine if a judgment is true? According to Bernard Lonergan, the self-transcending subject has a deep drive and thrust toward the truth. When the truth is achieved, it comes with the peace and joy that derives from a basic drive being fulfilled and finding its object. Moral judgments work in an analogous manner. The moral subject has a drive and thrust for value that is quieted only when value is achieved.[26]

This understanding of judgment corresponds to our own human experience. Examine your experience in this regard. How do you determine when you have come to a good decision or judgment? One always begins by asking pertinent questions. As long as there are unanswered questions, I am still seeking and not satisfied. However, when there are no more pertinent questions, I am satisfied and at peace. The human person has a God-given inclination to the true and the good, which grounds the questions we are constantly raising about moral action. When all the pertinent questions have been raised and settled, one is at peace precisely because no questions remain. The drive for the truth has found its proper object. Grace, reason, affectivity, and intuitions all cooperate in this thrust for the true and the good.

Without doubt, the manuals of moral theology operated on a different epistemology. Truth was the conformity of the mind to objective reality. Conscience was conformity to the objective law and the moral order established by God. In the approach developed here the primary emphasis is on the knowing subject. This emphasis incorporates the shift to the subject that has been so prominent in contemporary Catholic thought. It also coheres with a notion that has existed throughout Catholic tradition concerning the primacy of the subjective in matters of conscience. Such primacy does not reject the importance of the objective, but the ultimate criterion for judgment comes from the subject. Far from positing relativism or subjectivism, this approach affirms a radical identity between authentic subjectivity and objectivity.[27]

Connaturality or congeniality grounds the joy and peace of conscience as a criterion indicating that conscience is true. The Christian is striving to be a disciple of Jesus, seeking the true and the good. When a proposed course of action is placed before such a person, if the action is in accord with his or her basic thrust, one's inclination will have found its proper object. The person then experiences the joy and peace of having found what he or she had been searching for.

Such peace and joy as a criterion of conscience also coheres with the ethical model of relationality-responsibility with its recognition of the turn to the subject. A deontological model would interpret the criterion in terms of obedience to God's law. The extrinsic teleological model would make the ultimate criterion of true conscience the accomplishment of the greater good.

At times this criterion is somewhat difficult to apply and obviously can be readily abused. The possibility of abuse, however, does not deny the basic validity of the criterion, but does point to the need to recognize this possibility and employ the means to avoid or guard against such abuses. In the light of our stance, there are three possible reasons why this criterion might not function properly: finitude, sinfulness, and a lack of eschatological fullness.

Human beings are finite and limited. We do not see or know all that is involved in any decision and experience only limited aspects of reality. We are all familiar with the experience of looking back at past decisions that we now know were wrong and lamenting that, if we had only known then what we know now, things would have been different. Human sinfulness affects all of us to some extent. My unjustified anger toward a particular person will affect how I treat that person. On a social level, as I cannot in theory accept total nonviolence for nations in this imperfect world, I must accept some theory of justified wars. But why does our country always decide that its wars are just while those of our enemy are unjust? Finally, since we are all pilgrims in this world on the journey of faith, we continually fall short in our multiple relationships. We do not live in the fullness of the final kingdom. As a result, we can at times be deceived into believing that something is compatible with what we are striving to be.

SAFEGUARDS AGAINST ABUSE. In accord with an axiom of the spiritual life, the Christian should take steps to act against specific dangers and pitfalls that might arise. Above all the church community constitutes a very significant antidote against the three generic sources of error in our conscience decisions. However, the church should not be seen merely in terms of a means to help individuals. As I noted in chapter one, we come into the presence of God's salvific gift through Jesus in the Spirit in and through the community of the church.

As a universal community existing in all parts of the world and with a long history, the church community presents a strong antidote against our finitude and limitations. Although I disagree with some approaches taken by John Paul II, I believe he exercises the church's universal petrine office very well when he reminds first world countries of the needs and problems of the two-thirds world. The church, too, is sinful and not yet perfect, but the community strives to be more faithful to the work and word of Jesus and challenges its members in their own lives to be conscious of their sinfulness and strive for an ever deeper relationship with God and others.

There are many ways in which the church carries out its role in forming the conscience of the individual Christian. The experience of the ecclesial community, its liturgical celebrations, teaching, and living witness all contribute to the proper formation of the conscience and also supply some benchmarks and norms that are helpful. The church is also the locus for the proper interpretation of Scripture and this, too, contributes to the work of conscience formation.

The judgment of conscience is made by the individual person who always recognizes herself as belonging to the church and many other communities, especially the fundamental natural communities of family, neighborhoods, and nations. All these relationships contribute to the formation of conscience. The ultimate decision of conscience rests with the individual person who belongs to the community of Jesus' disciples and has other relationships. Three steps are very significant for the proper formation of the person and her or his response in conscience.

First, the fundamental disposition of Christians is openness to the word and call of God. Mary's response to the angel well exemplifies this fundamental openness—be it done to me according to your word. (Luke 1:28) We recognized the fundamental importance of this virtue in chapter five. The relationality-responsibility model reinforces the importance of openness to hear the call of God and act accordingly. Most of us would like to think we are truly open, but in reality many obvious and subtle influences stand in the way of true openness. One of the definitions of sin is to be self-centered. Looking out for myself as "number one" is the most obvious obstacle to true openness to

God's call which is mediated in and through the situation in which I find myself.

Second, theological and philosophical ethicists have proposed various ways over the years to insure that the person does not make self the center of all things and consequently make erroneous moral decisions. These practical proposals can help support the fundamental Christian relationships. The golden rule serves this purpose well. Do unto others as you would have them do unto you. Put yourself in the other's position. That is a practical way of insuring that I do not make easy exceptions for myself. The Kantian categorical imperative and principle of universalization can perform the same practical function.[28] You can do something in this situation if you would allow all other persons in the same situation to do the same.The veil of ignorance proposed in the theory of John Rawls is likewise a good practical way of striving to overcome the danger of self-centeredness.[29] Pretend you do not know what your role is in the community whose proper distribution of benefits and burdens you are discussing. These practical steps help to insure that one is truly open and is not acting out of one-sided individualism or self-centeredness. The third step involves the need to strive to live ever more fully and deeply the Christian life with its basic orientation toward God and its appropriate virtues. This striving is really the whole question of the proper formation of the person. One strives daily to become a good person and a Christian who makes good decisions.

The theory of conscience developed here recognizes the primacy of the subjective but also the importance of the objective. There are no infallible criteria to determine if the decision of conscience is true. But the peace and joy of conscience remains the best criterion. Other criteria involve all the virtues, values, norms, experiences, and examples promoted by the church community and people of good will. The individual decision maker must always be aware of the possibility of deception, lack of openness, and ways of short circuiting the process. But the dangers and possible abuses do not negate the fundamental role of the joy and peace of a good conscience.

The theory of conscience developed here has been based primarily on theological and philosophical foundations, but psychology has also contributed significantly to our understanding of conscience. Two brief comments should be made. First, Freudian psychology has highlighted the role of the superego which can be readily mistaken for the true conscience. In reality the superego, or the internal censor incorporating the command of an extrinsic authority, is directly opposed to the concept of conscience developed here. In theory and especially in practice, one must be aware that the superego is not the true moral conscience.[30] Second, in the past determinists and some psychologists have denied the free decision-making capacity of conscience. But many contemporary psychologists reject the view that we are programmed by our genes, manipulated by unconscious instinctual forces, or blindly responding to environmental stimuli. The findings of these nondeterministic psychologists can contribute much to our understanding of conscience.[31]

MEANING OF SIN

Also related to conscience and especially to the primacy of the subjective pole together with the importance of the objective pole is the question of sin in the Catholic tradition. Recall that one of the primary functions of the moral manuals was to point out acts that were sinful and their degree of sinfulness.

In keeping with its legal model, the manualist approach defines sin as a free transgression of the law of God.[32] A very significant distinction concerns the difference between mortal and venial sin. This distinction is based on the effect produced with regard to grace. Mortal sin turns the person away from God as the ultimate end, brings death to the soul by depriving it of sanctifying grace, and merits everlasting punishment. Venial sin is defined negatively with regard to the same three aspects. Venial sin does not turn the person away from God as the ultimate end, does not bring about the death of the soul by depriving it of sanctifying grace, and does not merit eternal punishment but only temporal punishment.[33]

The manuals generally propose three conditions necessary for a mortal sin. First, grave matter concerns an act or object that involves a grave deformity from the law. Second, full advertence requires that the sinner recognize both the moral malice of the act and its gravity. Third, full consent involves an act of the will which, knowing the malice and gravity of the act, freely determines—either through weakness or malice—to do the wrong act. Some mortal sins are always grave by reason of their objects or because they constitute a grave disorder and insubordination to God, such as sins directly against the three theological virtues. These actions do not admit parvity of matter—to use the technical term. No parvity of matter means that the matter is always grave, and the manuals called these mortal sins *"ex toto genere suo."* According to the manuals all sins against sexuality do not admit parvity of matter. Sometimes the sin is mortal or venial depending on the gravity of the matter involved. Thus, a grave injustice is a mortal sin, but a slight injustice is a venial sin. Some matter is always light and involves only venial sin such as actions involving excesses with regard to a good, for instance, too much sleep.[34]

Notice what is happening here. Strictly speaking the three conditions for mortal sin deal with both the objective aspect (the act) and the subjective aspects (advertence and consent). However, the heavier emphasis is on the objective aspect. Thus, we have mortal sins that are always mortal by reason of their object. The object or the act itself becomes the primary consideration. Strictly speaking, even by their own distinction, the manuals should have spoken about grave matter that is always such and not grave sins. For example, Noldin distinguished between mortal and venial sin based on the degree of opposition to the moral order.[35] However, he should have referred not to mortal or venial sin but to grave or light matter.

The overemphasis on the objective aspect to the extent that mortal sins are considered primarily on the basis of the object or the matter comes from the very nature of the manuals themselves. The manuals arose as a response to the Council of Trent's calling for a yearly confession of mortal sins according to number and species. The species of sin was determined by the object or the matter. The numbers were based on the reality of discrete acts that again put the emphasis on the object or the matter.[36] In discussing various specific acts the manuals focus solely on the matter under consideration. The presumption thus grew that usually the requirements of advertence and consent were present, and that the primary determining factor of mortal sin was grave matter. The neglected emphasis on the subject before Vatican II only exaggerated the importance given to the objective aspect in understanding and determining what constitutes mortal sins.

At the end of the nineteenth century, a very perceptive moral theologian in the United States, the Irish-born, French-educated John B. Hogan recognized the problem in the way the manuals distinguish between mortal and venial sin. Hogan insisted on the need to recognize many gray areas. The distinction between mortal and venial sin is at best rudimentary. Hogan, who served as rector of the seminary in Boston, astutely pointed out long before the renewal of moral theology in the middle of the twentieth century how too often in pastoral ministry the fear of hell connected to mortal sin was used to secure a more prompt and thorough obedience especially to positive laws of the church like Friday abstinence from meat. Even if it were possible to have a clear distinction between mortal and venial sin, this distinction would apply only to the objective side of the issue. But the moral value of human actions is derived primarily from the subjective side—the mental and moral condition of the agent that others can know only in a very imperfect way.[37] Hogan's position was not picked up by other theologians, but, with the renewal of moral theology since Vatican II, his position has become quite commonplace.

Given the primacy of the subjective, one should not refer to external acts as sinful or not, but as right or wrong. At best one could use "sin" analogously to describe the external act alone, but because of past distortions in the Catholic tradition, it is much better to describe the objective act in itself as "right" or "wrong." On the basis of the external act alone, one cannot determine whether or not sin exists. In the light of the relationality-responsibility model, sin is seen in terms of multiple relationships. Mortal sin is the breaking of our relationships with God and others while venial sin weakens these fundamental relationships. On the basis of the external act alone, one can never know whether the relationship with God and others has been severed or not. The manualist approach, with its legal model of sin as an act against the law of God, gave the impression that mortal sin was a rather common occurrence in the Christian life. However, since mortal sin involves the breaking of the relationship of friendship with God and others, it cannot be that frequent an occurrence. Thus the proper understanding of sin, like the proper understanding of conscience, gives primacy to the subjective aspect while still recognizing the importance of the objective. Sin refers primarily to the breaking of our multiple relationships with God, neighbor, world, and self.

THE "LAW OF GROWTH"

Some contemporary Catholic theologians have developed what has been called the law of gradualness or the law of growth. This concept owes much to the thought of Alphonsus Liguori.[38] The great accomplishment of Alphonsus was to bring peace to moral theology after the struggles between the rigorists and the laxists, the probabiliorists and the probabilists in the seventeenth and eighteenth centuries. Above all, his pastoral prudence guided him in his casuistry and discussion of particular cases. Alphonsus's significant pastoral and practical contributions were connected with his recognition of the primacy of the subjective pole without denying the reality of the objective pole in morality. One very significant controversy in his time concerned the possibility of invincible ignorance of the natural law. Could a person be ignorant of the demands of natural law and not be guilty of sin? The rigorists and one-sided objectivists denied the possibility of invincible ignorance of the natural law. Alphonsus, with his greater recognition of the role of the subject, defended the possibility that a person could be ignorant of the more remote aspects of the natural law without any guilt or culpability.[39] Recall how Alphonsus also moved beyond Aquinas in recognizing that a wrong act done in invincible ignorance was not only not imputed to the person but could also be good and meritorious.[40] His insight into the primacy of the subjective was intimately connected with his own pastoral prudence. This insight has been developed by some contemporary theologians into what has been called, perhaps unfortunately, the law of growth.

Bernard Häring, a spiritual son of Alphonsus, the founder of the Redemptorists, has developed this insight to support an important distinction between the work of moral theology and the work of pastoral counseling. Invincible ignorance refers to the one area of the lack of knowledge, but in the light of modern psychology an analogous approach refers to the existential state of the whole person. Häring correctly insists on the need for growth for all Christians as we are called to holiness, but there can be another implication of the need for growth. An individual might be existentially incapable of fulfilling the requirements of objective morality at a particular time in certain circumstances. In doing all that one existentially can do and in remaining open to a greater fullness, the person's act is actually formally good despite the material evil involved. (This helpful distinction between formal and material evil comes from the manuals themselves.) Pastoral counseling deals with a particular person in an existential situation and thus differs from moral theology. Prudence is most important in dealing on the level of pastoral counseling.[41] Häring applies this theory to a pastoral counseling case dealing with abortion in a very distressing situation.

In some ways the hierarchical magisterium itself has recognized the distinction between moral theology and pastoral counseling. The papal encyclical *Humanae vitae*, after dealing with "Doctrinal Principles" in Section II, discusses "Pastoral Directives" in Section III. This section does not explicitly accept the distinction between levels of moral theology and pastoral counseling, but it does at least implicitly recognize that those who practice contraception might not always be subjectively culpable.[42] Some episcopal conferences in their commentary on *Humanae vitae* developed these pastoral aspects more in the direction of the distinction between the levels of moral theology and pastoral counseling. The French bishops, for example, insist that contraception "can never be a good. It is always a disorder, but this disorder is not always culpable."[43] One resolution of the 1980 Synod of Bishops reminds pastoral ministers to keep in mind the law of gradualness in dealing with married couples while reconizing that there can be no false dichotomy between Catholic teaching and pastoral practice.[44] Pope John Paul II in *Familiaris consortio* somewhat defensively warns against confusing "the law of gradualness" with the "gradualness of the law."[45] The primacy of the subjective grounds the distinction between moral theology and pastoral counseling, but the importance of the objective aspect calls for great prudence on the level of pastoral counseling because of the material evil involved.

Conscience and moral decision making are very important realities in all ethical theories. The dilemma of conscience is recognized by almost everyone—I must follow my conscience, but my conscience might be wrong. This chapter has surveyed, analyzed, and criticized the Catholic tradition in the area of conscience and decision making and proposed a holistic theory of conscience. Both the subject pole and the object pole of morality have a role to play in conscience decisions. The most adequate criterion of a good conscience is one's peace and joy. This priority of the subject, while not negating the importance of the object, points again to the primary moral role of the Christian's basic orientation and virtues.

N O T E S

1. For a manualist approach to conscience, see Benedictus H. Merkelbach, *Summa theologiae moralis*, vol. 1, *De principiis*, 10th ed. (Bruges, Belgium: Desclée de Brouwer, 1959), pp. 186–99; I. Aertnys and C. Damen, *Theologia moralis*, 2 vols., ed. J. Visser, 17th ed. (Rome: Marietti, 1956), 1, pp. 75–89; Zalba, *Theologiae moralis summa*, 1, pp. 239–63.

2. Vereecke, *Ockham à Saint Alphonse*, pp. 553–60.

3. C. A. Pierce, *Conscience in the New Testament* (London: SCM, 1955).

4. Ibid., p. 109.

5. Ceslaus Spicq, *Théologie morale du Nouveau Testament*, 2 vols. (Paris: J. Galbada, 1965), 2, p. 603; Philippe Delhaye, *The Christian Conscience* (New York: Desclée, 1968), pp. 37–50.

6. For the development of this teaching in the scholastic period, see Odon Lottin, *Psychologie et morale aux XIIe et XIIIe siècles*, vol. 2 (Louvain, Belgium: Abbaye du Mont César, 1948), pp. 103–350. Lottin's six volumes are the classical study of Catholic moral theology at this time.

7. J. de Blic, "Syndérèse ou conscience?" *Revue d'ascétique et de mystique* 25 (1949): 146–57.

8. Hieronymus Noldin, *Summa theologiae moralis*, vol. 1, *De principiis*, ed. Godefridus Heinzel, 33rd ed. (Innsbruck, Austria: Rauch, 1960), p. 198.

9. Zalba, *Theologiae moralis summa*, 1, p. 242.

10. Aquinas, *IaIIae*, q.58, a.5; *IIaIIae*, q.45, a.2.

11. Joseph de Guibert, *The Theology of the Spiritual Life* (New York: Sheed and Ward, 1956), pp. 129–44; Jacques Guillet, et al., *Discernment of Spirits* (Collegeville, Minn.: Liturgical, 1970). This book is the authorized English translation of the article in the *Dictionnaire de spiritualité*.

12. de Guibert, *Theology of the Spiritual Life*, pp. 132–37.

13. See Jules J. Toner, *A Commentary on Saint Ignatius' Rules for the Discernment of Spirits: A Guide to the Principles and Practice* (St. Louis, Mo.: Institute of Jesuit Sources, 1982); Toner, *Discerning God's Will: Ignatius of Loyola's Teaching on Christian Decision Making* (St. Louis, Mo.: Institute of Jesuit Sources, 1991).

14. de Guibert, *Theology of the Spiritual Life*, pp. 131–44.

15. Ibid., pp. 139–40.

16. Jacques Maritain, *Man and the State* (Chicago: University of Chicago Press, 1956), pp. 84–94. For Thomas Aquinas's understanding of prudence, see especially *IaIIae*, q.57; *IIaIIae*, q.47–56. For an often cited commentary and explanation of Aquinas, see Josef Pieper, *The Four Cardinal Virtues* (Notre Dame, Ind.: University of Notre Dame Press, 1966), pp. 3–40.

17. For an interpretation of prudence in Aquinas which argues for the primacy of prudence over natural law, see Daniel Mark Nelson, *The Priority of Prudence: Virtue and Natural Law in Thomas Aquinas and the Importance for Modern Ethics* (University Park, Pa.: Pennsylvania State University Press, 1992).

18. Gilson, *Christian Philosophy*, p. 288.

19. Pieper, *Four Cardinal Virtues*, p. 8.

20. Merkelbach, *De principiis*, p. 102.

21. Daniel C. Maguire, *The Moral Choice*, (Garden City, N.Y.: Doubleday, 1978), pp. 128–88.

22. See the perceptive title of the popular moral theology textbook by Richard M. Gula, *Reason Informed by Faith: Foundations of Catholic Morality* (New York: Paulist Press, 1984).

23. For Aquinas's understanding of the gifts of the Holy Spirit and their role in moral life, see *IaIIae*, q.68.

24. Sidney Callahan, *In Good Conscience: Reason and Emotion in Moral Decision Making* (San Francisco: Harper, 1991).

25. Ibid., pp. 75–94.

26. Bernard Lonergan, *Insight: A Study of Human Understanding* (New York: Philosophical Library, 1957), pp. 279–316. Lonergan sees these judgments made in the context of three conversions of the self-transcending subject—intellectual, moral, and religious; see Bernard Lonergan, *Method in Theology* (New York: Herder and Herder, 1972), pp. 103–05, 239–41.

27. Lonergan, *Insight*, pp. 279–316.

28. For an introduction to Kant's ethics with emphasis on his political theory, see Sullivan, *An Introduction to Kant's Ethics.*

29. John Rawls, *A Theory of Justice* (Cambridge, Mass.: Belknap Press of Harvard University Press, 1971), pp. 136–42.

30. Gula, *Reason Informed by Faith*, pp. 123–30. For an appealing holistic theory of conscience with similarities to the approach taken here, see Richard M. Gula, *Moral Discernment* (New York: Paulist, 1997).

31. Callahan, *In Good Conscience.*

32. Noldin, *De principiis*, p. 266.

33. Ibid., pp. 270–78.

34. Zalba, *Theologiae moralis summa*, 1, pp. 618–25.

35. Noldin, *De principiis*, pp. 280–88.

36. Zalba, *Theologiae moralis summa*, 1, p 272.

37. John B. Hogan, *Clerical Studies* (Boston: Marlier, Callanan, 1898), pp. 257–59.

38. For the most recent biography of St. Alphonsus, see Frederick M. Jones, *Alphonsus de Liguori: The Saint of Bourbon Naples, 1696–1787* (Westminister, Md.: Christian Classics, 1992). For my fuller discussion of the role and contribution of Alphonsus, see Curran, *The Origins of Moral Theology in the United States*, pp. 27–39.

39. Charles E. Curran, *Invincible Ignorance of the Natural Law According to Saint Alphonsus* (Rome: Accademia Alfonsiana, 1961).

40. Vereecke, *Ockham à Saint Alphonsus*, pp. 555–60.

41. Bernard Häring, "A Theological Evaluation," in *The Morality of Abortion: Legal and Historical Perspectives*, ed. John T. Noonan, Jr. (Cambridge, Mass.: Harvard University Press, 1970), pp. 139–42; Häring, *Shalom: Peace—The Sacrament of Reconciliation* (New York: Farrar, Straus, and Giroux, 1968), pp. 39–49.

42. Paul VI, *Humanae vitae*, nn. 19–31, pp. 12–19.

43. William H. Shannon, *The Lively Debate: Responses to Humanae Vitae* (New York: Sheed and Ward, 1970), p. 136.

44. *National Catholic Reporter* 16 (December 12, 1980): 22.

45. Pope John Paul II, *The Role of the Christian Family in the Modern World: Familiaris Consortio* (Boston: St. Paul, 1982), n. 34, p. 56.

8

Church Teaching

The moral life and formation of its members constitute a large and essential part of the reality and meaning of the church. A pre-Vatican II theology distinguished between the teaching church (the hierarchical teaching office) and the learning church (all others). Most theologians today recognize that the whole church is both teaching and learning.[1] In light of the Constitution on the Church of Vatican II this chapter will consider first the role of the whole church, and then that of the hierarchical teaching office with regard to moral teaching and learning.

TOTAL CHURCH AS TEACHER

The total church and all its members are involved in teaching and learning the theory and practice of the moral life. The Holy Spirit guides the church in this mission, and every individual Christian through baptism shares in the threefold office of Jesus as priest, teacher, and ruler.

In going about its teaching and learning function with regard to the moral life, the whole church needs to be cognizant of the sources of moral wisdom and knowledge. In particular, the church will rely heavily on Scripture, recognizing both its importance but also its limitations in arriving at moral understandings. Tradition, reason, and experience are also necessary means for the church to use in striving to know and teach the Christian moral life.

The whole church must recognize the various levels involved in the moral life. The basic reality of conversion and continuing conversion constitutes the most fundamental level of the subject pole of morality. The proper characteristics of persons and the manifold Christian virtues must also be learned and taught. The object pole includes values, principles, and norms. The whole church can never reduce morality only to the comparatively small area of specific moral norms. Likewise the whole church helps the individual in concrete decision making.

How does the total church carry out its function of learning and teaching morality? A Catholic and inclusive approach recognizes many different ways in which the church fulfills its learning and teaching function. In the Catholic tradition the liturgy always plays a central role. The sacramental celebration of the saving encounter of God with human beings through the community of the church involves both God's gift and our response. The Christian is called to live the life of discipleship. The baptismal promises commit the Christian to live in accord with the newly given life-giving Spirit. Above all, the eucharist calls all participants to share bread and wine, love and life, mercy and forgiveness with one another—especially the poor and the needy—in response to Jesus who gave himself to us not because of our merits and accomplishments but because God in her graciousness has made a covenant with us. The eucharist is the covenant meal that celebrates this reality and renews our commitment to live in its accord.

The liturgical celebration exists in intimate connection with the daily life of the community of the baptized. Liturgy and life can never be separated. The witness of the members of the church furnishes an important way for the whole church to teach and learn the Christian moral life. From small ordinary aspects of daily life to the heroic actions of Christians in very difficult and trying circumstances, other Christians show us what it means to be a follower of Jesus. In accord with the contemporary emphasis on praxis, our involvement in what has traditionally been called the spiritual and corporal works of mercy brings us also to a better understanding of the reality of the Christian moral life. The church has always recognized the basic teaching role of the family as instructors in religious education.

The church also employs all the other teaching means at its disposal—preaching, catechizing, educating, and inviting all Christians to fully share and participate in the moral life of the community. All the members of the church in many different ways contribute to the learning and teaching of the Christian moral life. The activity of the whole church and all its members constitutes the most significant and important teaching function in the church. However, this teaching role receives little attention, in part because there is no controversy surrounding it.

THE HIERARCHICAL TEACHING OFFICE

In the Roman Catholic tradition a special teaching function has been given to pope and bishops to safeguard, protect, and properly develop the faith and moral life of the community of believers.[2] However, at the present time as John Paul II has said, "a genuine crisis" exists in the church on moral teachings. Especially in the last two centuries, the popes have proposed moral teachings regarding many specific issues involved in human life. But now, according to the pope, a new situation has arisen within the church with regard to the church's moral teaching. It is no longer a matter of limited and occasional dissent but an overall and systematic calling into question of traditional moral teaching which even exists in seminaries and theologates. John Paul II wrote his encyclical *Veritatis splendor* with the express purpose of dealing with this crisis.[3]

In recognizing the crisis over dissent from, or disagreement with, some hierarchical church teaching, the pope calls attention to a phenomenon that has often been mentioned in the secular press. Many Catholics in theory and in practice disagree with some hierarchical teachings dealing especially with sexual matters such as contraception, divorce, and homosexuality. Sociological surveys indicate the same reality to which the pope has called attention.[4] The contemporary situation is thus generally recognized, but the important question is how to evaluate this reality.

The discussion centers on the moral teaching role of the hierarchical magisterium (teaching office) in the Catholic Church. The issues are very complex and involve more that moral theology. The primary consideration is ecclesiological—the understanding of the church and the place of the hierarchical magisterium's moral teaching in the church. This book cannot develop a full ecclesiology or even a systematic theological understanding of the hierarchical teaching office in the church. Many ecclesiological considerations will be presumed in this chapter to explain and develop the role of the hierarchical teaching office in moral matters. The question is also intimately linked with the role of theologians in the church and how the theological enterprise and the hierarchical magisterium are related.

The question deals with the "magisterium" which only since the nineteenth century has been regularly understood as the body of pastors authoritatively exercising the function of teaching. This comparatively recent usage of the term is quite significant. The term magisterium in classical Latin means one who is an authority or a master in a particular area; for example, a commander of troops. In the Middle Ages it often referred to the role of teacher. Thomas Aquinas used the term to refer to the teaching role of both university professors and bishops. But in the last two centuries the term magisterium has been used to designate the office holders themselves—the pope and bishops who teach in the church.[5] I will generally accept this existing terminology with one significant modification. This book will use the term papal or hierarchical magisterium to refer to the pope and bishops who exercise this teaching function, precisely because the teaching function of the whole church is broader than the magisterial role of popes and bishops.

Our consideration assumes from ecclesiology that there exists an authoritative teaching role for bishops and pope in the Catholic Church that also involves moral matters. The problem resides in determining how this role is carried out and its precise function. Various distinctions have been proposed in this regard concerning the hierarchical teaching office. The major distinction in the exercise of the hierarchical magisterium is between the infallible and the noninfallible exercise of the hierarchical magisterium. Infallible teaching on the basis of the gift of the Holy Spirit claims to be free from error even though the teaching may not be perfect. Noninfallible teaching does not claim to be free from error even though it enjoys the assistance of the Holy Spirit. The infallible magisterium is exercised in an extraordinary or in an ordinary way. The extraordinary or solemn infallible hierarchical magisterium includes the definitive teaching of an ecumenical council or of the pope in an *ex cathedra* pronouncement on faith and morals. In *ex cathedra* pronouncements the pope uses a solemn wording indicating the infallible nature of the teaching. The ordinary infallible hierarchical magisterium involves the moral unanimity of all the bishops in the world down through the centuries together with the bishop of Rome on a matter of faith and morals to be held definitively by all the faithful. This is often called the ordinary universal magisterium.

The noninfallible exercise of the hierarchical magisterium involves the teaching of councils, the pope, and bishops. The most prominent aspect here is the noninfallible papal teaching which today is often called the ordinary papal magisterium, although this terminology was first proposed in an official church document only in Pius XII's encyclical *Humani generis* in 1950.[6] However, in this understanding of what is extraordinary and what is ordinary, different authors have used varying terminology at times. Despite some variations in terms, such basic distinctions have been accepted officially by the hierarchical magisterium and by theologians as well.[7] These basic distinctions are necessary to adequately evaluate and assess the proper role of the hierarchical magisterium in moral matters.

PRE-VATICAN II DEVELOPMENTS OF THE PAPAL MORAL MAGISTERIUM. Significant developments occurred in the Catholic Church with regard to the hierarchical magisterium's role in the church in general and in the area of morality in particular in the period preceding Vatican II. The involvement of the ordinary noninfallible papal magisterium in moral matters dramatically increased. The first detailed involvement in particular moral issues by the authoritative teaching role of the Holy Office, an office or dicastery of the Roman Curia now called the Congregation for the Doctrine of the Faith, occurred during the seventeenth-century controversy between laxists and tutiorists (see chapter three). In 1679 under Innocent XI the Holy Office condemned sixty-five propositions associated with moral laxism. Among the condemned laxist positions were the following: It is sufficient to elicit an act of faith only once in a lifetime. We can satisfy the precept of loving our neighbor by only external acts.[8] In 1690 the Holy Office under Alexander VIII condemned thirty propositions associated with the Jansenist position. One such proposition maintained that those who do not have in them the most uncontaminated pure love of God are to be excluded from Holy Communion.[9] Thus began a new level of involvement of the Holy Office in deciding the morality of particular questions, which continued to increase in the nineteenth and twentieth centuries.

In the nineteenth century moral questions were often sent by individual bishops to the pope and the congregations of the Roman Curia—the various offices that the pope uses to carry on the business of the church. Conflict situations involving abortion illustrate this recourse to Rome and Rome's responses to the particular moral dilemmas that were proposed.[10] Craniotomy as a means to save the life of the mother by crushing the skull of the fetus in the womb had become medically acceptable to many doctors in the nineteenth century. A question concerning the practice was proposed to the Sacred Penitentiary. The Penitentiary is the Roman congregation that deals with internal forum matters or questions of conscience. On September 2, 1869, the Sacred Penitentiary responded by advising the petitioner to consult the approved authors for an answer. "The authors" in this traditional phrase means the authors of moral theology manuals and cases of conscience that were used in seminaries and theologates. In the light of this response some theologians argued in favor of craniotomy on the basis that the fetus in this case is an unjust aggressor against the life of the mother.

On May 31, 1884, the Holy Office responded to the archbishop of Lyons in France that it cannot safely be taught that craniotomy is permitted to save the life of the mother. Some asked whether this response "was to be considered a doctrinal and definitive response or only disciplinary and prudential." General agreement arose that the response was doctrinal and "solved" the controversy over craniotomy in the Catholic Church.[11]

Other issues involving surgical procedures and pregnancy soon came to the fore. Six sets of cases were submitted by the bishop of Cambrai to the Holy See. In 1889, the year after their submission, the Holy Office responded, not with a solution to the individual cases as such, but with a principle—any direct killing of the fetus or the mother is wrong. T. Lincoln Bouscaren writing in 1944 comments that as a result of this response, "The question of the possible licitness of direct abortion in any form is thus, for Catholic moralists and physicians, forever closed."[12]

However, the response raised the obvious question of what is a direct killing. Some theologians claimed that to remove the fetus from the womb did not directly kill the fetus even though it would not be able to survive outside the womb. Soon this case was sent to Rome, and the Holy Office responded on July 24, 1895, that this medical action could not be safely used in accord with the earlier two responses. Then another related issue arose. In 1893, the *American Ecclesiastical Review* published discussions about ectopic pregnancies by eminent physicians and four moral theologians from around the world, including Aloysius Sabetti, an Italian-born Jesuit teaching moral theology at the Jesuit theologate in Woodstock, Maryland.[13] Others also discussed the same question. As might be expected, this question was also sent to the Holy Office. The 1898 response was somewhat guarded, but, in 1902, the Holy Office responded that one could not remove a nonviable ectopic pregnancy from the mother to save her life. The question was later solved by saying that the fallopian tube containing an ectopic pregnancy can be removed because it is infected and constitutes a danger for the mother. In this case the abortion is indirect.[14]

A quick historical overview of questions relating to abortion near the end of the nineteenth century shows how theologians and bishops appealed to Rome to respond to their doubts and provide them with answers that would definitively solve the question. One Catholic theologian raised some questions about this practice of recourse to Rome. The strongly propapal and neoscholastic professor of moral theology at the Catholic University of America, Thomas Bouquillon, cautioned against the abuse of referring questions to Roman congregations for decisions when there was no necessity for so doing. Bouquillon feared that moral theologians were relying either on extrinsic probabilism or on authoritative decisions from Rome to solve problems rather than doing the hard work of trying to ascertain the moral truth.[15]

In the nineteenth and twentieth centuries the Roman congregations, especially the Sacred Penitentiary and the Holy Office, responded to a number of questions about birth control dealing explicitly with questions of a wife cooperating in the marital act when the husband will withdraw and whether or not the confessor should question married penitents about the practice of birth control. The birth control movement began to grow in the early nineteenth century, and one would have expected some responses from Rome. The Catholic moral teaching against birth control remained the same, but the papacy showed no special inclination to combat birth control and also showed a surprising tolerance of the good faith of Catholic spouses. However, after 1876, the pope and the bishops throughout the world vigorously reacted to the growing international movement promoting birth control. The growing reaction culminated in the 1930 encyclical *Casti connubii* strongly condemning artificial contraception for spouses.[16]

Throughout the twentieth century, the Holy Office and Sacred Penitentiary continued to respond to moral issues and also to issue decrees and declarations concerning them. Papal teaching on specific moral issues reached its zenith with the many pronouncements of Pius XII (1939–1958) in regard to questions of medical ethics. Pius XII frequently addressed medical groups and was often asked to consider specific moral questions arising in medicine. The pope not only addressed Catholic groups but was often asked to speak to secular medical associations and groups especially when they happened to be meeting in Rome. Within a three year span, the pope spoke to the following groups: The First International Conference on the Histopathology of the Nervous System (1952), the Fifth International Congress of Psychotherapy and Clinical Psychology (1953), the Twenty-Sixth Congress of the Italian Society of Urology (1953), and the Eighth Assembly of the World Medical Association (1954).[17] In the process of talking to these groups and through other addresses, Pius XII considered many of the significant, biomedical moral issues including abortion, anesthesia to the dying, artificial insemination, blood transfusions, care for the dying, cosmetic surgery, experimentation, and extraordinary and nonnecessary means to preserve life. There were comparatively few issues of the times that were not directly addressed by this pope. A 1962 American manual of medical ethics in the index lists almost forty different issues that the pope addressed.[18] Thus before Vatican II (1962-1965) the papal teaching office had become heavily involved in proposing authoritative solutions to many particular problems. Catholics in general and moral theologians in particular expected the pope to solve authoritatively many of the moral issues facing human beings and society at large.

THE BROADER PRE-VATICAN II CONTEXT. This unprecedented growth in papal teaching on specific moral issues did not occur in a vacuum but must be understood in the light of the growing importance given to the papal office in the Catholic Church in the nineteenth and twentieth centuries. Historians often refer to the beginning of the modern papacy in the course of the nineteenth century, when the supreme role and power of the papacy within the church were highlighted and emphasized. In this period, the papacy became more monarchical and powerful than ever before in the history of the Catholic Church and the papacy.[19] Many factors influenced this development in the nineteenth and twentieth centuries.

Before the nineteenth century, the papacy was a spiritual and secular power engaged in relationships and power struggles on many different fronts. Gallicanism describes the multifaceted movement to limit the papacy in both its secular and spiritual aspects which began in France in the thirteenth century and continued until the nineteenth century. There were different degrees of spiritual Gallicanism but all sought to enhance the role of the church in France and limit the spiritual power of Rome.[20] In the eighteenth century Febronianism in Germany and Josephinism in Austria also tried to subordinate the church to national interests.[21]

The nineteenth century saw a strong reaction to such movements for more local church authority, and, in particular, the rise of ultramontanism, an intellectual and political movement which again had significant spiritual overtones. The word ultramontanism, meaning "beyond the mountains," refers to a movement in European countries beyond the Alps, especially in the north. The proponents of ultramontanism in the nineteenth century saw the papacy as the strongest defense against newer political, philosophical, and scientific developments that were threatening the older order. But the movement also had an important spillover in the spiritual realm. Ultramontanism gave greater importance and significance to the spiritual role of the papacy at the expense of local churches. Even more politically liberal Catholics such as Felicité Lammenais, whose thought was ultimately condemned by the papacy, supported a stronger spiritual role for the papacy. By the end of the nineteenth century ultramontanism triumphed with the strengthening of the spiritual role of the papacy in every respect.[22]

One slice of history at this time illustrates the stakes involved in this strengthening of the papacy. In 1829 with the assistance of political conservatives such as Klemens Metternich of Austria, Mauro Cappellari, a Camaldolese monk, was elected pope and took the name of Gregory XVI. He had earlier written (1799) a famous book in Italian— *The Triumph of the Holy See and of the Church against the Assaults of the Innovators Withstood and Defeated by Their Very Own Weapons.*[23] The book develops the power and role of the church over the power of the state. Christ established the church as a monarchy. While the forms of civil government are obviously subject to change, the church's own structure comes from God and cannot be changed. The church must be independent of the civil power, and the pope enjoys infallibility when he speaks as head of the church but not as a private theologian.

Gregory XVI (d. 1846) in theory and practice set the stage for the monarchical papacy which came to the fore in the nineteenth and twentieth centuries. In the latter part of the nineteenth century popes had lost their temporal power with the overthrow of the papal states. Ironically, the loss of temporal power resulted in more emphasis on the papacy's spiritual power and role. Gregory's successor, Pius IX, convened the First Vatican Council which defined the infallibility of the pope. The Council was cut short because of the danger of military attack against Rome and never considered a total theology of the church as had been its original agenda, but dealt only with the role of the papacy. As a result the monarchical nature of the church under the papacy became the primary way of understanding the internal life of the church.[24] Vatican II, with its emphasis on the role of bishops and the local church together with the collegiality of all the bishops with the bishop of Rome, would later correct the monarchical overemphasis on the role of the papacy in the church.

Thus the nineteenth century Catholic Church was very defensive about new developments that were occurring in the world and affecting the church. Opposition to the ideas and practices of the Enlightenment characterized the nineteenth-century papacy. In his encyclical *Mirari vos* in 1832, Gregory XVI condemned modern liberties including religious liberty and the separation of church and state.[25] In 1864, his successor, Pius IX, issued the *Syllabus of Errors* which condemned eighty modern errors affecting the church. Among these errors were pantheism, naturalism, relativism, and political liberalism. The Catholic Church could not be reconciled with contemporary liberal culture.[26]

The condemnation of modernism by Pius X in 1907 emphasized the defensive mentality in the church and the unwillingness to dialogue with contemporary thought.[27] Some Catholic scholars had begun to appeal to contemporary ideas in their approach to Scripture, tradition, ecclesiology, and philosophy by giving greater importance to historicity and development. In a sense these thinkers were truly wrestling with modernity. The term and common understanding of modernism come primarily from papal condemnations. The basic charge was that modernists often went too far in their embrace of modern ideas and repudiated truths of the faith related to the inspiration and inerrancy of Scripture, the meaning of the evolution of dogma, the reality of Christ, the very constitution of the church, and the immutability of religious teaching. At this same time, the Biblical Commission condemned in general the use of historical criticism with regard to Scripture and insisted, for example, on the literal historical sense of the first three chapters of Genesis.[28]

The complex story of modernism cannot be told here.[29] There were some extreme tendencies in some modernists, but the need to dialogue with contemporary thought was later basically accepted by Vatican II. The condemnation of modernism, the need for all clerics to take an oath against modernism, the establishment of vigilance committees in dioceses, and the unwillingness of the Biblical Commission to accept the use of the historical method all contributed to a very defensive attitude toward theological renewal or development. The neoscholastic emphasis on essentialism and unchanging metaphysics had no room for historical consciousness or the move to the subject. The condemnation and investigations of some scholars created a climate that effectively cut off creative theological thinking in the first part of this century. The atmosphere created by these condemnations and actions early in the twentieth century continued down to the time of Vatican II. Although some interesting theological stirrings did occur as time went on, Catholic theology in general and moral theology in particular were at a low ebb at this time, too often merely repeating the presentations of the manualists. Manualistic theology reigned supreme and creativity was suspect. Conformity, continuity, and the handing on of the unchanging tradition characterized Catholic thought and theology.

The Catholic Church was thus more authoritarian, more defensive, and more centralized in the twentieth century than it had ever been in its history. The papacy, operating in a monarchical way, governed the whole church and gave the church its direction and ethos. Developing technologies in transportation and communication fostered the move toward greater papal centralization in the church.

Given this background, one can better appreciate the important role assigned to papal moral teaching in the church and the authoritative character of such teaching during this period. As the nineteenth and twentieth centuries progressed, the hierarchical teaching role took on a greater juridical coloring with the teaching role often seen in terms of the power of jurisdiction.[30] What is the precise authority of the ordinary papal magisterium in moral matters? Pius XII's 1950 encyclical *Humani generis* deals precisely with the authority of the ordinary papal magisterium as distinguished from the extraordinary, *ex cathedra*, infallible papal magisterium. These ordinary teachings do not involve the supreme power of the papal magisterium, but they still demand assent. The words of Jesus in Luke 10:16 also apply to the ordinary papal magisterium—He who hears you, hears me. When the pope goes out of his way to speak on a controverted subject, the subject can no longer be regarded as a matter for free debate among theologians.[31] In 1952 Franz Hürth, the influential Roman Jesuit moral theologian, discussed the proper response of Catholics to what the pope teaches in an address or allocution, which is a lesser type of document than an encyclical and the format in which most of Pius XII's medical moral teaching appeared. In such cases the pope is speaking in an official capacity and not simply as a private teacher, but he is not teaching in the full and highest degree of his teaching office. The faithful must give internal and external assent to such teaching. It must be admitted and held as true but not with an absolute and irreformable assent.[32] Thus in the middle of the twentieth century the ordinary papal magisterium, more frequently than ever in the past, proposed moral teachings on specific issues, and these teachings were to be accepted by all Catholics.

VATICAN II. The Constitution on the Church (*Lumen gentium*) of Vatican II dealt with the question of authoritative church teaching and the proper response of the Catholic faithful. Vatican II repeated what had become the standard understanding in the twentieth-century manuals of dogmatic theology. To infallible teaching, the faithful owe the assent of faith. To noninfallible teaching, the faithful owe the religious *obsequium* of will and intellect.[33] *Obsequium* has been translated as submission, allegiance, or respect.[34] Vatican II thus simply repeats the words that had become standard but only in the twentieth century.

However, the historical background of the Constitution on the Church indicates two points that help interpret what was said. First, the fathers of the council rejected the original proposed schema on the church which, among other things, included the sentence from *Humani generis* that whenever the pope in his ordinary magisterium goes out of his way to speak on a controverted issue, it is no longer a matter for free debate among theologians. The final document does not include this sentence found in *Humani generis*.[35]

Second, the issue of dissent or not accepting such an authoritative noninfallible teaching was raised in discussions of the council.[36] One proposed emendation (*modus* 159) raised the case of an educated or knowledgeable person (*eruditus quidam*) who cannot give internal assent to a noninfallible teaching. The council's Doctrinal Commission responded that the approved theological explanations should be consulted. Another emendation (*modus* 161) wanted the document to point out that after such a teaching, there was still freedom to pursue further investigation. The Doctrinal Commission recognized that observation as true but concluded that it did not need to be brought up at this time.

In the light of the first response, what were these approved theological explanations and what did they say? They are the positions of the authors of manuals in dogmatic theology dealing with ecclesiology. In general these manualists recognized the assent of faith to infallible teaching as absolute because the motive of faith is the unfailing authority of God. The religious *obsequium*, however, which is owed to noninfallible teaching rests on the authority of the teaching office. Such an assent is thus conditional even though most manualists thought it was morally but not absolutely certain. Some manualists discussed the nature of this condition. All admitted a presumption in favor of authoritative noninfallible teaching as true, but some recognized that past papal teachings had been wrong and later corrected. Ludwig Lercher went further than the others by saying that ordinarily the Holy Spirit protects the church from error through assisting the pope, but it is possible that the Holy Spirit could protect the church from error by guiding others to detect error in the papal teaching. The small print in the manuals recognizes the comparatively rare, but real, possibility of the legitimacy of disagreeing from such teaching. However, in the defensive and more authoritarian atmosphere of a monarchical papacy in the early and middle twentieth century, this possibility of dissent had been neglected and forgotten.

The Constitution on the Church of Vatican II definitely changed the primacy of the institutional model in the church and the monarchical understanding of papacy that had been so strong in the earlier part of the twentieth century. Yes, the church is an institution, but this aspect is not the only or even the most important model of the church. *Lumen gentium* in its first chapter describes the church primarily as a mystery not an institution. The second chapter understands the church as the community or the people of God. In the original proposal the hierarchy was to be considered in the second chapter, but then all agreed that the hierarchy exists to the serve the people of God who are the church. The hierarchical office is discussed in the third chapter.[37] The council emphasizes the role of the local bishop and the local church and also the collegiality of all the bishops together with the bishop of Rome in their common solicitude for the church universal. Such an approach superseded the concept of a monarchical papacy which had flourished in theory and even more so in the practice and general understanding of most Catholics before Vatican II.

The council recognized that the Holy Spirit fulfills its teaching role, not only through the hierarchical teaching office, but also in other ways. Through baptism all Christians share in the threefold function of Jesus as priest, teacher, and ruler. The Holy Spirit distributes special graces and gifts among the faithful of every rank. These charismatic gifts are to be used for the good of the total Christian community. The body of the faithful, anointed as they are by the Holy One, cannot err in matters of belief.[38] The Declaration on Religious Liberty acknowledged the contemporary consciousness and demand for responsible use of freedom including religious freedom. The council declares these desires to be greatly in accord with truth and justice.[39] In other words, the fathers of the council learned their new teaching on religious liberty from the peoples' experience.

Vatican II made Catholics more conscious of the possibility and even need for change in the church. Not only did great changes occur in liturgy and pastoral practice, but also with regard to significant teachings such as religious liberty, the relationship between the Catholic

Church and other churches, and the understanding of Scripture and tradition and their role in the life of the church.[40] Such an approach to change made people more conscious of the changes that had already occurred in authoritative teachings in the past on subjects such as torture, usury, slavery, and the Catholic understanding of sexuality. Thus Vatican II in many ways contributed to a more nuanced interpretation of the role of the ordinary papal magisterium in moral matters.

HUMANAE VITAE. The role of the ordinary papal magisterium in moral matters came to the fore in the discussion over Paul VI's 1968 encyclical *Humanae vitae,* which reaffirmed the papal condemnation of artificial contraception for spouses. Birth control was the most talked about issue in Roman Catholicism in the middle 1960s. In accord with the pre-Vatican II atmosphere, no Catholic theologian explicitly questioned the papal teaching before 1963. In that year John XXIII formed a small group to study the matter—The Pontifical Commission for the Study of Population, Family, and Birth, but he died before the group had its first meeting in October 1963. Paul VI continued the commission and continually increased its membership. In June 1964 Paul VI publicly announced the existence of the commission but maintained that the present teaching of the church was valid and binding. Consideration of the issue was removed from the Vatican Council debates and left with the pope and his commission. Meanwhile the debate grew ever more intense in Catholic circles. The commission met on five occasions, with the last meeting taking place over an extended period of time from April to June 1966. In April 1967, the *National Catholic Reporter* and *Le Monde* published documents showing that the majority of the commission favored a change in the teaching.[41]

On July 29, 1968, Paul VI released his encyclical *Humanae vitae* in which he reiterated the teaching that "every action, which either in anticipation of the conjugal act, or in its accomplishment, or in the development of the natural consequences, proposes either as an end or as a means, to render procreation impossible" is morally wrong.[42] The pope stated that the conclusions of the commission could not be definitive or dispense him from his own examination, thus implying that he disagreed with them. The pope then goes on to give the primary reason for his teaching. Some of the proposed solutions had "departed from the moral teaching on marriage proposed with constant firmness by the teaching authority of the church."[43] The encyclical develops the reasons against contraception,[44] but the pope's own words reveal that his position rests primarily on the fact that the teaching authority of the church has constantly and firmly taught this position. The pope felt he could not change this authoritative church teaching.

Paul VI even referred to the "lively discussion" occasioned by his encyclical.[45] A good number of Catholic theologians maintained that one could dissent from the teaching in theory and practice and still be a good Catholic.[46] The discussions reverberated throughout the world. Individual conferences and groups of bishops gave their own commentaries on the encyclical. Three distinct positions emerged from these episcopal documents. No episcopal document disagreed with the teaching. Many supported it without further nuance; some hedged; a third group was willing in some way to accept the legitimacy of dissent. The Belgian, Canadian, German, Austrian, Swiss, and Scandinavian bishops all recognized the possibility of legitimate dissent in this case.[47] The U.S. bishops addressed the proper response of theologians and proposed norms for theological dissent from noninfallible teaching even though there is a presumption in favor of that teaching. "The expression of theological dissent from the magisterium is in order only if the reasons are serious and well-founded, if the manner of the dissent does not question or impugn the teaching authority of the church, and is such as not to give scandal."[48]

AFTER HUMANAE VITAE. Since *Humanae vitae* dissent by theologians has spread to many issues other than contraception. Chapter six has shown that the primary areas of dissent tend to be questions of sexuality and other areas in which the problem of physicalism arises. (The human act is identified with the physical structure of the act.) Thus, considerable dissent by Catholic theologians exists on issues such as contraception, masturbation, sterilization, divorce, artificial insemination with the husband's seed, homosexual acts, in vitro fertilization, and the meaning of direct and indirect. The questioning of the immorality of premarital sexuality has been raised, but most Catholic theologians do not want to abandon the need for sexual expression to be seen within the context of marriage or a true personal commitment. Some moral theologians have also dissented from the hierarchical teaching on the beginning of human life as it relates especially to abortion, and a few have argued in favor of euthanasia. There can be no doubt that dissent from, and public disagreement with, hierarchical church teaching has continued to deepen on many issues and to encompass other issues as time goes on. In practice many Roman Catholics seem to be acting in the same way. However, other Catholic theologians strongly defend the existing hierarchical teachings. In addition those theologians who dissent on one or more particular issues do not necessarily dissent on other issues.[49]

The 1993 papal encyclical *Veritatis splendor* clearly gives the authoritative papal response to this growing dissent. There is a grave crisis in the church of unprecedented proportion which needs to be corrected.[50] This encyclical did not come out of the blue but was the culmination of many actions and declarations of the pope and the Roman congregations. A period of "restoration" or tightening up has been going on in the Catholic Church on many fronts, especially in the papacy of John Paul II.[51]

Our focus is on moral theology, but there have been tensions across the board between theologians and the authoritative magisterium on a number of issues. Some theologians have been under suspicion and disciplinary actions have been taken against a few.[52] The renowned German moral theologian Bernard Häring, who taught in Rome for many years at the Alphonsian Academy and has influenced Catholic moral theology more than any other figure in this century, revealed that he had been under investigation by the Congregation for the Doctrine of the Faith from 1975 to 1979. However, after his battle with cancer, the investigation did not continue.[53] In this period church authorities intervened and took action also against moral theologians Ambroggio Valsecchi in Italy and Stephan Pfürtner in Switzerland.[54] In the area of moral theology much of the hierarchical attention has recently centered on the United States and Canada. Cardinal Joseph Ratzinger, the prefect or head of the Congregation for the Doctrine of the Faith, in a famous 1984 interview later published as a book, claimed that North American theologians are primarily engaged in ethics or moral theology, and it is here that the crisis of morality exists. The North American ethos differs considerably from the Catholic ethos. In his judgment, North American moral theologians believe they are forced to choose between dissent from the society or dissent from the magisterium. Many choose this latter dissent, adapting themselves to compromises with a secular ethic which ends up denying men and women the most profound aspect of their nature, leading them to a new slavery while claiming to free them.[55]

The actions taken against moral theologians and others in North American center on disputes over sexuality. Jesuit John McNeil, author of *The Church and the Homosexual*, was silenced by church authorities and later dismissed from the Society of Jesus when he publicly criticized the 1986 Vatican document on homosexuality. The Vatican pressured the archbishop of Seattle to take away the imprimatur he had given in 1977 to Philip S. Keane's *Sexual Morality: A Catholic Perspective.* In 1977 a committee appointed by the Catholic Theological Society of American published *Human Sexuality: New Directions in Catholic Thought,* a book that proposed different pastoral directives for sexuality. Church authorities in Rome and in the United States published their disagreements but also took disciplinary action against Anthony Kosnik, the chair of the committee that produced the volume.[56] In 1986 after a seven year investigation the Congregation for the Doctrine of the Faith concluded that I was neither suitable nor eligible to teach Catholic theology and eventually I was dismissed from my tenured professorship at the Catholic University of America. The reason for this Vatican action was my dissent from hierarchical teachings on contraception, sterilization, masturbation, divorce, and homosexuality.[57] In early 1992 the Congregation for the Doctrine of the Faith asked Ottawa moral theologian André Guindon to explain how his book *The Sexual Creators: An Ethical Proposal for Concerned Christians* can be faithful to Catholic teaching.[58] Unfortunately, Guindon died while the investigative process from Rome was going on.

In addition, the Sisters of Mercy were forced to back down from attempts to allow some sterilizations in their hospitals in the United States. Agnes Mary Mansour, a Sister of Mercy, was forced by the Vatican to request a dispensation from her religious vows if she wished to continue as Director of the Michigan Department of Social Services which included programs involving funding abortions for poor women. Twenty-four religious women, who signed an advertisement in 1984 in *The New York Times* maintaining that direct abortion, although tragic, can at times be a permissible moral choice, also came under Vatican investigation. All but two worked out some private agreement with the Vatican without retracting their public statement.[59] All these actions are illustrative of the tensions existing on matters of moral teaching in the Catholic Church today.

Official documents have continued to be issued by the hierarchical magisterium repeating and reinforcing the moral teaching in the areas where some dissent exists. In addition, in this same time frame, other Vatican documents and actions have insisted that the hierarchical magisterium have greater control over theologians. John Paul II in 1979 promulgated the apostolic constitution *Sapientia Christiana,* which insisted on hierarchical control of Catholic theologians teaching in pontifical schools and faculties (those that grant academic degrees accredited by the Vatican).[60] In 1990 the pope's apostolic constitution *Ex corde ecclesiae* called for greater control by the hierarchy over teachers of theology in all Catholic colleges and universities.[61] The U.S. Catholic bishops are still trying to work out with Rome the norms to be applied in this country. The 1983 Code of Canon Law,[62] the 1989 Profession of Faith and Oath of Fidelity promulgated by the Congregation for the Doctrine of the Faith,[63] and the Congregation for the Doctrine of the Faith's 1990 "Instruction on the Ecclesial Vocation of the Theologian (*Donum veritatis*)"[64] all emphasize the decisive role of the hierarchical magisterium and the submission required by theologians.[65] This brief historical overview shows the continuing and growing tensions between the hierarchical magisterium and some Catholic theologians today.

What is the exact position of the hierarchical magisterium with regard to the possibility of theological dissent from authoritative noninfallible papal teaching? The 1990 "Instruction on the Ecclesial Vocation of the Theologian" considers in some detail the proper response of theologians to authoritative noninfallible teaching. The document spells out the meaning of the religious *obsequium* of intellect and will. The theologian is officially charged with the task of presenting and illustrating the doctrine of the faith in its integrity and with full accuracy.[66] "The willingness to submit loyally to the teaching of the magisterium on matters per se not irreformable must be the rule."[67] If after serious study and true openness to the teaching the theologian cannot give internal intellectual assent, the theologian has the obligation to remain open to a deeper examination of the question. In this situation the instruction deals with three ways of acting. First, the theologian has the duty in this case to make known to the magisterial authorities, with no recourse to the mass media, the problems involved in the teaching. Second, the theologian can suffer in silence and prayer with the certainty that truth will ultimately prevail. Third, dissent, which is described as public opposition to the magisterium of the church and involves serious harm to the community of the church, cannot be justified.[68]

Note the one-sided and very prejudicial description of dissent as public opposition involving grave harm to the church. I know no Catholic theologian who would describe dissent in this way. The document goes on to give the false bases for this unacceptable type of dissent.[69]

Again, the reasons proposed are often caricatures of the reasons that have been proposed by theologians to justify their understanding of dissent.

The instruction explicitly recognizes no option between private recourse to the magisterial authorities and public opposition to the magisterium of the church. But implicitly there might be room for something else. The instruction maintains that one who has a disagreement with such authoritative teaching should show "a readiness, if need be, to revise his [*sic*] own opinions and examine the objections which his colleagues might offer him."[70] Criticism from colleagues presupposes some publication so they are aware of one's positions. The instruction also comments that the theologian will refrain from giving *untimely* (emphasis added) public expression to his or her divergent hypotheses.[71] This statement seems to recognize some possibility of timely expression. In sum, the instruction is very defensive. It never deals with the strongest arguments in favor of some theological dissent, and it does not develop the teaching role of other members in the church or the entire church. Loyal acceptance of noninfallible teaching is the rule for theologians. There is no explicit condemnation, however, of some type of public dissent that does not involve public opposition to the magisterium of the church. Implicitly, the document seems to leave open the possibility of some publication of dissenting positions.

JUSTIFICATION OF DISSENT

This section will briefly synthesize the justification and explanation of dissent from authoritative noninfallible teaching. In theory and in practice one can disagree with such teaching and still be a Roman Catholic.[72] Perhaps the word "dissent" is too strong, but it indicates what is happening vis-à-vis the particular hierarchical teaching in question and expresses some presumption in favor of that particular teaching. The hierarchical papal teaching is not simply another opinion within the Catholic Church. However, this understanding of dissent has none of the pejorative connotations of dissent found in the explicit understanding of dissent recently proposed by the hierarchical magisterium.

POSSIBILITY OF PUBLIC DISSENT. The possibility of such dissent rests on historical, ecclesiological, and moral considerations. Historically, change has occurred in church teaching on the rights of defendants, torture, slavery, usury, religious freedom, democracy, and the meaning and justification of marital relationships.[73] Ecclesiologically, the teaching function of the church is broader than the hierarchical teaching office. All Christians share in some way in the teaching role of the church. Some have explained the possibility of dissent from authoritative noninfallible teaching on the basis of reception or nonreception by the whole church. Reception is ultimately grounded in the reality that teaching in the church involves more than the hierarchical magisterium.[74] The very word "noninfallible" recognizes that the teaching is fallible. It might be wrong. The Catholic tradition, even before Vatican II, used what were called "theological notes" to recognize the various levels of hierarchical teaching so that not all teachings were core and central to the faith.[75]

The understanding of morality presented here also supports the possible legitimacy of dissent. Morality deals with the contingent and not the necessary. The more specific one becomes, the more circumstances may enter and change specific principles and norms of morality. The shift to historical consciousness, experience, and induction, together with an appreciation of cultural diversity, increases the difficulty of claiming absolute certitude on specific moral issues. All these perspectives thus justify the possibility of dissent from authoritative, noninfallible papal teaching on morality.

The official hierarchical reaction seems to be directed especially against public dissent or disagreement. Only private dissent to the appropriate authorities is explicitly recognized. The issue of organized and public dissent became the focus of the 1968–1969 inquiry at the Catholic University of America into the declarations and actions that I and other professors at the University took to solicit scholars to sign a statement of dissent from the encyclical *Humanae vitae*.[76] Once one recognizes the teaching role of the whole church, then the church itself truly becomes a community of moral discourse which by definition calls for a public discussion of positions. The theologian's responsibility to the whole church grounds the need for such public discussion. In the older tradition the school or faculty of theologians formed an important mediating structure or institution in the church, but in recent times the hierarchy has seen the theologian only as an isolated individual.[77] A faculty or school of theologians requires public discussion to function properly. All these aspects point to the need for, and legitimacy of, public dissent in the church—provided, as the American bishops recognized, that the dissent is based on good reasons and does not impugn the teaching authority of the church.

The encyclical *Veritatis splendor* seems to imply that occasional private dissent is acceptable, but the encyclical identifies widespread dissent on many issues present even today in seminaries and theologates as a genuine crisis for the church.[78] Can such apparently widespread dissent be legitimate? Some of the reasons underlying dissent point to the possibility of its being more than occasional. The very nature of noninfallible teaching recognizes that by definition the matter is fallible and could be wrong. As one descends to the more specific, Thomas Aquinas recognized that the secondary principles of the natural law might not always oblige because of the new and different circumstances that arise. Moral truth deals with the particular and contingent not the necessary as in speculative truth. The shift to historical consciousness, the recognition of greater pluralism and diversity, and a more inductive approach all point to the greater difficulty in achieving certitude about particular norms and judgments. In addition earlier discussions have pointed out the common problem of physicalism found in many areas under dispute such as contraception, homosexual acts, artificial insemination, in vitro fertilization, and the solution of conflict situations by the principle of the double effect. In all these situations, the same basic problem of identifying the human moral act with the physical structure of the act has strongly affected the papal teaching. All these reasons indicate why disagreement with or dissent from hierarchical teaching is not just an isolated and rare phenomenon today but occurs in a number of different areas.

At the same time one should not exaggerate the areas today in which many Catholic people in practice and theological ethicists in theory disagree with hierarchical papal teaching. John Paul II in the encyclical *Veritatis splendor* definitely seems to overstate the differences between contemporary revisionist Catholic moral theologians and the papal magisterium. The pope makes no distinction between Catholic revisionist moral theologians and the proponents of absolute freedom, conscience separated from truth, individualism, subjectivism, and relativism.[79] No fair minded interpreter of the present state of Catholic moral theology would readily recognize that revisionist Catholic moral theologians are absolutizing freedom or conscience and supporting individualism, subjectivism, and relativism. Indeed, Catholic revisionist moral theologians agree with the pope in opposing these positions.

Is more than occasional dissent compatible with the recognized presumption in favor of the hierarchical teaching, the attitude of docility to papal teaching, and the sincere effort to give intellectual assent that are often cited by theologians as required by the religious *obsequium* of intellect and will?[80] Frankly, I still continue to use the word dissent to indicate a posture that can be genuinely compatible with these attributes. The general theological understanding of the requirements of religious *obsequium* of intellect and will rests on the Catholic belief that the Holy Spirit assists the hierarchical teaching office. Yes, a Catholic should make every effort to accept the teachings, but the fact remains that the teachings are fallible and often come from a time in which the epistemological understandings related to moral truth and certitude differ somewhat from those prevailing today as illustrated by the contemporary recognition of historical consciousness.

It is interesting that during and immediately after Vatican II there was a greater recognition, although somewhat implicit and muted, of the legitimacy and even the possible frequency of dissent. Recall the response of the Doctrinal Commission of Vatican II in the discussion on authoritative church teaching. The Declaration on Religious Liberty states that "in forming their consciences the faithful must pay careful attention to the sacred and certain teaching of the church."[81] An emendation was proposed to replace "must pay careful attention to" to "ought to form their consciences according to." The Doctrinal Commission responded that the proposed formula seems excessively restrictive. The obligation binding on the faithful is sufficiently expressed in the text as it stands.[82]

The German bishops in a letter explaining the Constitution on the Church of Vatican II understand the noninfallible papal teaching office in this way. "In order to maintain the true and ultimate substance of faith she must, even at the risk of error in points of detail, give expression to doctrinal directives which have a certain degree of binding force and yet, since they are not *de fide* definitions, involve a certain element of the provisional even to the point of being capable of including error."[83] Recall that the U.S. bishops had recognized the legitimacy of public theological dissent in 1968. There definitely was an undercurrent at the time of Vatican II and later in the discussion of *Humanae vitae* which recognized the possibility of forms of dissent similar to some that are occurring at the present time. But this understanding has never been officially accepted by the papal magisterium and has become less prominent in the ensuing years in the documents of various bishops' conferences.

RELUCTANCE TO ADMIT DISSENT. The papal magisterium has been unwilling to change its teaching on any issue even on the question of contraception. Contraception is no longer a significant issue in the life of most Catholics. The vast majority of Catholic spouses disagree with the papal teaching and continue to consider themselves good Catholics.[84] The papal teaching office, however, continues to defend staunchly the older papal teaching and resolutely fails to recognize the legitimacy of dissent here. Why is the papal teaching office so adamant about not changing any teaching or not even explicitly recognizing the legitimacy of dissent from noninfallible papal teaching?

A number of factors have contributed to the reluctance on the part of the papal teaching office to change any of its teachings today or even explicitly to recognize and approve the legitimacy of dissent. An earlier section of this chapter described the increasing centralization, defensiveness, and authoritarianism of the Catholic Church which continued right up to Vatican II in the early 1960s. In such a context the noninfallible teaching tended to become closely assimilated to infallible teaching. Public theological dissent did not occur and was explicitly prohibited. In reacting to such an understanding and its continuing influence today, André Naud has published a book with a captivating title—*The Uncertain Magisterium.*[85] The hierarchical magisterium in the pre-Vatican II period claimed to be much too certain. Despite some developments and changes at Vatican II, this understanding of the papal magisterium has continued. The papal teaching office today still functions very much in continuity with the pre-Vatican II approach.

Theological factors also affected this historical development toward a more centralized and authoritarian papacy. First of all there was a misuse of the traditional Catholic emphasis on mediation. The church mediates the work of the risen Jesus, but it is not totally identified with it. Too often in the pre-Vatican II period the church became practically identified with the risen Jesus. Likewise the papal teaching office was seen as the vicar of Christ, and it was too easy to forge an identity between the pope's role and the role of Jesus as exemplified by applying to the pope the scriptural text that the one who hears you hears me.[86] The juridical understanding of the church at this time also affected our understanding of the teaching office of the church. Teaching became very much associated with a command and obey approach. The words "authoritative teaching" indicate the great emphasis on authority. In this theological and ecclesial context, the understanding of teaching itself was modified.

The reluctance of the hierarchical magisterium to admit error in its teaching is strongly entrenched today but was present even at the time of Vatican II. The Declaration on Religious Liberty was one of the most important documents from Vatican II. Before that time the hierarchical teaching called for the denial of religious liberty and the union of church and state as the best approach to the problem. At the time of the council the question was not so much the substantive issue of religious liberty but the development of doctrine. Many of those commenting on the issue at the time of the council, including Bishop Émile-Joseph de Smedt of Bruges, who introduced the document to the council assembly,[87] and John Courtney Murray, the American Jesuit whose thinking and writing influenced the document more than anyone else,[88] did not admit error in the Catholic teaching. They espoused a theory of development that insisted on continuity in the midst of changing historical circumstances. Put boldly, their argument was that the teaching denying religious freedom in the nineteenth century was correct and the teaching accepting religious liberty in the twentieth century is correct.

The Declaration on Religious Liberty itself nowhere acknowledges that the teaching denying religious liberty, which had been repeated until just before the council, was ever in error. The document addresses the issue by recognizing, that although "through the vicissitudes of human history there has at times appeared a form of behavior which was hardly in keeping with the spirit of the Gospel and was even opposed to it, it has always remained the teaching of the church that no one is to be coerced into believing."[89] At best this statement is disingenuous. It recognizes that forms of behavior were wrong but not that the teaching of the church was wrong. It explicitly claims that the church has always taught that no one is to be coerced into believing. In one sense this is generally true. However, coercion was accepted in theory and in practice against heretics and schismatics who had at one time belonged to the true faith. Likewise coercion could be used against infidels who impeded or persecuted the faith as it was proposed to them—an approach taken by many to justify the treatment of Native Americans by European colonizers. But no mention is made of the fact that the papal magisterium had explicitly denied religious liberty or that the teaching of Vatican II marked a clear change.[90] Even Vatican II could not admit that church teaching was in error on a recent teaching. In this climate one can better understand how for Paul VI the ultimate determining factor in his reiteration of the condemnation of artificial contraception for spouses was the argument from already existing, authoritative papal teaching.

PRESENT SITUATION

Why is the papal magisterium unwilling to admit that its moral teaching has been wrong? and why is it so reluctant to admit the legitimacy of explicit theological and personal dissent from noninfallible teaching? I find no single or easy answer to these questions. Undoubtedly control and power have some role here. However, in disagreeing with someone I think it is important to recognize the strongest reason for their position if only to refute that reason. So what is the best argument for not changing church teaching on these issues and not explicitly acknowledging dissent? The Catholic Church believes that the Holy Spirit assists the hierarchical teaching office. Could the Holy Spirit allow the teaching office to be wrong on such important matters? Contraception in the Catholic tradition was always a grave moral matter which meant it involved a grave or mortal sin if the subject had sufficient knowledge and consent. Instead of helping people, was the Catholic Church really hurting people by its teaching? Would the Holy Spirit allow the church to be wrong on such a significant and important matter and thus be a source of harm for its members? The argument cast in these terms has some force. It goes to the heart of the church's self-understanding and is not just a peripheral matter. The promise of the Holy Spirit's assistance would seem to be negated if papal teaching on such a significant point could be in error.

What is the nature of the Spirit's assistance to the hierarchical magisterium and its moral teaching function? The Catholic Church has traditionally insisted that most of its specific moral teachings (e.g., against contraception or opposition to *laissez-faire* capitalism) are based on natural law. They are per se intelligible to all human beings. Today we recognize more explicitly the limitations and sinfulness that affect all human knowledge. Social location obviously influences our human understandings and we appreciate that affectivity, intuition, and "gut feelings" have a role in our discussions of moral truths. None of these realities undermines the presumption in favor of hierarchical teaching with the assistance of the Holy Spirit and the need for Catholics to try to accept such teaching. However, the principle of mediation reminds us that the Holy Spirit works in and through the human, without short-circuiting the human process of trying to arrive at moral truth. The Holy Spirit does not do away with human processes or substitute for them. The Holy Spirit works in and through the human in the search for moral truth. The Spirit's assistance can help to correct human limitations and sinfulness and to intensify the truly human search for moral truth. In short, the Holy Spirit is not something magic or impervious to the human.[91]

I am afraid that the hierarchical magisterium has done much to create the present problem. If it had recognized explicitly and at all times that noninfallible moral teachings are truly fallible, many problems concerning dissent would not exist. The hierarchical magisterium has claimed too great a certitude for its specific moral teachings. One cannot appeal to the assistance of the Holy Spirit to claim a greater certitude than the matter itself is capable of having. Here again one sees the abuse of mediation—the effect of identifying the church and the papal teaching office too closely with the work of Jesus—and the problems resulting from a very juridical and legalistic understanding of what teaching is.

Another preoccupation of the hierarchical magisterium at the present time appears to be the fear that, once change is admitted in a church teaching, the door is open to accepting other changes including many seemingly far out proposals that circulate in today's world. This fear is a version of the wedge argument; if you give them an inch, they will take a mile. Obviously, however, this argument is not always true and is often used to justify the status quo. Each issue has to be discussed on its own merits. Catholic moral theologians do not and should not espouse subjectivism, relativism, and individualism. Some of us would recognize the goodness of genital homosexual relations between committed partners, but no one is supporting casual sex or the so-called one night stand.

The hierarchical teaching on the beginning of truly individual human life cannot be absolutely certain. In theory even in the twentieth century some Catholics accepted the delayed animation theory of Thomas Aquinas.[92] In fact for the greater part of its history Catholic theology accepted the delayed animation theory but did not accept abortion. However, in practice Catholic teaching maintains one must always follow the safer course and practically recognize that truly individual human life exists from the moment of conception.[93] Catholic theologians before Vatican II acknowledged that we were uncertain about when death actually occurs. Much of this discussion about the time of death was in the context of when a priest could or should "administer" the sacrament of "extreme unction." The aim was to permit reception of the sacrament in doubtful cases.[94] But doubt about the time of death indicates that there may also be some doubt about the time of the beginning of truly individual human life. There is much in the Catholic tradition moving toward an early beginning of human life (e.g., the fact that life is a free gift from God, not based on our merits, and concern for the helpless and the innocent), but one cannot claim absolute certitude about the beginning of truly individual human life today. Yes, there are limits to dissent, but each issue must be considered in itself.

The discussion thus far has assumed that we are dealing with the category of noninfallible teaching. However, some claim that the teaching on contraception belongs in the category of infallible teaching which is irreformable. After *Casti connubii* (1930) very influential moral theologians, for example, the Jesuits Felix Cappello and Arthur Vermeersch, maintained that the condemnation of artificial contraception in that encyclical was an *ex cathedra* papal teaching and therefore infallible.[95] Marcellino Zalba in his manual is not certain if Pius XI infallibly condemned contraception. However, on the basis of the constant teaching of the ordinary and universal magisterium condemning contraception as a teaching certainly to be held, the faithful ought to accept it as infallibly true without doubt.[96] Germain Grisez and John Ford have also maintained that the teaching is infallible on the basis of the ordinary and universal magisterium of all the bishops throughout the world.[97]

What about these positions? Despite the reputations of both Cappello and Vermeersch (who reputedly had a significant hand in drafting *Casti connubii*), their position has not been generally accepted by the vast majority of Catholic theologians. The hierarchical magisterium has never claimed that this teaching is infallible. Regarding the possibility of its being infallible as a teaching of the ordinary and universal magisterium, one important condition for such infallibility is that the teaching must be proposed as something to be held definitively by the faithful.[98] (Note that Zalba substitutes "certainly held" for the acknowledged requirement of "definitively held.") This condition is the precise

problem. It would be very difficult to prove that all the bishops proposed this teaching as something to be held *definitively* by all Catholics.

Another question arises. Can a position based on natural law and
not found in revelation (which is the case with artificial contraception
but not necessarily with other moral teachings) be infallibly taught?
Francis Sullivan maintains that in this case we could be dealing with
what theologians call the secondary object of infallibility.[99] Many official
church documents refer to the capacity of the magisterium to speak
definitively and infallibly on matters that are not revealed but are
"necessarily" or "strictly and intimately" connected with revealed
truth. Such matters are referred to as the "secondary objects of infallibility." To such infallible teaching, one owes not the irreformable assent
of faith, but such teachings are to be "firmly accepted and held."
However, the question is whether the moral wrongness of contraception
is "necessarily" or "strictly and intimately" connected with revealed
truth.

Contraception, at the very minimum, seems somewhat removed
from revelation. The 1917 Code of Canon Law maintained: "Nothing
is understood to be infallibly defined or declared unless this is clearly
established." However, the 1983 Code omits the words "or declared."
On this basis Grisez concludes that the fact of infallibility has to be
clearly established only when it is a question of judging when a doctrine
has been infallibly defined and not in the case of the infallible ordinary
and universal magisterium. Yet it seems that the intent of this statement,
from a theological perspective, applies to any type of infallibility. Thus,
if the infallibility is not clearly established, the particular teaching is
not infallible.[100] In addition the very nature of specific moral norms
argues strongly against the possibility of any infallible teaching in this
area. The possibility of certitude decreases as one descends to the more
specific and complex. Consequently, the secondary principles of the
natural law can at times admit of some exceptions. Thus, in my judgment there has never been an infallible teaching on a specific moral
norm based on natural law and never can be.

However, in June 1998, new fuel was added to the fire of this
debate. John Paul II, to safeguard Catholic faith against errors coming
especially from theologians, introduced into the Code of Canon Law
some changes that had first appeared in the Profession of Faith proposed by the Congregation for the Doctrine of the Faith in 1989. The
1983 Code of Canon Law referred to two categories of teaching—the
infallible teaching of a divinely revealed truth which must be believed

by divine and Catholic faith and the noninfallible teaching to which the faithful owe the religious *obsequium* of intellect and will. The new second category, inserted between these two existing categories, refers to definitive (i.e., infallible) teaching by the magisterium of a doctrine concerned with faith or morals that is not directly revealed but is necessarily connected with revelation. The faithful must firmly and definitively hold this teaching.[101] The second category seems to be identical to what theologians have previously called the secondary object of infallibility which includes aspects necessarily connected with revelation which are not themselves revealed, such as the existence of the soul.

There is no doubt that by this addition the pope intended to protect the church against theological errors. The new Profession of Faith proposed in 1989 and this insertion into the Code of Canon Law were done without any consultation or discussions among the bishops of the church. They are both unilateral actions coming from Rome. The fact that just punishments are also prescribed for those who teach such a condemned position adds a punitive element to the matter. However, the second category itself is not really new. It has been recognized by theologians as the secondary object of infallibility.

Together with the papal apostolic letter the Vatican released a "Commentary on Profession of Faith's Concluding Paragraphs" signed by Cardinal Joseph Ratzinger and Archbishop Tarcisio Bertone, the two top officials in the Congregation for the Doctrine of the Faith. Note that the commentary is not on the papal letter itself. This commentary gives examples of what fits under the three categories of teaching that are now part of canon law. As examples of the second category (not directly revealed but necessary for defending and safeguarding revelation) that have been infallibly taught by the ordinary and universal magisterium the commentary mentions the ordination of women, the invalidity of Anglican orders, and the moral teaching on euthanasia, prostitution, and fornication.[102]

This commentary possesses little or no standing as an official church document. Instead, it is a fallible judgment that certain teachings are infallible by reason of being taught by the ordinary and universal magisterium of all the bishops together with the pope. If the moral teachings proposed in this commentary are necessarily connected with revelation, then many other moral teachings would likewise be infallibly taught. In fact, in light of the circumstances, I was somewhat surprised that contraception, abortion, and genital homosexual acts were not included. The commentary seems to be an example of creeping infallibility and of growing authoritarianism in the church.

The arguments mentioned above are applicable to show that a specific moral teaching such as euthanasia is not infallible by reason of the ordinary and universal magisterium. To meet the criteria for infallibility one has to show that all the bishops over time and throughout the world together with the pope have proposed this teaching to be held *definitively* by the faithful. Obviously, they have taught these matters, but to be infallibly taught one must prove they were taught as definitive. This is practically impossible to prove. Recall the basic principle: Nothing is understood to be infallible unless it is clearly established.

Even more significantly, the teaching on euthanasia is not necessarily connected with revelation. One can safeguard and expound revelation no matter what is taught about euthanasia. Respect life is a general moral principle accepted by all. The condemnation of euthanasia is a specific moral teaching. Hierarchical teaching recognizes that extraordinary means (e.g., a respirator) may be removed from a dying person even though death will follow. The condemnation of euthanasia rests on the philosophical difference between allowing death and directly causing death. Many strong arguments can be made against euthanasia, but they are far removed from revelation.

CONCLUSION

How should the hierarchical magisterium in the church function? A full answer to that question lies beyond the scope of this book. John Boyle has succinctly summarized the shift that needs to occur. We must move from a juridical model of teaching authority in an institutional model of the church to an understanding of the church as a community of religious and moral discourse with a special assistance of the Holy Spirit given to the hierarchical teaching office.[103] The hierarchical magisterium must recognize, and dialogue with, the lived experience of all God's people and with the various prophetic voices existing in and outside the church. Papal teachings should emerge only after a broad consultation that aims to discern the truth in the church community, with special importance given to the role of bishops in the church. The consultation involved with the pastoral letters of the U.S. bishops on peace and the economy indicate how well broad consultation can work.

Above all, the hierarchical magisterium must honestly recognize that it has an obligation to learn the moral truth. The papal magisterium does not merely possess the truth but must seek it out. As Yves Congar perceptively pointed out, too often the issue is discussed in two terms— magisterium vis-à-vis theologians or magisterium vis-à-vis the faithful. But in reality we must begin with moral truth, which the hierarchical magisterium with the special assistance of the Holy Spirit, along with all the Christian faithful, including theologians, is striving to discover.[104] The hierarchical magisterium both learns and teaches moral truth. The papal and hierarchical magisterium must accept pluralism within the church and not base its teaching on only one theological or philosophical school as tends to happen at the present time. The hierarchical magisterium needs to recognize the limits involved in the nature of specific moral teaching and the fallible nature of such teaching.

The need for the hierarchical magisterium to learn moral truth seems greater than its need to learn the truths of faith. Truths of faith are based on revelation; moral truth is based on reason and experience. The condemnation of contraception or the criticism of *laissez-faire* capitalism are not found in what has been called the deposit of faith entrusted to the apostles and then to the hierarchical magisterium. Over time the hierarchical magisterium learned these teachings. That some moral and social teachings have changed over time proves that the hierarchical magisterium learns before it teaches.

Many of the positions and concepts proposed here came to the fore at or since Vatican II. However, church structures have not changed. The 1983 Code of Canon Law is in basic continuity with the older code. The new code still supports a juridical model of the church's teaching authority in an institutional model of the church in which too much power is concentrated in the papacy. Until church structures and institutions change to reflect the church as a community of religious and moral discourse with a special role for the hierarchy, the existing tensions will persist and grow.

What about the situation in the church that John Paul II calls the genuine crisis of widespread dissent? There are obvious limits to dissent, but dissent is more frequent today than it was in the past. A positive aspect in the present situation is that the Catholic faithful recognize in practice that they can dissent on some moral issues and still be loyal Catholics. The negative aspect concerns the obvious tensions existing in the situation and the deterioration of the credibility of the papal magisterium. Yes, some dramatic changes must be made in the self-understanding and operating procedures of the papal teaching office, but the papal teaching office can and should exercise a great service for the church and the world. It is important, for example, that the pope can still get a worldwide hearing when he speaks out for the poor, the marginalized, and the oppressed.

The tension between the papal magisterium and the faithful in moral matters can be mitigated somewhat in the forum of conscience. People who dissent in practice can continue to celebrate their participation in the Christian community and the Catholic Church. Ordinarily no one is going to stop them. The tension between the papal magisterium and theologians cannot be ameliorated that easily. The most serious tension or conflict exists in those areas of dissent that call for structural change. The present conflict between the teaching of the hierarchical magisterium and the attitude of many in the church about the ordination of women cannot be resolved pastorally in the forum of conscience. Recent events indicate a strong unwillingness on the part of the hierarchical magisterium to change on this issue. As these differences illustrate, the next years will not be easy. Tensions and conflicts will continue. The transition from a juridical model of teaching authority and an institutional model of the church to an understanding of the church as a community of religious and moral discourse with a hierarchical teaching office that has the special assistance of the Holy Spirit will not be easy. But eventually it will occur.

The sharp controversy over the hierarchical magisterium's role on specific moral issues has called for an extended discussion of this function. However, the role of the hierarchical magisterium is much less significant and important than the role of all God's people in the total moral formation of the community and its members.

NOTES

1. Ladislas Orsy, *The Church Learning and Teaching: Magisterium, Assent, Dissent, Academic Freedom* (Collegeville, Minn.: The Liturgical Press, 1991).

2. For a balanced overview of the hierarchical teaching function, see Francis A. Sullivan, *The Magisterium: Teaching Authority in the Catholic Church* (New York: Paulist, 1983); for a very perceptive recent treatment, see Richard B. Gaillardetz, *Teaching with Authority: A Theology for the Magisterium in the Church* (Collegeville, Minn.: Liturgical, 1997); see also Charles E. Curran and Richard A. McCormick, eds., *Readings in Moral Theology No. 3: The Magisterium and Morality* (New York: Paulist, 1983).

3. John Paul II, *Veritatis splendor*, nn. 4–5, *Origins* 23 (1993): 299–300.

4. D'Antonio, et al., *Laity, American and Catholic*, pp. 43–64.

5. Yves Congar, "A Semantic History of the Term 'Magisterium'," and "A Brief History of the Forms of the Magisterium and Its Relations with Scholars," in *Readings in Moral Theology No. 3*, ed. Curran and McCormick, pp. 297–331.

6. John P. Boyle, *Church Teaching Authority: Historical and Theological Studies* (Notre Dame, Ind.: University of Notre Dame Press, 1995), p. 190, fn. 30.

7. Gaillardetz, *Teaching with Authority*; Sullivan, *Magisterium*.

8. Denzinger, *Enchridion*, nn. 2101–69, pp. 457–66.

9. Ibid., nn. 2301–32, pp. 480–84.

10. For a detailed history of the theological discussion of the issues and the responses from Rome, see John Connery, *Abortion: The Development of the Roman Catholic Perspective* (Chicago: Loyola University Press, 1997), pp. 225–303; for an earlier study briefly dealing with craniotomy but concentrating on the ectopic pregnancy issue, see T. Lincoln Bouscaren, *The Ethics of Ectopic Operations*, 2nd ed. (Milwaukee: Bruce, 1944).

11. Connery, *Abortion*, p. 285.

12. Bouscaren, *Ethics of Ectopic Operations*, p. 13.

13. Joseph Aertnys, et al., "Casus de conceptivis ectopicis, seu extrauterinis," *American Ecclesiastical Review* 9 (1893): 343–360.

14. Bouscaren, *Ethics of Ectopic Operations*, pp. 17–171.

15. Thomas Bouquillon, "Moral Theology at the End of the Nineteenth Century," *Catholic University Bulletin* 5 (1899): 267.

16. John T. Noonan Jr., *Contraception: A History of Its Treatment by the Catholic Theologians and Canonists*, enlarged ed. (Cambridge, Mass.: Belknap Press of Harvard University Press, 1986), pp. 404–32.

17. The official version of these documents can be found in *Acta Apostolicae Sedis*. English translations of the later documents can be found in *The Pope Speaks* which began with volume one in 1954. The beginning of this journal illustrates the increasing role played by the papacy in the life of the church at that time.

18. John P. Kenny, *Principles of Medical Ethics*, 2nd ed. (Westminster, Md.: Newman, 1962).

19. For an acclaimed historical overview of nineteenth-century Catholicism, see Roger Aubert, et al., *The Church in the Age of Liberalism*, History of the Church, vol. 8, ed. Herbert Jedin and John Dolan (New York: Crossroad, 1981); William J. LaDue, *The Papacy: A Sign of Contradiction? A Short History of the Evolution of the Papal Office* (Maryknoll, N.Y.: Orbis, 1999), Chapter 8: The Installation of the Absolutist Model—1869 to the Present.

20. M. Dubruel, "Gallicanisme," *Dictionnaire de théologie catholique*, 6, cols. 1095–1137.

21. T. Ortolan, "Febronius," *Dictionnaire de théologie catholique*, 5, cols. 2115–24.

22. Aubert, *Church in the Age of Liberalism*, pp. 304–30.

23. Mauro Cappellari, *Il trionfo della Sancta Sede e della chiesa contro gli assalti dei novatori combattuti e respinti colle stesse loro armi* (Rome, 1799).

24. Cuthbert Butler, *The Vatican Council, 1869–1870* (Westminster, Md.: Newman, 1962).

25. Pope Gregory XVI, *Mirari vos*, in *The Papal Encyclicals 1740–1878*, ed. Claudia Carlen (Wilmington, N.C.: McGrath, 1981), pp. 235–41.

26. Denzinger, *Enchiridion*, nn. 2901–80, pp. 576–84.

27. Ibid., nn. 3475–3500, pp. 675–83; Gabriel Daly, *Transcendence and Immanence: A Study in Catholic Modernism and Integralism* (New York: Oxford University Press, 1980).

28. Denzinger, *Enchiridion*, nn. 3512–19, pp. 684–85.

29. See Daly, *Transcendence and Immanence*; Marvin O'Connell, *Critics on Trial: An Introduction to the Catholic Modernist Crisis* (Washington, D.C.: Catholic University of America Press, 1994); David G. Schultenover, *A View from Rome: On the Eve of the Modernist Crisis* (New York: Fordham University Press, 1993); R. Scott Appleby, *Church and Age Unite: The Modernist Impulse in American Catholicism* (Notre Dame, Ind.: University of Notre Dame Press, 1992).

30. T. Howland Sanks, *Authority in the Church: A Study in Changing Paradigms*, American Academy of Religion Dissertation Series, 2 (Missoula, Mont.: American Academy of Religion and Scholars Press, 1974).

31. Denzinger, *Enchiridion*, n. 3855, pp. 775–76.

32. Franciscus Hürth, "Annotationes," *Periodica de re morali, canonica, liturgica* 41 (1952): 245–49. It was well known that Hürth wrote and drafted most of Pius XII's addresses on moral issues. He authored a commentary on the September 29, 1949, papal allocution condemning artificial insemination in the September 15, 1949, issue of *Periodica* 38 (1949): 282–95.

33. Constitution on the Church, n. 25, in *Vatican Council II*, ed. Flannery, pp. 379–80.

34. Sullivan, *Magisterium*, pp. 158–68; Orsy, *Church Learning and Teaching*, pp. 85–89; Boyle, *Church Teaching Authority*, pp. 63–78; Gaillardetz, *Teaching with Authority*, pp. 263–70; Richard A. McCormick, *Corrective Vision: Explorations in Moral Theology* (Kansas City, Mo.: Sheed and Ward, 1994), pp. 82–99. Most of these sources provide discussions of the meaning of *obsequium* and the possibility of dissent.

35. Charles E. Curran, Robert E. Hunt, et al., *Dissent in and for the Church: Theologians and Humanae Vitae* (New York: Sheed and Ward, 1969), pp. 114–15.

36. Here I am following the original research of Joseph A. Komonchak, "Ordinary Papal Magisterium and Religious Assent," in *Contraception: Authority and Dissent*, ed. Charles E. Curran (New York: Herder and Herder, 1969), pp. 101–26.

37. Gérard Philips, "History of the Constitution" in *Commentary on Documents of Vatican II*, ed. Vorgrimler, 1, p. 110.

38. Constitution on the Church, n. 12, in *Documents of Vatican II*, ed. Flannery, pp. 363–64.

39. Declaration on Religious Liberty, n. 1, in *Documents of Vatican II*, ed. Flannery, p. 799.

40. See, for example, Timothy E. O'Connell, ed., *Vatican II and Its Documents: An American Reappraisal* (Wilmington, Del.: Michael Glazier, 1986); John W. O'Malley, *Tradition and Transition: Historical Perspectives on Vatican II* (Wilmington, Del.: Michael Glazier, 1989).

41. For the history of the papal commission, see Robert Blair Kaiser, *The Politics of Sex and Religion: A Case History in the Development of Doctrine, 1962–1984* (Kansas City, Mo.: Leaven, 1985); Robert McClory, *Turning Point: The Inside Story of the Papal Birth Control Commission and How Humanae Vitae Changed the Life of Patty Crowley and the Future of the Church* (New York: Crossroad, 1955).

42. Paul VI, *Humanae vitae*, n. 14, p. 9.

43. Ibid., n. 6, p. 4.

44. Ibid., nn. 7–18, pp. 4–12.

45. Paul VI used the expression *la vívida discussión* in a speech delivered to the Second General Conference of Latin American Bishops (CELAM) held at Medellín, Colombia, on August 24, 1968. *Acta apostolicae sedis* 60 (1968): 644.

46. For my involvement in and defense of the dissent from *Humanae vitae*, see Curran, Hunt, et al., *Dissent in and for the Church*.

47. Joseph A. Selling, "The Reaction to Humanae Vitae: A Study in Special and Fundamental Theology," (STD Diss., Catholic University of Louvain, 1977), pp. 1–139; Shannon, *Lively Debate*, pp. 117–46.

48. Catholic Pastoral Letter of the American Hierarchy, *Human Life in Our Day* (Washington, D.C.: U.S. Catholic Conference, 1968), p. 18.

49. For an overview providing all sides in the church on the discussion about dissent, see Charles E. Curran and Richard A. McCormick, eds., *Readings in Moral Theology No. 6: Dissent in the Church* (New York: Paulist, 1988).

50. John Paul II, *Veritatis splendor*, nn. 4–5, *Origins* 23 (1993): 299–300.

51. Giancarlo Zizola, *La restaurazione di papa Wojtyla* (Rome: Laterza e Figli, 1985); André Naud, *Un aggiornamento et son éclipse: La liberté de la pensée dans la foi et dans l'Église* (Montreal: Fides, 1996).

52. For many recent cases involving theologians, see Küng and Swidler, eds., *The Church in Anguish*.

53. Bernhard Häring, *Fede, storia, morale: Intervista di Gianni Licheri* (Rome: Borla, 1989), pp. 86–117, with full documentation on pp. 229–78. For a less complete English version, see Häring, *My Witness for the Church* (New York: Paulist, 1992).

54. Ludwig Kaufmann, *Ein Ungelöster Kirkenkonflikt: Der Fall Pfürtner: Documente und Zeitgeschichtliche Analyzen* (Freiburg, Switzerland: Exodus, 1987).

55. Vittorio Messori, Colloquio con il cardinale Josef Ratzinger, "Ecco Perché la fede é in crisi," *Jesus* (November 1984), p. 77. The later book developing this interview including the English translation softened the original somewhat—Joseph Cardinal Ratzinger with Vittorio Messori, *The Ratzinger Report: An Exclusive Interview on the State of the Church* (San Francisco: Ignatius, 1985), p. 83.

56. For an overview of the following cases, see Leslie Griffin, "American Catholic Sexual Ethics, 1789–1989," in *Readings in Moral Theology No. 8*, ed. Curran and McCormick, pp. 471–77; for separate reactions of the Congregation for the Doctrine of the Faith to the work of Kosnik, McNeill, and André Guindon see *Readings in Moral Theology No. 8*, ed. Curran and McCormick, pp. 485–510.

57. For documentation and my analysis, see Charles E. Curran, *Faithful Dissent* (Kansas City, Mo.: Sheed and Ward, 1986). For other analyses, see

William W. May, ed., *Vatican Authority and American Catholic Dissent: The Curran Case and Its Consequences* (New York: Crossroad, 1987).

58. Congregation for the Doctrine of the Faith, "Note," *Origins* 21 (1992): 573–79. For Guindon's response, see André Guindon, "L'éthique sexuelle qu'en Église je professe: apropos de The Sexual Creators," *Église et théologie* 24 (1993): 5–23.

59. Patrick, *Liberating Conscience*, pp. 45–48, 118–28.

60. Pope John Paul II, *Apostolic Constitution Sapientia Christiana: On Ecclesiastical Faculties and Universities* (Washington, D.C.: U.S. Catholic Conference, 1979).

61. Pope John Paul II, *Ex corde ecclesiae, Origins* 20 (1990): 265–76.

62. James A. Coriden, Thomas J. Green, and Donald E. Heintschel, eds., *The Code of Canon Law: A Text and Comentary* (New York: Paulist, 1985).

63. Congregation for the Doctrine of the Faith, "Profession of Faith and Oath of Fidelity," *Origins* 18 (1989): 661–63.

64. Congregation for the Doctrine of the Faith, "Instruction on the Ecclesial Vocation of the Theologian," *Origins* 20 (1990): 117–26.

65. For commentaries on these documents, see many of the citations to works on the magisterium, but especially Naud, *Un aggiornamento et son éclipse*, pp. 73–175 and Boyle, *Church Teaching Authority*, pp. 95–123, 142–60.

66. "Instruction on the Ecclesial Vocation of the Theologian," n. 22, *Origins* 20 (1990): 122.

67. Ibid., n. 24, p. 122.

68. Ibid., nn. 30–32, pp. 123–24.

69. Ibid., nn. 33–41, pp. 124–25.

70. Ibid., n. 29, p. 123.

71. Ibid., n. 27, p. 123.

72. For earlier in-depth developments of my position on dissent, see Curran, Hunt, et al., *Dissent in and for the Church* and Curran, *Faithful Dissent*.

73. Noonan, *Theological Studies* 54 (1993): 662–77; J. Robert Dionne, *The Papacy and the Church*.

74. Gaillardetz, *Teaching with Authority*, pp. 227–273; Hermann J. Pottmeyer, "Reception and Submission," *Jurist* 51 (1991): 262–92.

75. Sixtus Cartechini, *De valore notarum theologicarum et de criteriis ad eas dignoscendas* (Rome: Gregorian University Press, 1951).

76. Curran, Hunt, et al., *Dissent in and for the Church*, pp. 133–53.

77. Boyle, *Church Teaching Authority*, pp. 171–75.

78. *Veritatis splendor*, n. 5, *Origins* 23 (1993): 300.

79. Ibid., nn. 32–34, pp. 308–9.

80. Sullivan, *Magisterium*, p. 78.

81. Declaration on Religious Liberty, n. 1, in *Documents of Vatican II*, ed. Flannery, p. 811.

82. Sullivan, *Magisterium*, p. 169.

83. Karl Rahner, "The Dispute Concerning the Teaching Office of the Church," in *Readings in Moral Theology No. 3*, ed. Curran and McCormick, p. 115.

84. Archbishop John R. Quinn, "New Context for Contraception Teaching," *Origins* 10 (1980): 263–67.

85. Naud, *Le magistère incertain*.

86. Pius XII, *Humani generis*, in Denzinger, *Enchiridion*, n. 3885, p. 776.

87. Émile-Joseph de Smedt, "Religious Freedom," in *Council Speeches of Vatican II*, ed. Yves Congar, Hans Küng, and Daniel O'Hanlon (London: Sheed and Ward, 1964), pp. 161–68. For commentaries on this speech, see Richard J. Regan, *Conflict and Consensus: Religious Freedom and the Second Vatican Council* (New York: Macmillan, 1967), pp. 41–46; Xavier Rynne, *The Second Session: The Debates and Decrees of Vatican Council II, September 29–December 4, 1963* (New York: Farrar, Straus, 1964), pp. 223–34.

88. For Murray's summary judgment on the nineteenth-century teaching of Leo XIII in relation to the newer approach, see John Courtney Murray, *The Problem of Religious Freedom* (Westminster, Md.: Newman, 1965), pp. 52–64; for my analysis and criticism, see Charles E. Curran, *American Catholic Social Ethics: Twentieth Century Approaches* (Notre Dame, Ind.: University of Notre Dame Press, 1982), pp. 202–11, 228–30.

89. Declaration on Religious Liberty, n. 12, in *Documents of Vatican II*, ed. Flannery, p. 809.

90. For my analysis of these changes, see Charles E. Curran, "Commentary on Religious Liberty," in *Rome has Spoken: A Guide to Forgotten Papal Statements and How They Have Changed Through the Centuries*, ed. Maureen Fiedler and Linda Rabben (New York: Crossroad, 1998), pp. 46–54.

91. Richard A. McCormick, *Notes on Moral Theology 1965–1980* (Washington, D.C.: University Press of America, 1981) pp. 262–66.

92. Hyacinth M. Hering, "De tempore animationis foetus humani," *Angelicum* 28 (1951): 18–29; Joseph Donceel, "Immediate Animation and Delayed Hominization," *Theological Studies* 31 (1970): 76–105. For one journal's recent debates about delayed hominization, see Thomas A. Shannon and Allan B. Wolter, "Reflections on the Moral Status of the Preembryo," *Theological Studies* 51 (1990): 603–26; Mark Johnson, "Reflections on Some Recent Catholic Claims for Delayed Hominization," *Theological Studies* 56 (1995): 743–63; Jean Porter, "Individuality, Personal Identity, and the Moral Status of the Preembryo: A Response to Mark Johnson," *Theological Studies* 56 (1995): 763–70; Thomas A Shannon, "Delayed Hominization: A Response to Mark Johnson," *Theological Studies* 57 (1996): 731–34; Mark Johnson and Thomas A. Shannon, "*Questio Disputata*: Delayed Hominization," *Theological Studies* 58 (1997): 708–17.

93. For the historical development, see Connery, *Abortion*.

94. Edwin F. Healy, *Medical Ethics* (Chicago: Loyola University Press, 1956), pp. 380–83.

95. Felix Cappello, *De sacramentis*, vol. 5, *De matrimonio*, 7th ed. (Rome: Marietti, 1960), n. 816, p. 752. For a long study reviewing the literature and defending the *ex cathedra* and infallible nature of the condemnation of artificial contraception by Pope Pius XI and Paul VI, see Ermenegildo Lio, *Humanae vitae e infallibilità* (Vatican City: Libreria Editrice Vaticana, 1986).

96. Zalba, *Theologiae moralis summa*, 3, p. 742, fn. 70.

97. John C. Ford and Germain Grisez, "Contraception and Infallibility of the Ordinary Magisterium," *Theological Studies* 39 (1978): 258–312.

98. Constitution on the Church, n. 25, in *Vatican Council II*, ed. Flannery, p. 379. For some ambiguity about the meaning of "definitively" in other official documents, see Francis Sullivan, "New Claims for the Pope," *Tablet* 248 (June 18, 1994): 767–769.

99. Francis A. Sullivan, "The 'Secondary Object' of Infallibility," *Theological Studies* 54 (1993): 536–50.

100. For Grisez's response to Sullivan's position and a further dialogue between the two, see Germain Grisez and Francis A. Sullivan, "The Ordinary Magisterium's Infallibility," *Theological Studies* 55 (1994): 720–38.

101. Pope John Paul II, *Ad Tuendam fidem,* in *Origins* 28 (1998): 113–16.

102. Cardinal Joseph Ratzinger and Archbishop Tarcisio Bertone, "Commentary on Profession of Faith's Concluding Paragraphs," *Origins* 28 (1998): 116–19.

103. Boyle, *Church Teaching Authority,* pp. 161–78.

104. Congar, *Readings in Moral Theology No. 3,* ed. Curran and McCormick, p. 238.

Afterword

This book has proposed a systematic Catholic moral theology and recognized the important difference between the systematic study of Christian morality and living the Christian moral life in the Catholic community. When teaching moral theology classes, I begin by asking the students what they expect to get out of the course and raise some questions to trigger the conversation. One question is this: Will the study of moral theology make you a better practicing Christian? The first reaction is usually affirmative. After all, what we learn in the classroom or in books should have some relevance to, and influence on, our daily lives.

But there is another important side to the issue. What about the over 99 percent of Christians who have never studied theology? Do you think that moral theologians are the best practicing Christians and the best decision makers? You may not know enough moral theologians to answer that question, but I do. Knowing myself and others, the answer is obvious. Moral theologians are not necessarily the best Christians in the world. Almost all the saints and friends of God in history and in contemporary life have never studied theology or ethics.

Then why study moral theology? What is its purpose? Moral theology seeks systematic and thematic understanding of the Christian moral life. The Catholic tradition has always appreciated the role of human reason in trying to understand all reality better and deeper, including our understanding of God. Theology plays an important role in the Catholic Church. Systematic knowledge is something good in itself and as human beings we are called to increase and deepen our knowledge and understanding.

Moral theology is also very helpful in clarifying complex realities and disputed issues. Think of the subjective and objective aspects of human action and the many discussions going on today about bioethics or the just distribution of wealth in our global economy.

The study of moral theology can have some effect on the decisions and life of the believer. Systematic knowledge is never totally separated from life. However, the moral theologian as a Christian must existentially appropriate and live out this understanding. On this existential level of Christian life in the Catholic community, the moral theologian is no better than anyone else.

The foregoing discussion illustrates the understanding of moral theology as a second-order discourse which stands back from the lived reality of the Christian moral life in order to study it thematically. As second-order discourse, moral theology is closely related to, but different from, the daily living of the Christian life although there is considerable overlap. This book illustrates the differences and the overlap. First, two long chapters dealt with the most controversial questions in moral theology today—the existence and role of moral norms and the papal teaching function in the Catholic Church. These are important topics for scientific analysis and criticism, but the issues they raise are not that common in daily life.

Second, the discussions of stance, model, the basic orientation of the person in conversion, and the virtues that affect the person as subject and agent did relate directly to the daily life of the disciples of Jesus. But again, the systematic understanding of these realities is different from the life of Christian discipleship. The personal and existential appropriation of stance or model will have consequences for Christian living, but many exemplary Christians have never even thought about their stance or moral model.

Third, the closest relationship between the systematic study of moral theology and the life of Christians involves the reality of conscience. The theory of conscience proposed in this book is based on the experience of Christian people. Peace and joy as the ultimate criterion of a good conscience seems to be in accord with Christian and human experience. Chapter seven tried to systematically understand and develop that experience and how this criterion of peace and joy actually functions.

The synthesis presented here, like any synthesis, has sought to identify and integrate the various parts of moral theology. Only at the very end of the book can the reader come to understand and evaluate the synthesis. By definition each of the chapters has developed an important aspect or part of the whole. The discussion of the individual parts relates them to some other parts and to the whole. A brief overview of how each part fits into the whole will help the reader to see more clearly the synthesis that has been proposed.

Catholic moral theology is rooted in the life of the Roman Catholic Church, so an ecclesial understanding is needed to give direction and guidance to the systematic study of moral theology. The Catholic Church embraces both saints and sinners in its internal life and also works with others for a better human society. The Catholic emphasis on inclusivity and "both-and" approaches rather than "either-or" approaches can be seen in the fact that the Catholic tradition recognizes the need for virtues, principles, and casuistry. Some philosophical and theological approaches appeal to just one of these, but the Catholic tradition has rightly seen a place for all three. Likewise the inclusivity of the Catholic tradition insists on holding together the subject pole (the person) and the object pole (the world in which we live) in its analysis of moral life and action. The Catholic theological tradition itself has encouraged attempts to synthesize and systematically present the Catholic moral tradition in a comprehensive and adequate manner.

The logical first step in the proposed synthesis involves a characterization of the stance of moral theology since it is the perspective from which one views and understands the moral life of the Christian. The stance based on the fivefold Christian mysteries of creation, sin, incarnation, redemption, and resurrection destiny can be understood as the Christian horizon that enables us to perceive all that is occurring in the world and our role in it. But to fully understand morality, one also needs a model to organize its different aspects. In the light of theological, philosophical, and ethical concerns, the relationality-responsibility model seems most appropriate for understanding how the moral life unfolds.

The moral life includes both a subject and an object pole. The subject pole of morality is the human person whose fundamental conversion to the Triune God establishes the basic orientation of the person and affects his or her multiple relations with God, neighbor, world, and self. The virtues, systematically developed in terms of this fourfold relationship, affect the person as subject by making one a better moral person. But the virtues also affect the person as agent by disposing one to act in multiple relationships according to these virtues and their corresponding values. The person as agent is the bridge moving from the subject pole to the object pole. Thus, the virtues are related to both. The object pole includes all moral realities but especially the values and human goods that should be preserved and developed. Principles and norms exist to protect and promote these goods.

The subject and the object pole of morality come together in the concrete decision making of conscience. In addition, all the aspects mentioned here—especially one's basic orientation and virtues, values and goods existing in the world, and the principles that protect and promote them—influence and affect the decision of conscience. By my individual decisions I make myself the moral person I want to become, and I influence the world in which I live. In a true sense authentic subjectivity and genuine objectivity for the Christian come together in good conscience decisions. The peace and joy of a good conscience constitutes the basic criterion for decision making (i.e., for perceiving and grasping what is compatible with and fulfilling to one as subject and agent). The fundamental option and virtues are necessary for this criterion of a good conscience to work properly. Yes, principles and norms have a role to play, but the fundamental orientation and virtues of the person are most important. The peace and joy of the person, despite all the possibilities of abuse, remains the most adequate criterion for knowing and doing the good.

In its own way, this synthesis illustrates the moral methodology associated with the Catholic tradition. Any synthesis of this tradition must be very familiar with the past, but it should not merely repeat the past. The tradition has to be understood in the light of contemporary realities and the signs of the times. A Catholic moral theology can and should use insights and concepts from non-Catholic sources to more adequately propose the Catholic tradition today.

One final consideration is appropriate. It concerns the writer's social location. Each of us comes from a particular social location that definitely affects our understanding and approaches. None of us is totally neutral. Readers have a right to know my social location.

I have been teaching and writing in the area of Catholic moral theology since 1961. My approach is usually identified as belonging to the school of liberal or revisionist moral theology. These terms are typically used to describe moral theologians who disagree with or dissent from some teachings of the papal magisterium, especially in the area of sexual morality. However, these terms like many others in moral theology, tend to reduce moral theology to quandary ethics—the consideration of specific acts that are debated in the church community today. This book has pointed out that moral theology must consider not only quandaries but all possible human acts and all other aspects of moral theology. Note that a comparatively small part of this book deals directly with controversial particular issues. This book has attempted a systematic understanding of all the aspects of moral theology, and quandary ethics involves only a small part of the whole.

Many contemporary Catholic moral theologians, as John Paul II recognized in *Veritatis splendor*, disagree with some of the specific moral teachings of the hierarchical magisterium. In this volume I tried to show how and why such dissent is justified and in keeping with the best of the Catholic tradition. However, here again, this effort constitutes only a small part of the present venture.

But another factor affecting my social location needs to be mentioned. In 1986 after a seven year investigation, the Vatican Congregation for the Doctrine of the Faith declared that I was "neither suitable nor eligible to exercise the function of a professor of Catholic theology." The reasons for the action taken by the Congregation for the Doctrine of the Faith were my positions on specific issues such as contraception, masturbation, sterilization, divorce, homosexual acts in committed relationships, and the concept of direct and indirect actions.[1]

In this matter too I respectfully disagree and dissent. Yes, I personally have been hurt by the judgment of the Congregation for the Doctrine of the Faith, but I have also been heartened by the support of many in the Catholic Church today. Many theologians have pointed out that my theology and my positions are very much in keeping with what other Catholic moral theologians are writing and saying today.[2] Anyone with an understanding of the Catholic tradition and its history knows there have always been and always will be tensions and differences in its development.

I write as a person deeply committed to the Catholic Church and to the Catholic moral tradition. I have a few disagreements with the hierarchical teaching on some specific issues, but these disagreements and the tensions are part of living in the Catholic Church today and do not put me outside the pale of Roman Catholicism. The Vatican Congregation for the Doctrine of the Faith made no judgment about my situation as a believing member of the church and even as a Catholic priest.

I appreciate the Catholic theological tradition; it is the tradition that makes most sense to me. As a living tradition that recognizes the four sources of theology and the inclusiveness and universality often associated with a "both-and" approach, the Catholic tradition is most helpful in dealing with individual moral issues but also in analyzing and synthesizing all the aspects involved in doing moral theology. The methodological approaches embedded in the living Catholic tradition provide the basis even to dissent at times from some comparatively few hierarchical teachings.

This volume comes, then, from a committed Catholic Christian. The synthesis developed in this volume tries to integrate into moral theology all aspects of the Catholic tradition that bear on morality. This synthesis builds on, appreciates, and appeals to the Catholic understanding of the church community and its life, the centrality of liturgy, especially the eucharist, the spiritual tradition, and other aspects dealing specifically with morality in the Catholic tradition. And all these aspects must be seen in dialogue with other Christians, philosophers, ethicists, and the signs of the times.

Thus, I have tried to make this synthesis both comprehensive and adequate in the light of the living tradition of Catholic moral theology and my own social location. The estimate of its success, I leave, as I must, to the readers' discernment.

NOTES

1. For official documentation and my analysis and reflections, see Curran, *Faithful Dissent.*

2. For different evaluations of my dissent see William W. May, ed., *Vatican Authority and American Catholic Dissent;* and Curran and McCormick, eds., *Readings in Moral Theology: No. 6.*

Index

Abelard, Peter, 88

actions, xii, 3, 62, 70, 73, 93, 110, 172; and agent-subject, 88, 89, 150; and categorical freedom, 97, 106, 143; and consequentialism, 70–71; and intention, 155; and intrinsic evil, 139, 141, 144, 150, 155, 160; and law, 64, 175; and physical structure, 150, 152–155, 166; and sinful, 39, 65, 79, 150, 192; and subjective conscience, 174, 192; and Thomistic system, 67–69

Acts, 26, n. 5; 89, 91

Adam, 18; and Eve, 74–76

Aertnys, I., 194, n. 1; 229, n. 13

agent, xii, 88; and actions, 88, 130; community of, 73; and intentionality, 70, 150, 192; and power, 130; and subject, 70, 88, 97, 98, 118, 127, 132, 182, 192, 194

Alexander VIII, 201

Allen, Joseph L., 84, n. 13

Allenson, Alec R., 170, n. 102

Allsopp, Michael E., 167, n. 4; 168, n. 39

Altizer, Thomas J. J., 57, n. 35

Ambrose, 122

Andrew, Maurice Edward, 170, n. 102

Angelini, Guiseppe, 25, n. 1; 84, n. 19

Appleby, R. Scott, 230, n. 29

Aquinas, Thomas, x, 14, 25, n. 3; 33, 74, 195, nn. 10, 23; 217, 222, and

Aristotelian-Thomistic tradition, 23, 32, 87, 99, 100, 117, 121, 123, 160; and Dominican tradition, 62, 111; and faculties and powers, 111, 113, 114; and human acts, 67, 88, 155, 174, 182; and natural law, 35, 68, 138, 139, 143, 150, 152, 154, 156, 158, 159, 175, 179–180, 186; and relational model, 113; and *Summa theologiae*, 1, 27, 28, n. 49; 56, nn. 10–12, 14; 61, 67, nn. 35, 38; 84, nn. 16, 17, 19; 85, nn. 35, 36; 108, n. 39; 133, nn. 1, 5, 7, 15; 135, nn. 44, 45, 54; 136, n. 61; 167, n. 13; 169, nn. 71, 74, 75, 177; and teleology, 66–69, 71–73, 137, 140, 158; and Thomistic philosophy, 11, 38; and virtues and habits, 68, 87, 110, 111–113, 120

Aristotle, x, 14, 23, 66, 67, 99, 108, n. 38; 117, 121–122, 126, 136, n. 60; and virtues, 110, 111, 180

artificial contraception or birth control, 3, 36, 82, 142–144, 146, 150, 152, 153, 156, 157, 158, 159, 160, 163, 164, 199, 203, 210–211, 213, 217, 219, 223, 224, 225, 239

Aubert, Roger, 229, n. 19, 22

Augustine, 67, 71, 74, 111, 115, 120

von Balthasar, Hans Urs, 27, n. 37

baptism, and community, 3, 76; and mediation, 11

241

Barth, Karl, 11, 27, n. 37; 39, 40, 56, n. 8; 85, n. 31

Bauer, Johannes B., 134, n. 23

Bauman, Zygmunt, 28, n. 61

Bernard of Clairvaux, 88

Bernardine, Joseph Cardinal, 28, n. 51

Berry, Thomas, 135–136, n 59

Bertone, Tarcisio, 225, 234, n. 102

Billy, Dennis J., 28, n. 49; 107, n. 30; 168, n. 51

bioethics, xi, 64, 99

bishop, of Rome, 9; college of, 9, 13; collegiality, 13; role, 14; teaching in communion, 141

Böckle, Franz, 57, n. 26

Bouquillon, Thomas, 84, n. 9; 203, 229, n. 15

Bouscaren, T. Lincoln, 169, n. 70; 202, 229, nn. 10, 12, 14

Bouvier, L., 135, n. 45

Boyle, John, 226, 229, n 6; 230, n. 34; 232, nn. 65, 77; 234, n. 103

Boyle, Joseph, 170, nn. 89, 93

Boyle, Philip, 169, n. 77

Brown, Raymond, 85, n. 33

Butler, Cuthbert, 230, n. 24

Cahill, Lisa Sowle, 23, 29, n. 70

Cahill, Thomas, 18, 28, n. 56

Call to Action, 99

Callahan, Daniel, 57, nn. 21, 35

Callahan, Sidney, 195, nn. 24, 25; 196, n. 31

Calvin, John, 37, 57, n. 23; and Calvinism, 39

Camp, Richard L., 168, n. 56

Campaign for Human Development, 15, 131, 136, n. 67

Campbell, Ted A., 58, n. 46

Cappellari, Mauro, 229, n. 23

Cappello, Felix, 223, 233, n. 93

Carrillo de Albornoz, Angel F., 56, n. 16

Cartechini, Sixtus, 232, n. 75

casuistry, 137, 164–165

Catechism of Catholic Church, 74–75, 82–83, 85, n. 34; 86, n. 56

Catholic moral theology, 30, 40–41, 49–50, 60, 95, 110, 111, 181; dealing with persons, institutions, actions, xii, 87–88, 89, 153; and ecology, 125–126; extremes of laxism and rigorism, 53, 62, 63, 193; and hermeneutic problem, 53; and obligation, 70, 137; and physicalism, 150, 152–155; and relativism, 161; and sources, 47–55, 182; and systematic approach, 181

Catholic moral tradition, x, ix, xi, 8, 9, 66, 70, 110, 111, 152, 173; and catholicity, x, 4, 8, 48, 76; embodied in church community, ix, 1, 30, 48; and goodness of creation, 33, 34, 54, 131; as inclusive, x, 4, 5, 18, 51; and killing, 42–43, 49, 118, 137, 141, 144, 150, 152–153, 155, 157, 162, 164–165; and object of act, 182; and power, 130–132; not monolithic, xiii, 138; and Scripture as interpreted by church, ix, 2, 12, 48; and social nature of person, 99–100, 121, 123; and universal ethics, 20, 21–24, 66, 68, 76

Catholic sexual teaching, xi, 82, 129, 163; and artificial contraception, 3, 36, 82, 142–144, 145, 146, 150, 152–153, 156, 157, 158, 159, 160, 163, 164, 199, 203, 210–211, 213, 217, 219, 223, 224, 225, 239; and artificial insemination, 142–143, 144, 146, 150, 152, 156, 158, 204, 211, 217; and deontological model, 146; and faculties, 82–83, 112, 144, 145, 146, 152, 211; and homosexual acts, 143, 144, 146, 150, 152–153, 156, 157, 158, 199, 211, 213, 225, 239; and in vitro fertilization, 142–144, 211, 217; and masturbation, 143, 144, 146, 150, 152–153, 156, 160, 211, 213; and pre-marital relations, 153, 166, 211, 225

Catholic social ethics, xi, 9, 83, 122, 130, 131, 160, 172

Centesimus annus, 78, 86, n. 46; 122, 135, n. 40; 170, n. 101

Cessario, Romanus, 106, n. 2; 111, 133, nn. 6, 16

Champlin, Joseph M., 86, n. 48

character, 87, 106; and virtues, 110–112

Chavannes, Henry, 57, n. 27

Christ, Carol, 107, n. 20

Christiansen, Drew, 135, n. 59

Christology, 21, 31, 53, 92; from above, 22; from below, 21–22, 92; and Chalcedonian formula 92; and Logos, 22

church, as Catholic, 14, 16, 33; and community action, 15; as community of disciples, 2, 3, 12, 16, 112, 127; as community mediating God's presence, 2, 3, 9, 10, 13, 188, 198; as inclusive, 4, 9–10, 15, 16, 24; as moral ethos and ground for ethics, 5, 30, 116, 184, 188; as people of God, 3, 14, 52; as pilgrim, 16, 116; as post-Constantinian, 7; as prophetic, 17; as sinful, 24, 116, 188; as teaching and learning community, 3, 14, 197, 197–198; as voluntary society, 3, 4

classicism, 100, 130, 149; and family, 100, 101; and hierarchical teaching, 80, 147; and moral manuals, 20, 21

Clifford, Richard, 85, n. 33

Code of Canon Law, 9, 65, 67, 227

Coleman, John A., 28, n. 54; 108, n. 48

Collins, Mary, 59, n. 60; 86, n. 49; 134, n. 19

Collins, Raymond, 59, n. 57

Colossians, 50

common good, x, 99, 102–103, 124, 130, 160

communitarians, 137

Congar, Yves, 229, n. 5; 233, n. 87; 234, n 104

Congregation for the Doctrine of the Faith or Holy Office, 62, 81, 82, 86, n. 51; 150, 201, 202, 203, 212, 213, 214, 224, 225, 232, nn. 58, 63; 239; and Declaration on Sexual Ethics, 81, 142, 145, 150, 167, nn. 28, 29; and Instruction on Respect for Human Life, 143, 167, nn. 33, 34; and Instruction on the Ecclesial Vocation of Theologians, 232, nn. 66–71; and Joseph Cardinal Ratzinger, 83; and Letter on Pastoral Care of Homosexual Persons, 146, 168, n. 50

Congregation of Divine Worship, 79, 86, n. 48

Conn, Walter, 96, 107, n. 28

Connery, John, 229, nn. 10, 11; 233, n. 93

Connolly, Hugh, 84, n. 4

conscience, xiii, 36, 166, 172–196, 236; antecedent, 174–175; and consequent, 174–175, 186; examination of, 128; and imagination, 183–184; and interior peace, 177–179, 186; and intuitions, 178–179, 184–185; and invincible ignorance, 88, 173; and reason, 183–184; and sincere and insincere, 173; as subjective norm, 62, 173–174, 186; and superego, 189–190; true or erroneous, 173, 185–187, 189 consequentialism, 69–72, 118, 144, 157

Constitution on the Church, 2, 25, n. 4; 26, nn. 6, 8; 27, nn. 25, 26; 42, 43, 44, 46, 107, n. 15; 230, nn. 33, 38; 233, n. 98; 197, 207–208, 209

Constitution on the Liturgy, 10, 27, nn. 33, 34; 57, n. 30

contract theory, 102, 121, 124

conversion, 16, 17, 47, 80, 98, 127, 182; and basic orientation, 95, 236; and Lonergan, 95–96

Coriden, James A., 27, n. 48; 232, n. 62

Corinthians, 52

Council of Trent, 1, 62, 106, n. 1; 191

Counter Reformation, 53

Cowdin, Daniel M., 135–136, n. 59

creation, 10, 11, 47, 69, 74, 116, 126, 131, 160; and ecology, 73, 94, 125, 126; and goods of, 122; and sacramentality, 126; and sin, 37–38, 44; and stance, 33, 35, 36, 41, 42, 43, 51, 128

Crocco, Stephen D., 84, n. 12

Cromartie, Michael, 57, n. 23

Cronin, John F., 168, n. 56

Crossan, John Dominic, 56, n. 7

Crowe, Frederick, 85, n. 40

Cummings, Charles, 107, n. 19

Curran, Charles E., 25, n. 2; 27, n. 24; 28, nn. 50, 64; 29, n. 68; 56, n. 13; 59, n. 58; 84, n. 12; 86, nn. 53, 54; 108, n. 43; 109, n. 57; 134, n. 34; 135, n. 51; 136, n. 64; 166, n. 2; 167, n. 27; 168, n. 40; 169, nn. 73, 74; 170, n. 82; 196, nn. 38, 39; 228, n. 2; 229, n. 5; 230, nn. 35, 36; 231, nn. 46, 49, 56, 57; 232, nn. 72, 76, 83; 233, nn. 88, 90; 240, nn. 1, 2

Dallen, James, 86, n. 47; 134, n. 31

Daly, Gabriel, 230, nn. 27, 29

Damen, C., 194, n. 1

D'Antonio, William V., 26, n. 14; 229, n. 4; 230, nn. 26–28, 31

de Blic, I., 195, n. 7

Declaration on Religious Liberty, 7, 26, n. 21; 36, 56, nn. 16–18; 105, 109, n. 63; 148, 163, 168, n. 43; 209, 220, 230, n. 39; 232, n. 81; 233, nn. 87–90

Decree on the Training of Priests, 57, n. 32

de Guibert, Joseph, 195, nn. 11, 12, 14, 15

Delhaye, Philippe, 107, n. 25; 168, n. 51; 194, n. 5

Deman, T., 84, nn. 5, 8

Denzinger, Henricus, 106, 229, nn. 8, 9

deontological model, 60, 61–66, 74, 76, 77, 118, 146, 158, 187; and hierarchical teaching, 80–81, 146; or legal, 64; and manuals, 61, 67; and right vs good, 66; strengths of, 65–66; strict vs modified, 65

de Smedt, Émile-Joseph, 220, 233, n. 87

Dionne, J. Robert, 171, nn. 105, 106; 232, n. 73

discernment, 53; of Spirits, 55, 72, 177–178, 183–184, 186

Dogmatic Constitution on Divine Revelation, 48, 57, n. 31; 59, n. 60

Doherty, J.J., 108, n. 46

Dolan, John, 229, n. 19

Donahue, James, 108, n. 47

Donceel, Joseph, 233, n. 92

Dorr, Donal, 135, n. 47

Dorszynski, Julius A., 86, n. 55; 170, n. 83

Douglass, R. Bruce, 28, n. 62; 109, n. 54; 168, n. 57; 169, n. 58

Downey, Michael, 94, 107, nn. 14, 22

Dublanchy, E., 84, n. 5

Dubruel, M., 229, n. 20

Duffy, Stephen, 56, n. 3; 57, n. 39

Dulles, Avery, 58, n. 47; 133, n. 15
Dwyer, Judith A., 136, n. 65

Eastern Orthodoxy, 53, 59, n. 63
Egan, Marie, 136. n. 70
Ellington, James, 83, n. 2
Engelen, William J., 109, n. 56
Enlightenment, 19, 20, 23, 104, 115,
    145, 148
Ephesians, 50
epistemology, 22, 123, 160, 161, 186,
    218
Erickson, Erik, 96
Ervin, Sam, 61, 84, n. 3
eschatology, 44, 49–50, 52, 115, 116,
    128; tensions, 34, 42, 91
essentialist approaches, 19–20, 24,
    100, 142
eucharist, 9, 10–11, 120, 128; and
    Holy Thursday, 94, 95
Evangelium vitae, 141–142, 147, 150,
    167, nn. 22–25; 169, nn. 66, 67;
    171, n. 110
experience, x, 44, 54–55, 143, 162,
    164; of God, 55; moral, 185, 189;
    of oppressed, 19, 54; as source for
    ethics, 12, 20, 23, 48, 137

Fahey, Michael A., 25, n. 4; 26, n. 7;
    27, nn. 28, 47
faith, 8, 12, 41, 54, 138, 183, 184; as
    virtue, 41, 51, 68, 90, 113, 114, 115
Faley, Roland J., 84, n. 13
Farley, Margaret, 22, 29, n. 68; 108,
    n. 43
feminist ethics and theology, 19–23,
    50, 115, 131; and African-
    American theologies, 20, 131; and
    ecofeminism, 126; and *mujeristas*,
    20
fidelity, 113, 118
Fiedler, Maureen, 233, n. 90

Finnis, John, 157, 158–160, 170,
    nn. 89, 93
Fiorenza, Elizabeth Schüssler, 59,
    n. 55
Fiorenza, Francis Schüssler, 25, n. 4;
    27, nn. 28, 47; 58, n. 47; 106, nn. 8,
    9; 133, n. 15
Fitzmyer, Joseph A., 85, n. 33
Fletcher, Joseph, 69, 85, n. 22
Ford, John C., 223, 233, n. 97
fortitude, 112–113
Francis de Sales, 178–179
freedom or liberty, 36, 77, 81, 116,
    118, 140, 145, 148, 149; categori-
    cal, 96; and fundamental option,
    96–98; and intrinsic approaches
    65; transcendental, 97
Freud, 181, 189
Freyne, Sean, 171, n. 102
Fuchs, Josef, 96, 106, n. 6; 107, n. 31;
    108, n. 36
Fuerth, Patrick, 26, n. 11
fundamental moral theology, xi, 68,
    98, 99

Gaffney, James, 168, n. 39
Gaillardetz, Richard B., 228, n. 2;
    229, n. 7; 230, n. 34; 232, n. 74
Galatians, 4
Galileo, 7
Galvin, John P., 25, n. 4; 26, n. 7; 27,
    nn. 28, 47; 58, n. 47; 106, n. 9; 133,
    n. 15
Gannon, Thomas, 109, n. 53
Gelin, Albert, 134, n. 29
Genesis, 18, 33, 44, 74–75, 125
Gilleman, Gérard, 56, n. 11
Gilligan, Carol, 88, 106, n. 5
Gilson, Etienne, 25, n. 3; 84, n. 16;
    109, n. 58; 180, 195, n. 18
Glover, Jonathon, 85, n. 26
Gnosticism, 129

God, 2, 44, 66, 99; in Aquinas, 71, 72,
113, 186; and creation, x, 10, 11,
33, 34, 35, 36, 40, 69, 139; faith in,
7, 115; image of, 127; law of, 79,
139–140; as mother and father, 18,
40, 64, 95; people of, 14, 115; and
poor, 19, 21, 123; and reign of, 13,
34, 42, 43, 45, 95, 115, 116, 119; re
lationship with, xii, 4, 10, 12, 32,
44, 73, 74–75, 80, 97, 113–114, 118,
119, 122, 127; saving grace, 3, 71,
76, 87–88, 89, 90, 110, 116, 119;
Triune, 32, 53, 76, 92; wills holiness, 3, 5, 16, 111
Goodall, Norman, 26, n. 11
Gorman, Rosemarie, xiii
Gospel, 8, 64, 73, 93, 119, 148, 149,
177; Synoptic, 32, 73, 89
grace, 36, 41, 42, 46, 53, 54, 68, 76,
87, 97, 138, 182, 183, 185, 190; and
works, 11, 12, 13, 112; and soteriology, 91–92, 97; and virtue, 110,
111–112
Grazen, Walter, 135, n. 59
Greeley, Andrew M., 12
Green, Thomas, 232, n. 62
Gregory XVI, 163, 205–206, 230,
n. 25
Griffin, Leslie, 170, n. 98; 231, n. 56
Grisez, Germain, 157, 158–160, 170,
nn. 85–87, 89–95; 223, 224, 233,
n. 97; 234, n. 100
Gudorf, Christine E., 108, n. 43; 136,
n. 64
Guenther, Titus F., 108, n. 33
Guillet, Jacques, 195, n. 11
Guindon, André, 213, 231, n. 56; 213,
232, n. 58
Gula, Richard M., xiii, 28, n. 63; 195,
n. 22; 196, n. 30
Gurr, J.E., 84, n. 18
Gustafson, James, 30, 31, 56, nn. 2, 5,
6; 125, 135, n. 55

Gutiérrez, Gustavo, 28, n. 58; 58,
n. 44; 92, 94, 106, n. 11; 107, n. 18

Habermas, Jürgen, 170, n. 97
Haight, Roger, 106, n. 9
Hall, Pamela, 167, n. 5; 170, n. 88
Hallahan, Kenneth P., 26, n. 18
Hamilton, William, 57, n. 35
Happel, Stephen, 96, 107, n. 29
Harakas, Stanley Samuel, 59, n. 63
Häring, Bernard, 49, 58, n. 53; 85,
n. 38; 95, 107, nn. 25, 26; 118, 134,
n. 25; 168, n. 48; 193, 196, n. 41;
212, 231, n. 53
Hauerwas, Stanley, 6, 26, n. 19; 58,
n. 45; 133, n. 3; and particular
community, 46–47; and stance, 47;
and universal ethic, 6; and virtues, 47
Hay, Leo C., 134, n. 30
Hayes, Diana L., 28, n. 59
Healy, Edwin, 233, n. 94
Hebrew Bible, 16, 48, 64, 115, 123;
and Abraham and Sarah, 64, 119;
and covenant, 64, 76; and good
and evil spirits, 177; and heart,
184; and Moses, 64, 90, 119; and
Saul, 177; and Torah, 64
Heintschel, Donald E., 232, n. 62
Hering, Hyacinth M., 233, n. 92
hermeneutic circle, 55
hierarchical magisterium or teaching
office, xiii, 3, 8, 14, 35, 36, 55, 93,
141, 155, 158, 199–201, 209, 212,
216, 222, 227, 239; and deontological model, 80–81; and infallible
and non-infallible teaching, 200,
205, 208, 215, 216, 218, 219, 221,
223–226; and ordinary magisterium, 201, 207, 208, 210, 214; and
papal magisterium, 14, 53, 104,
139, 141, 142, 152, 163, 201–204,

207–208, 210, 214–215, 218–221, 227–228

Hiers, Richard, 59, n. 54

Hill, William, 57, n. 28

Hillman, Eugene, 27, n. 30

Himes, Kenneth, 28, n. 54

Hinze, Christine Firer, xiii, 131–132, 136, nn. 68, 69, 71, 72

historical consciousness, 21, 76, 78, 112, 118, 131, 138, 140, 147–149, 152

Hogan, John B., 191–192, 196, n. 37

Hollenbach, David, 28, n. 62; 109, n. 54; 168, n. 57; 169, n. 58

Holocaust, 15

Holy Spirit, xi, 2, 48, 52, 53, 55, 76, 93, 97, 114, 119, 177, 184, 197, 200, 209, 218, 221, 222, 227, 228

Hoose, Bernard, 170, n. 84

hope, 51, 68, 113, 115–117

human dignity, 36, 145, 148, 164

Humanae vitae, 31–37, 56, nn. 19, 20; 86, n. 54; 142, 147, 150, 167, nn. 30, 31; 168, n. 52; 193–194, 196, n. 42; 231, nn. 41–44; 210–211, 216, 218,

Humani generis, 200, 207,

Hunt, Robert E., 230, n. 35; 231, n. 46; 232, n. 72

Hürth, Franciscus, 207, 230, n. 32

Hutchinson, D.S., 84, n. 15

Ignatius of Loyola, 178–179, 195, n. 13

infallibility, 9

Innocent XI, 49

International Synod on Justice in the World, 12, 27, n. 39; 93, 99, 107, n. 17

Irwin, Kevin, 135, n. 56

Isasi-Diaz, Ada Maria, 28, n. 60

Jans, Jan, 106, n. 7

Jansenism, 129

Jesuits, and *Institutiones theologiae moralis*, 62, 65

Jerome, 175

Jesus, 5, 6, 10, 11, 13, 48, 64, 69, 114, 138, 140, 147, 177, 198, 206, 207, 219, 222; and body of Christ, 9; and community of disciples, 2, 12, 16, 89, 90–91, 94, 119, 127, 187–188; embodying God's love, 97; and gift of peace, 36; and Incarnation, 33–34; and metaphysical and ontological aspects, 21, 92; and Paschal Mystery, and cross, 32, 34, 43, 72, 92, 115; and poor, 22; as priest, teacher, ruler, 14; and principles, 45, 147; and relationality, 76; and saving work, 21, 52, 94; as stance for ethics, 31, 41, 44, 64;

Joachim of Fiore, 115

John, and faith, 90; and First Letter of, 177

John of the Cross, 88, 106, n. 3

John XXIII, 35, 56, n. 15; 77–78, 85, nn. 41, 42; 103, 108, n. 49; 145, 148, 168, nn. 41, 42; 169, nn. 59, 60; 170, n. 99; 171, n. 113

John Paul II, 138–144, 146, 160, 188, 224, 227; and *Centesimus annus*, 78, 86, n. 46; 122, 135, n. 40; 170, n. 101; and *Evangelium vitae*, 141–142, 147, 150, 167, nn. 22–25; 169, nn. 66, 67; 171, n. 110; and *Familiaris consortio*, 194, 196, n. 45; and *Laborem exercens*, 145, 149, 168, nn. 45, 53; and *Sapientia Christiana*, 213; and *Sollicitudo socialis*, 170, n. 100; and United Nations Address on Fabric of Relations Among Countries, 63–65; and *Veritatis splendor*, 81, 86, n. 52; 88, 98,

106, n. 7; 108, n. 35; 138, 144, 147,
149, 150, 152, 154, 155, 159, 166,
n. 1; 167, nn. 3, 6–12, 14–21, 26,
35–37; 168, nn. 38, 39, 53; 169,
nn. 76, 78, 80, 81; 170, n. 96; 199,
213–214, 217, 229, n. 3; 231, n. 50;
232, nn. 60, 61, 78, 79; 234, n. 101;
239
Johnson, Elizabeth, 106, n. 10; 135,
n. 57
Johnson, Luke Timothy, 56, n. 7
Johnson, Mark, 233, n. 92
Johnstone, Brian V., 106, n. 7; 107,
n. 30
Jones, Frederick, 196, n. 38
Jonsen, Albert R., 58, n. 52; 171,
nn. 107, 108
Judeo-Christian tradition, 16, 19
just war theory, 38, 43, 187
justice, 15, 24, 90, 99, 105, 113, 132,
145, 149, 156, 172; and almsgiving, 123; commutative, 121, 124,
162; distributive, 3, 121–124, 162;
and forgiveness, 112; legal or contributive, 124; and peace, 17, 116;
social, 8, 47, 93, 124, 162; and taxation, 123–124; as virtue, 112, 120,
121, 123–125, 162

Kaiser, Robert Blair, 231, n. 41
Kant, Immanuel, 61, 77, 83, n. 2; 128,
189, 196, n. 28
Kaufmann, Ludwig, 231, n. 54
Keane, Philip S., 134, n. 24; 213
Keenan, James, 106, n. 6; 133, nn. 9,
12; 171, n. 107
Kelly, Gerald, 86, n. 50
Kennedy, Robert J., 86, n. 49
Kennedy, Terence, 28, n. 49
Kenny, John P., 27, n. 45; 229, n. 18
killing, 42–43, 49, 118, 144, 150, 152–
153, 155, 157, 162, 164–165; and

abortion, 141–142, 144, 150–151,
152, 162, 201–202, 204, 213, 222,
225; and capital punishment, 137;
and euthanasia, 141, 144, 226
King, Martin Luther, 45, 58, n. 42
Klubertanz, George P., 133, nn. 10,
11, 14
Kohlberg, Lawrence, 88, 96, 106, n. 5
Komonchak, Joseph A., 59, n. 60;
134, n. 19
Kosnik, Anthony, 213, 231, n. 56
Kung, Hans, 26, nn. 7, 10; 29, n. 71;
171, n. 112; 231, n. 52; 233, n. 87
Kuschei, Karl-Josef, 29, n. 71

Laborem exercens, 145, 149, 168, n. 45
LaCugna, Catherine Mowry, 85,
n. 37; 92, 107, n. 13
LaDue, William J., 229, n. 19
Lammenais, Felicité, 205
Lane, Dermot A., 59, n. 60; 133,
n. 17; 134, n. 19
Langan, John, 170, n. 84
Langford, Thomas G., 58, n. 46
Larkin, E.E., 106, n. 4
Las Casas, Bartolomé, 96
law, 117, 166; in Aquinas, 68–69; and
deontological model, 64, 68, 146;
and legal models, 61, 63, 65, 68,
79, 80, 81, 137, 140, 146, 175, 176,
190, 192; of neighbor love, 32; as
objective norm, 62; and probabilism vs probabiliorism, 63, 65;
and rigorism vs laxism, 53, 62, 63;
and teleological model, 68; written in human nature, 36, 146, 148
Lazareth, William H., 108, n. 45
Leo XIII, condemnations of freedom,
105; and social encyclicals, 18, 78,
104–105; 109, nn. 58–61; 120,
144–145
Lercher, Ludwig, 208

liberalism, 104

liberation theologies, 18–20, 25, 46, 115, 123, 131, 132; emphasis on particular, 21; and salvation, 46, 92; and stance, 46; and spirituality, 94

Liguori, Alphonsus, 63, 173–174; and actions, 88; and law of growth, 192, 196, n. 38; and ultramontanism, 63

Lio, Hermenegildus, 135, n. 46; 233, n. 95

Little, David, 57, n. 23

Lombard, Peter, 122, 123, 135, n. 43; 175

Lonergan, Bernard, 21, 77, 95, 107, n. 27; 186, 195, n. 26; 196, n. 27

Lottin, Odon, 133, n. 8; 135, n. 44; 195, n. 6

love, or charity, 2, 11, 32, 34, 43, 87, 145, 149, 184; Christian, 64, 69; God's love, 3, 10, 12, 32, 44, 73, 75, 113; for God, friendship with, 97, 111, 114; and neighbor, 12, 32, 73, 97, 111, 114, 125; in New Testament, 49, 90; for poor, 19, 123; as theological virtue, 32, 51, 68, 113

Lovin, Robin, 56, n. 8; 58, n. 43

Luke, 119, 188; and beatitudes, 89

Lutheran tradition, and gift of salvation, 110, 112; on political society, 101–102; and power of sin, 101–102

lying, 82, 83, 166

MacNamera, Vincent, 58, n. 40

Maguire, Daniel, 134, nn. 24, 34; 183, 195, n. 21

Mahoney, John, 27, n. 29

Mansour, Agnes Mary, 213

manuals of dogmatic theology, 21, 53

manuals of moral theology, 53, 88, 145, 164, 207–208; and Aquinas, 67, 154, 174, 176; and canon law, 65; and Council of Trent, 1, 62; and deontological approach, 61, 67, 186, 192; and essentialism, 20; and killing, 49; and Liguori, 63, 174, 192–3; and physicalism, 152–153; and principles, 137; and quandary ethics, 51, 110, 164; and reason, 49, 65; and sacrament of penance, 1, 62, 65, 87, 190; and virtues, 110, 117

Maritain, Jacques, 131, 179, 183, 195, n. 16

Mark, 89, 119

Martensen, Daniel F., 59, n. 61

Mary, 11, 63, 119, 188

Mater et magistra, 108, n. 49; 145, 168, n. 41

Matthew, 52, 73, 119, 125, 127, 140, 177; and divorce and remarriage, 52, 147; and poor in Spirit, 89–90

May, William W., 232, n. 57; 240, n. 2

Mayes, A. D. H., 170, n. 102

McBrien, Richard, 27, nn. 31, 36

McClory, Robert, 231, n. 41

McCormick, Richard A., 27, n. 24; 29, n. 68; 56, n. 13; 86, n. 54; 108, n. 43; 166, n. 2; 167, n. 27; 169–170, nn. 73, 82; 170, n. 84; 228, n. 2; 229, n. 5; 230, n. 34; 231, nn. 49, 56; 232, n. 83; 233, n. 91; 240, n. 2

McDonagh, Enda, 85, n. 38

McInerny, Ralph M., 57, n. 25; 167, n. 5; 168, n. 39

McNeil, John, 212, 231, n. 56

mediation, 10, 12, 13, 35, 40, 43, 53, 69, 139, 183–184, 189; and analogy, 11–12, 39; and Catholic worldview, 44

Meier, John P., 56, n. 7

Meilander, Gilbert, 110, 133, n. 4

Merkelbach, Benedictus H., 194, n. 1; 195, n. 20

Merton, Thomas, 18, 134, n. 28

Messner, Johannes, 108, n. 46; 109, n. 55; 136, n. 65

Messori, Vittorio, 231, n. 55

Metternich, Klemens, 205

Metz, Johann Baptist, 97

Mick, Lawrence, 107, n. 24

Miller, Donald A., 108, n. 42

Miller, Richard B., 171, n. 107

Minus, Paul M., 58, n. 41

Misner, Paul, 134, n. 32

model for interpreting moral life, xii, 60–86; and ethical models, 138; not exclusive, 60

modernism, 19–20

Mondin, Battista, 57, n. 27

Moo, Douglas J., 58, n. 49

Moore, Gareth, 136, n. 64

morality, extrinsic and intrinsic, 65; and global ethic, 166; and particular actions, 54; and social location, ix; and systematic study, xi

moral knowledge and wisdom, x, 35, 37, 38, 40, 49, 50, 54, 55, 69, 95, 138

moral self, 22, 87, 88, 153; and moral subject, 65, 127, 172; and unencumbered self, 110

moral theory, 138, 139; and John Paul II, 138–144

Moser, Mary Theresa, 108, n. 47

Mouw, Richard J., 84, n. 14

Mueller-Volmer, Kurt, 170, n. 97

Murphy, Charles, 135, n. 59

Murphy, Roland E., 85, n. 33

Murray, John Courtney, 115, 133, n. 18; 134, n. 36; 220, 233, n. 88

National Catholic Reporter, 196, n. 44

National Conference of Catholic Bishops, Challenge of Peace, 28, n. 53; 78; 85, n. 44; 152, 169, n. 72

National Conference of Catholic Bishops, Committee on Biblical Fundamentalism, 58, n. 50

National Conference of Catholic Bishops, Pastoral Letter on Economy, 6–7, 26, n. 20; 85, n. 45; 103–104, 109, nn. 50–53; 124

Native Americans, 19, 126, 220

natural law, 8, 23, 36, 81, 138; and Aquinas, 68–69, 137, 138, 143, 151, 154, 159, 176, 179–180; classicist version, 100, 130, 147; diversity of 138–139; participation in divine law, 35, 68–69, 139; physicalism, 152, 155; Protestant objections, 37; and sexual teachings, 82–83, 142–143; and Vatican II, 40–42

Naud, André, 219, 231, n. 51; 219, 232, n. 65; 233, n. 85

Nelson, Daniel Mark, 195, n. 17

Nevenzeit, Paul, 134, n. 23

New Testament, 32, 48, 49–50, 119, 123, 177

Newman, Jeremiah, 134, n. 34

Nicene-Constantinopolitan Creed, 4

Niebuhr, H. Richard, 28, n. 55; 83, n. 1; 85, nn. 29, 30; and person as maker, 72; and relational approach, 60, 73

Niebuhr, Reinhold, 45, 131

Noldin, Hieronymus, 195, n. 8; 196, nn. 32, 33, 35

Noonan, John T., 171, nn. 103–105; 196, n. 41; 229, n. 16; 232, n. 73

norms, 64, 68, 139, 143, 146, 149, 188, 189; absolute, 142, 147, 165–166; and concrete, 141, 150, 159, 163, 164; and intrinsic evil, 141; and

objective, 147; and practical vs
theoretical, 138; and universal,
140, 141–143, 166

Nygren, Anders, 85, n. 31

objective pole of morality, xii, 62, 64,
66, 83, 89, 132, 137, 162, 172, 182,
190, 193, 237

O'Brien, David, 27, n. 39; 57, nn. 36–
38; 85, nn. 41–44; 86, n. 46; 107,
n. 17; 108, nn. 47, 49; 109, n. 64;
135, nn. 38, 40–42; 168, nn. 39, 41,
42, 44, 45; 169, nn. 59–62, 72

O'Connell, Marvin, 230, n. 29

O'Connell, Timothy, 96, 108, n. 32;
230, n. 40

Octogesima adveniens, 78, 85, n. 43;
99, 105, 109, n. 64; 145, 149, 168,
n. 44; 169, n. 62

O'Hanlon, Daniel, 233, n. 87

O'Keefe, John J., 167, n. 4; 168, n. 39

O'Keefe, Mark, 107, n. 14; 136, n. 73

O'Malley, John W. 230, n. 40

O'Meara, Thomas F., 25, n. 3; 111,
133, n. 7

O'Rourke, Kevin D., 169, n. 77

Orsutu, Donna L., 107, n. 30

Ortolan, T., 229, n. 21

Orsy, Ladislas, 228, n. 1; 230, n. 34

Outka, Gene, 29, n. 68; 57, n. 23; 85,
n. 31

Outler, Albert, 58, n. 46

Pacem in terris, 8, 35, 36, 38, 40, 77,
78, 85, nn. 41, 42; 145, 148, 160,
168, n. 42; 169, nn. 59–61; 170,
n. 99; 171, n. 113

pacifism, 17, 43, 112

Pastoral Constitution on Church in
the Modern World, 6, 7, 26,
nn. 15, 22, 23; 40, 41, 57, nn. 33,

34, 36–38; 107, n. 16; 108, n. 47;
122, 135, n. 38; 142, 144, 145, 168,
nn. 39, 41, 42, 44, 45, 46, 48, 51

Patrick, Anne E., 22, 29, n. 69; 232,
n. 59

Paul, 32, 129, 174, 175, 177, 178

Paul VI, 36, 231, n. 45; and *Humanae
vitae*, 36–37, 56, nn. 19, 20; 86,
n. 54; 142, 147, 150, 167, nn. 30,
31; 168, n. 52; 210–211, 221, 231,
nn. 41–44; and *Octogesima adveniens*, 78, 85, n. 43; 99, 105, 109, n.
64; 145, 149, 168, n. 44; 169, n. 62;
and *Populorum progressio*, 122,
135, nn. 41, 42

peace, 17, 116, 149

Pelagianism, 110, 111; and semi-
pelagianism, 13

Pelikan, Jaroslav, 37; 57, n. 22

Pellegrino, Edmund D., 135, n. 56

person, 12, 83, 87–109, 88, 146, 153;
dignity of, 36, 145; fundamental
and basic orientation, 51, 89, 90,
95, 96, 98, 105, 113, 238; goodness
of, 15; and relationality, 77, 92, 99,
123; and social nature, 99–100,
121, 123, 160, 162; as subject and
agent, xii, 70, 88, 97, 118, 127, 132,
154, 237

Petrá, Basilio, 26, n. 12

Pfürtner, Stephan, 212

Philibert, Paul J., 106, n. 5

Philips, Gérard, 134, n. 20; 230, n. 37

philosophical ethics, 64, 161; and
Aristotle, 66; and consequentialism, 69–70; and principle of universalizability, 61; and Kant, 61;
two models, 60, 72, 76, 138; and
virtue, 110, 111

Piaget, Jean, 96

Pieper, Josef, 134, n. 34; 136, n. 63;
195, n. 19

Pierce, C.A., 174, 194, nn. 3, 4

Pius IX, 163

Pius XI, *Quadragesimo anno*, 147–148, 168, nn. 54, 55; 233, n. 95

Pius XII, 14, 105, 148, 160, 163, 200, 203–204, 233, n. 86; and prolongation of life, 169, n. 77

Plaskow, Judith, 107, n. 20

Poole, William T., 28, n. 51

poor, 54; cry of, 16, 19; material and poor in spirit, 89–90, 119; and marginalized, 94, 132; option for, 6, 18, 21, 93, 103, 123, 131

Pope, Stephen J., 28, n. 65

Populorum progressio, 122, 135, nn. 41, 42

Porter, Jean, 111, 133, n. 5; 167, nn. 4, 5; 155, 169, n. 79; 233, n. 92

postmodernism, 18–21, 23, 25, 54, 137

Pottmeyer, Hermann J., 232, n. 74

Power, David, 86, n. 49

power, 130–132

praxis, 23, 46, 198

pre-Vatican II church, 13, 14, 44, 62, 100, 138, 197; and natural-supernatural, 39–40; and sin, 39, 54; and triumphalism, 13, 47, 116

principles, 132, 133, 137–171; absolute, 147; conflicts of, 65; general, 141, 151, 165, 176, 177; intermediate, 159; and intrinsic evil, 139, 141, 155, 160, 198, 238; and natural inclinations, 140; and norms, 64, 68, 139, 160, 164, 172, 182, 183; and object pole, xii, 137; prima facie, 65

private property, and sin, 44; and social purpose, 122

probabilism, 63, and probabiliorism, 63, 192

prophet, 16–17, 119

proportionalism, 144, 155–158; and direct-indirect, 157; and premoral evil, 155–156

Protestant approaches, 2, 17, 36, 37; and ethics, 30, 125; and grace, 11–12, 110, 112; and reason, 37; and Scripture, 48, 49, 53, 175; and sin, 38, 39, 41, 45, 130, 131, 175

prudence, 23, 68, 112, 113, 177, 180, 183, 193

Quinn, Bishop John, 232, n. 84

Rabben, Linda, 233, n. 90

Rahner, Karl, 77, 92, 96, 97, 106, n. 12; 108, n. 34; 232, n. 83

Ramsey, Paul, 57, n. 23; 64, 84, n. 12; 170, n. 84

Ratzinger, Joseph Cardinal, 86, n. 57; 231, n. 55; 234, n. 102

Rauschenbusch, Walter, 45, 58, n. 41; 69, 84, n. 21; and sin 45

Rawls, John, 160, 170, n. 98; 189, 196, 197, n. 29

reason, 12, 34–35, 36, 40, 49, 138, 139, 162, 183, 185; in Aquinas, 68–69, 137, 144, 151, 154, 179–180; and experience, 12, 44, 48, 54–55, 162; goodness of, 34, 54; practical, 68, 151, 179–180; and sin, 38, 54

Reeder, John P., 29, n. 68

Reformation, 2, 4, 37

Regan, Richard J., 233, n. 87

relationality-responsibility model, xii, 55, 60, 73–80, 81–83, 117, 132, 146–149, 160, 166, 187, 188, 237; and faculties, 82–83; and fundamental option, 98; and multiple relationships with God, neighbor, self, world, xii, 73, 74–75, 77, 79, 80, 93, 105, 113, 118–119, 122, 125, 127, 133, 182, 192; and sin, 73–75, 76, 192; and social encyclicals, 77–79; and turn to subject, 187

relativism, 22, 23, 25; and subjectivism, 65, 160

resurrection destiny, and eschatologies, 34, 91; and stance, 34, 41–42, 44, 45, 87

Robertson, A. H., 29, n. 72

Rodger, P.C., 59, n. 59

Rohr, Richard, 107, n. 21

Roman Catholicism, 2, 13, 55; and catholicity, 8, 10, 14, 76; and divine, 40; and natural theology, 11, 42; and sin, 33, 38; and state, 100–102

Romans, 44

Rommen, Heinrich A., 108, n. 44

Ross, Susan A., 29, n. 67

Ryan, John A. 85, n. 27; 122, 123, 134, n. 37; 135, n. 48

Rynne, Xavier, 233, n. 87

Sabetti, Aloysius, 202

sacrament of penance and reconciliation, 1, 12, 39, 61, 79–80, 94, 120, 128; and history of, 61–62

sacraments, 11, 12, 40, 65, 94–95, 120

salvation, 5, 46; and community, 76; and morality, 110; and orientation, 89, 91, 97–98; and redemption, 22, 34, 36, 42–43, 88; as stance, 31, 43

Samples, John, xiii

Sanks, T. Howland, 230, n. 30

Scanlon, Michael, 134, n. 19

Scarre, Geoffrey, 85, n. 24

scholasticism, 8, 158, 175; and neo-scholasticism, 67

Schubeck, Thomas, 131; 136, n. 66

Schultenover, David G. 230, n. 29

Schweiker, William, 85, nn. 30, 39; 136, 74

Scripture, 7, 33, 44, 73, 114, 138, 162; and biblical morality, 51, 177; and Revelation, 48; and tradition, ix, 11, 13, 21, 48, 53, 55; as understood, interpreted, lived in community, ix–x, 48–49, 175, 188; and Vatican II, 40, 79

Sellers, James, 30, 31, 56, nn. 1, 4

Selling, Joseph, 106, n. 7; 168, n. 51; 231, n. 47

Sermon on the Mount, 6, 16, 51–52, 90

Shannon, Thomas, 27, n. 39; 57, nn. 36–38; 85, nn. 41–44; 86, n. 46; 107, n. 17; 108, nn. 47, 49; 109, n. 64; 135, nn. 38, 40–42; 168, nn. 39, 41, 42, 44, 45; 169, nn. 59–62; 171, n. 107; 233, n. 92

Shannon, William H. 28, n. 57; 196, n. 43; 231, n. 47

Shaw, Russell, 170, nn. 85–87, 90–92, 94, 95

Shriver, Donald W., 133, n. 13

Sigmund, Paul E., 109, n. 62; 169, n. 58

signs of the times, 23, 148

Siker, Jeffrey, 51, 59, n. 56

sin, 33, 37–39, 62, 65, 79–80, 99, 127, 138, 163, 188; and consumerism, 126–128; and Council of Trent, 1, 62; and finitude, 16, 54, 113, 128, 187; and goodness of creation, 38, 74–75; and individualism, 125–127; mortal, 1, 5, 74, 98, 190, 191, 192; and natural law, 38, 154; and power of, 34, 39, 101, 131; personal and structural, 42–43, 44–46, 132, 187; and sinful church, 16, 24, 116; and Vatican II, 41; and venial, 5, 109, 191

Skillrud, Harold C., 59, n. 61

Slamps, Mary E., 107, n. 23

Sobrino, Jon, 28, n. 66

Social Gospel School, 45, 69

social teaching, 83, 122; and individualism, 104; and papal social encyclicals, x, 18, 77, 80, 81, 104–105, 120–121, 144–146, 163

Sokolowski, Robert, 27, n. 40; 59, n. 64

Sollicitudo socialis, 170, n. 100

Southern Methodist, xiii

Sparks, Richard C., xiii

special moral theology, xi, 68, 99

Spicq, Ceslaus, 194, n. 5

Stafford, J. Francis, 59, n. 61

Stamm, Johann Jakob, 170, n. 102

stance or horizon, xii, 30–59, 60, 116; and five-fold mysteries, 33–34, 138, 237; and limits on Christian ethics, 46–47; limits on violence, 43; as source, 30, 128

Stein, Edith, 96

Stone, Jana, 135, n. 58

subject pole of morality, xii, 83, 172, 182, 190, 193, 197; and fundamental orientation, 90, 95, 96, 98, 105; and intentionality, 70, 88; and person and subject, xii, 70, 88, 97, 118, 127 132, 186

subsidiarity, 9, 103

Sullivan, Francis A. 26, n. 9; 224, 228, n. 2; 230, n. 34; 232, nn. 80, 82; 234, nn. 98, 99, 100

Sullivan, Roger, 136, n. 62; 196, n. 28

Summas, xi, 61

Swartz, Carol, xiii

Swidler, Leonard, 26, n. 10; 231, n. 52

Tavard, George H., 59, n. 60

Taylor, Charles, 133, n. 2

Taylor, Christopher (C.C.W.), 108, n. 38

teleological model, 60, 64, 65, 66–73, 76, 144, 146, 158; and Aristotle, 66; and Aquinas, 66–69, 71–73, 137, 140; and Catholic sexual teaching, 82; and consequential-

ism, 69–72; extrinsic, 69, 71, 72, 187; intrinsic, 71

temperance, 112–113, 128–129

Ten Commandments, 5, 61, 62, 64, 141, 162–163, 172

Teresa of Avila, 88, 106, n. 3

theologians, xiii, 117, 132; and Counter Reformation, 53; and dissent, 152; Medieval, 111, 175

Thessalonians, 50

Thielicke, Helmut, 57, n. 24; 108, n. 45

Thorsen, Donald A.D., 58, n. 46

Tillich, Paul, 132

Toner, Jules, 85, n. 28; 195, n. 13

Toulmin, Stephen, 58, n. 52; 171, n. 107

Tracy, David, 23, 27, n. 32

tradition, ix, 52, 55, 162; inheritance of particular church, 53; as source, 52–54; transmission of community's faith, ix, 48

Tremblay, Réal, 168, n. 51

Troeltsch, Ernst, 6, 26, n. 16; 84, n. 11

truth, x, 23, 66, 81, 105, 113, 118, 127, 140, 145, 149, 151, 160, 186

Udoidem, S. Iniobong, 27, n. 30

United Nations Address, Fabric of Relations Among Countries, 149, 169, nn. 63, 64, 65

U.S. Catholic Conference, Human Life in Our Day, 231, n. 48

U.S. Catholic Conference, Renewing the Earth, 135, n. 59

utilitarianism, 69–72; extrinsic, 72, rule, 71

Vacek, Edward Collins, 56, n. 9; 85, n. 32

Valsecchi, Ambrogio, 25, n. 1; 84, n. 19, 212

value, xii, 7, 17, 32, 132, 133, 149, 156, 182, 189, 197; basic goods, 140, 160, 162; comparison of goods, 158; existential and substantive goods, 159, 161

Varacalli, Joseph A., 108, n. 37

Vass, George, 85, n. 40

Vatican Council I, 9

Vatican Council II, xi, 1, 2, 5, 13, 116, 163, 191, 205, 206, 207–210, 219, 220, 227; and historical consciousness, 21; and natural law, 40–42, 139, 144, 145; and natural-supernatural dichotomy, 41–42; and pluralism of methods, 67; and social mission of church, 15; pilgrim church, 44, 116; and Scripture, 40, 49, 53, 79; and universal call to holiness, 16, 93

Vereecke, Louis, 25, n. 1; 59, n. 62; 84, nn. 6, 8; 106, n. 6; 194, n. 2; 196, n. 40

Veritatis splendor, 81, 86, n. 52; 88, 98, 106, n. 7; 108, n. 35; 138, 144, 147, 149, 150, 152, 154, 155, 159, 166, n. 1; 167, nn. 3, 6–12, 14–21, 26, 35–37; 168, nn. 38, 39, 53; 169, nn. 76, 78, 80, 81; 170, n. 96; 199, 213–214, 217, 229, n. 3; 231, n. 50; 232, nn. 60, 61, 78, 79; 234, n. 101; 239

Vermeersch, Arthur, 223

Vidal, Marciano, 84, n. 10

virtues, xii, 18, 62, 65, 89, 98, 105, 110–136, 182, 189, 194, 197, 237, 238; cardinal, 68, 112, 128, 180; content, 32; ecological steward-ship, 125–126; happiness, 66, 111; imagination, creativity, 117–118; infused, 11–113; integrity, 127–128, 156; as mean, 117, 118, 125, 194; modify subject-agent, 97, 127, 130; openness, 119; piety, 125; tensions with Protestant ethics, 110, 112; theological, 32, 51, 68, 113, 190; and voluntary poverty, 18, 112

Vischer, L., 59, n. 59

Vorgrimler, Herbert, 134, n. 20; 168, n. 48

Walter, James, 96, 107, n. 29; 170, nn. 82, 84

Wawrykow, Joseph P., 27, n. 38

Weisbord, Robert G., 28, n. 52

Weisheipl, J.A., 84, n. 18

Werpehowski, William, 84, n. 12

Wesleyan Quadrilateral, 48, 58, n. 46

Westberg, Daniel, 28, n. 49

Wilkins, John, 108, n. 36

Wogaman, J. Philip, 84, n. 14

World Council of Churches, 4, 52

World Parliament of Religions, 24

Yoder, John Howard, 6, 26, n. 18

Zalba, Marcellinus, 26, n. 13; 84, n. 7; 85, n. 25; 108, nn. 40, 41; 145, 168, n. 47; 169, n. 69; 171, nn. 109, 111; 177, 194, n. 1; 195, n. 9; 196, nn. 34, 36; 223, 233, n. 96

Zizola, Giancarlo, 231, n. 51